Are Liberty and Equality Compatible?

Are the political ideals of liberty and equality compatible? This question is of central and continuing importance in political philosophy, moral philosophy, and welfare economics. In this book, two distinguished philosophers take up the debate. Jan Narveson argues that a political ideal of negative liberty is incompatible with any substantive ideal of equality, while James P. Sterba argues that Narveson's own ideal of negative liberty is compatible, and in fact leads to the requirements of a substantive ideal of equality. Of course, they cannot both be right. Thus, the details of their arguments about the political ideal of negative liberty and its requirements will determine which of them is right. Engagingly and accessibly written, their debate will be of value to all who are interested in the central issue of what are the practical requirements of a political ideal of liberty.

Jan Narveson is Distinguished Professor Emeritus at the University of Waterloo. His previous publications include *The Libertarian Idea* (1989), *Moral Matters, Second Edition* (1999), *Respecting Persons in Theory and Practice* (2002), and *You and the State* (2008). In 2003, Professor Narveson was made an Officer of the Order of Canada in recognition of both his scholarly work and his lifelong promotion of music in his home cities of Kitchener and Waterloo, Ontario.

James P. Sterba is Professor of Philosophy at the University of Notre Dame. His previous publications include *Justice for Here and Now* (1998), *The Triumph of Practice over Theory in Ethics* (2005), *Does Feminism Discriminate Against Men? A Debate* (2008 – co-authored with Warren Farrell), and *Affirmative Action for the Future* (2009). Professor Sterba is past president of the American Philosophical Association (Central Division) and of several other philosophical associations.

For and Against

General Editor: R. G. Frey

For and Against offers a new and exciting approach to the investigation of complex philosophical ideas and their impact on the way we think about a host of contemporary moral, social, and political issues. Two philosophical essays explore a topic of intense public interest from opposing points of view. This approach provides the reader with a balanced perspective on the topic; it also introduces the deep philosophical conflicts that underpin the differing views. The result is both a series of important statements on some of the most challenging questions facing our society and an introduction to moral, social, and political philosophy. Each essay is compact and nontechnical, yet avoids a simplistic, journalistic presentation of the topic.

Other books in the series:

Are Liberty and Equality Compatible?

Jan Narveson

and

James P. Sterba

CAMBRIDGE
UNIVERSITY PRESS

CAMBRIDGE UNIVERSITY PRESS
Cambridge, New York, Melbourne, Madrid, Cape Town, Singapore,
São Paulo, Delhi, Dubai, Tokyo

Cambridge University Press
The Edinburgh Building, Cambridge CB2 8RU, UK

Published in the United States of America by
Cambridge University Press, New York

www.cambridge.org
Information on this title: www.cambridge.org/9780521883825

First published 2010

Printed in the United Kingdom at the University Press, Cambridge

A catalogue record for this publication is available from the British Library

Library of Congress Cataloging-in-Publication Data

Narveson, Jan, 1936–
     Are liberty and equality compatible? / Jan Narveson, James P. Sterba.
        p.   cm. – (For and against)
     ISBN 978-0-521-88382-5 (Hardback)
     1. Liberty.   2. Equality.   3. Social justice.   4. Social ethics.
I. Sterba, James P.   II. Title.   III. Series.
     JC575.N37 2010
     320.01′1–dc22
                                                                    2009051491

ISBN 978-0-521-88382-5 Hardback

Contents

Acknowledgments

Practically, this book would most likely never have been conceived except for the efforts of Peter Bornschein, at the time an undergraduate student at Albion College, now a promising graduate student in philosophy, who decided that he and his classmates could benefit from a debate about the ideals of liberty and equality. After this debate at Albion gave birth to the idea that Jan Narveson and I should do a book together, we took a proposal to Hilary Gaskin, Philosophy Editor at Cambridge University Press, who skillfully helped us turn our proposal into the book that you have before you.

Philosophically, my argument in the book has been developing for many years and has benefited enormously from interactions with many different people. Let me thank just some of those who have personally had a significant impact on my thinking: Gillian Brock, John Christman, Jerry Gaus, Carol Gould, John Hospers, Eric Mack, Tibor Machan, Thomas Nagel, Robert Nozick, Susan Okin, Thomas Pogge, Douglas Rasmussen, John Rawls, Jeffrey Reiman, Daniel Shapiro, Henry Shue, John Simmons, Peter Singer, A. Tara Smith, and Philippe Van Parijs. Of course, Jan Narveson deserves special thanks for his deep generosity over the years in helping me to better understand his own libertarian view, which has, I believe, thereby enabled me to better conceive and defend my own. And, as always, my partner and fellow philosopher, Janet Kourany, bears some responsibility for the strengths and weaknesses of my argument.

James P. Sterba

Philosophically, my part of this book owes its origins to my acquaintance with many writers, classic and modern: especially to David Gauthier, who stoutly denies that he is a Libertarian, and to Thomas Hobbes.

I would also like to thank Jim Sterba, with whom I have had so many lively exchanges and who engages unfailingly and with admirable civility on this important issue. Otherwise, I am sure that my views were influenced in some general way by my parents, assorted uncles and aunts – honest, hard-working people who asked little of others, and gave much – and to my brother Robert (Bud, to all who know him) whose opposition on almost everything has continually challenged my views. And finally, to Jean, my wife and partner of nearly four decades now, to whom I owe greatly.

Jan Narveson

1 Introduction

Jan Narveson and James P. Sterba

ARISTOTLE held that equals should be treated equally and unequals unequally. Yet Aristotle's ideal of equality was a relatively formal one that allowed for considerable inequality. Likewise, Thomas Hobbes, John Locke, and Jean-Jacques Rousseau all maintained that the equality in the state of nature could be reconciled with significant inequalities in social life. Immanuel Kant too held a view that justified considerable inequalities. In the nineteenth and twentieth centuries, however, more substantive ideals of equality, including ideals of economic and social equality, began to be defended by socialists, Marxists, welfare liberals, and feminists alike. As a result, the compatibility of the political ideals of liberty and equality has been seriously brought into question: how could such substantive ideals of equality be reconciled with an ideal of liberty?

Some contemporary political philosophers have sought to resolve the apparent conflict by simply endorsing an ideal of positive rather than negative liberty – one that can clearly be seen to impose the same requirements as a substantive ideal of equality. But this strategy simply begs the question unless we can demonstrate the moral or rational superiority of an ideal of positive liberty in the first place, which seems very difficult, if not impossible, to do.

In this book, Jan Narveson will argue for the incompatibility of the political ideals of liberty and equality, while James P. Sterba will argue for their compatibility. More specifically, Narveson will argue that a political ideal of negative liberty is incompatible with any substantive ideal of equality, while Sterba (in order not to beg the question against Narveson's view) will argue that Narveson's own ideal of negative liberty is compatible, and, in fact, leads to the requirements of a substantive ideal of equality. Throughout this essay, it bears noting that when Sterba speaks of an ideal of liberty or equality, he intends those ideals to include both supererogatory and obligatory requirements, the latter of which correlate with rights that are taken to be fundamental. So this debate is centrally about what fundamental rights people should have and what those rights require.

More on Narveson's argument

Narveson defines negative liberty to be the absence of factors that prevent a person from doing something. He takes the political ideal of negative liberty to be that each person's negative liberty should be constrained in the least possible way compatible with the same constraint on the negative liberty of everyone else. Narveson argues that commitment to this ideal of negative liberty will lead to free-market capitalist institutions without any right to welfare, let alone any requirement to secure economic or social equality. Nor do we violate the rights of distant peoples or future generations, he claims, by using up resources that they need, or will need, to survive, since distant peoples and future generations have no right to welfare. Narveson further argues that his political ideal of negative liberty can be supported by contractarianism. Thus, he maintains that his political ideal of negative liberty provides everyone with reason to abide by the ideal provided others do so as well, and, in this way, he claims, it can be given a contractual foundation.

More on Sterba's argument

Sterba accepts Narveson's definition of negative liberty. He also accepts Narveson's view that each person's negative liberty should be constrained in the least possible way compatible with the same constraint on the negative liberty of everyone else.

However, he maintains that this political ideal of negative liberty, under certain conditions, favors the liberty of the poor not to be interfered with in taking from the surplus of the rich what they require to meet their basic needs (a negative liberty) over the liberty of the rich not to be interfered with in using their surplus for luxury purposes (another negative liberty). Sterba further argues that the recognition of this negative liberty-right to welfare will give rise to a positive right to welfare. Agreeing with Narveson that basic rights are universal rights, Sterba extends this derived right to welfare to distant peoples and future generations. He further argues that respecting this right requires that we use no more resources than we need for a decent life so that distant peoples and future generations will also, as much as possible, have the resources they need for a decent life. And this, he claims, will lead to an equality in the use of resources over space and time. In short, Sterba argues that Narveson's own negative ideal of liberty leads to the requirements of a substantive ideal of equality.

Sterba disagrees with Narveson's claim that his political ideal of negative liberty is supported by contractarianism. Assuming the form of contractarianism in question is Hobbesian rather than Rawlsian, Sterba does not think that it will necessarily support either Narveson's interpretation of the political ideal of negative liberty or his own interpretation of that ideal.

More on our arguments together

Both of us recognize that we need to present a nonquestion-begging argument – one that should be acceptable to all parties – supporting one or the other of our different interpretations of the political ideal of negative liberty. Accordingly, Narveson seeks to provide a nonquestion-begging argument supporting his no-welfare, no-required-equality interpretation of the ideal, and Sterba seeks to provide a nonquestion-begging argument supporting his welfare-leading-to-substantive-equality interpretation of the ideal.

Of course, we both cannot be right. The details of our arguments about the political ideal of negative liberty and its requirements will determine which of us is right. Nevertheless, we will try to show that other arguments for the conclusions we support either are not as good as our own or are really equivalent with our own. We will also address the main objections to our views, including those objections that we have made to each other. In this way, we hope to leave the reader with no doubt about who wins this debate.

Part I

2   Equality is compatible with and required by liberty[1]

James P. Sterba

Is liberty compatible with equality? Following out the strategy proposed in the general introduction, I will seek to answer this question by starting with the libertarian's own ideal of negative liberty and then try to show that that ideal, when correctly interpreted, leads to substantial equality. I will then turn to an examination of other arguments that have sought to support similar conclusions and explain why those arguments are not as effective as my own. Finally, I will consider the main objections to my argument that have been raised by libertarians and my replies to those objections, where I will take up, in particular and at length, Jan Narveson's own objections to my argument from liberty to equality.

1   The practical requirements of liberty

From liberty to welfare

Libertarians like to think of themselves as defenders of liberty. F. A. Hayek, for example, sees his work as restating an ideal of

---

1 This essay draws and considerably improves upon earlier attempts of mine to construct an argument from liberty to equality and to deal with critiques that have been raised against these attempts found in *How To Make People Just* (Lanham, MD: Rowman and Littlefield, 1988), chs. 2, 7, and 11; *Justice for Here and Now* (New York: Cambridge University Press, 1998), chs. 2 and 3; *The Triumph of Practice Over Theory in Ethics* (New York: Oxford University Press, 2005), chs. 2 and 3; and "Completing the Kantian Project: From Rationality to Equality," *APA Presidential Addresses: Proceedings of the American Philosophical Association* 82, 2 (November 2008), pp. 47–83. Material from these earlier works is used with permission.

liberty for our times. "We are concerned," says Hayek, "with that condition of men in which coercion of some by others is reduced as much as possible in society."[2] Similarly, John Hospers believes that libertarianism is "a philosophy of personal liberty – the liberty of each person to live according to his own choices, provided that he does not attempt to coerce others and thus prevent them from living according to their choices."[3] And Robert Nozick claims that, if a conception of justice goes beyond libertarian "side-constraints," it cannot avoid the prospect of continually interfering with people's lives.[4]

Yet while libertarians endorse an ideal of liberty, they interpret it in different ways. For some, liberty is defined as follows:

> *The want conception of liberty*: Liberty is being unconstrained by other persons from doing what one wants.[5]

This conception limits the scope of liberty in two ways. First, not all constraints, whatever their source, count as a restriction of liberty; the constraints must come from other persons. For example, people who are constrained by natural forces from getting to the top of Mount Everest do not lack liberty in this regard. Second, constraints that have their source in other persons, but that do not run counter to an individual's wants, constrain without restricting that individual's liberty. Thus, for people who do not want to hear Beethoven's Fifth Symphony, the fact that others have effectively proscribed its performance does not restrict their liberty, even though it does constrain what they are able to do.

Of course, some may wish to argue that even such constraints can be seen to restrict a person's liberty once we take into account the fact that people normally want, or have a general desire, to be unconstrained by others. But others have thought

---

2 F. A. Hayek, *The Constitution of Liberty* (Chicago: University of Chicago Press, 1960), p. 11.
3 John Hospers, *Libertarianism* (Los Angeles: Nash Publishing, 1971), p. 5.
4 Robert Nozick, *Anarchy, State, and Utopia* (New York: Basic Books, 1974), p. ix.
5 Hospers, *Libertarianism*, p. 5.

that the possibility of such constraints points to a serious defect in this conception of liberty,[6] which can only be remedied by adopting the following broader conception of liberty:

The ability conception of liberty: Liberty is being unconstrained by other persons from doing what one is able to do.

Applying this conception to the above example, we find that people's liberty to hear Beethoven's Fifth Symphony would be restricted even if they did not want to hear it (and even if, perchance, they did not want to be unconstrained by others) since other people would still be constraining them from doing what they are able to do.

Moreover, it is important to note that being unconstrained from doing what one is unable to do does not constitute a liberty. Of course, some philosophers would object to this account, claiming, for example, that people might be free or have the liberty to run a four-minute mile even when they are unable to do so. However, if we allow that people can have the liberty to do what they are unable to do, then, presumably, they can also lack the liberty to do or be constrained from doing what they are unable to do, which seems absurd.

One reason why some philosophers have held that people can have the liberty to do what they are unable to do is that they believed that something of value is lost even when such a "liberty" is taken away.[7] Hayek, for example, suggests that penniless vagabonds who live precariously dependent on their own wits have more liberty than conscripted soldiers with all their security and relative comfort, despite the fact that the vagabonds lack the ability to derive much benefit from their liberty.[8] Yet although it is true that the vagabonds would lack the ability to derive much benefit from their liberty, it is also true that they would have the

---

6 Isaiah Berlin, *Four Essays on Liberty* (New York: Oxford University Press, 1969), pp. xxxviii–xl.
7 John Gray, "On Negative and Positive Liberty," *Political Studies* 29 (1980), pp. 507–26.
8 Hayek, *Constitution of Liberty*, p. 18.

ability to exercise that liberty, however unsuccessfully, and it is this ability which is presupposed by the possession of any liberty whatsoever. Thus, in general, while it is possible to confuse having a liberty with having certain sorts of abilities (for example, having the liberty to run a four-minute mile with the ability to succeed in doing so), at the same time, it should be recognized that having a liberty does presuppose the ability to exercise that liberty in some fashion or other, however unsuccessfully. As a consequence, all liberties determined by the Want Conception of Liberty will turn out to be liberties according to the Ability Conception as well.

Of course, there will also be numerous liberties determined by the Ability Conception that are not liberties according to the Want Conception. For example, there will be highly talented students who surprisingly do not want to pursue careers in philosophy, even though no one constrains them from doing so. Accordingly, the Ability Conception but not the Want Conception would view them as possessing a liberty. And even though such liberties are generally not as valuable as those liberties that are common to both conceptions, they still are of some value, even when the manipulation of people's wants is not at issue. This seems, therefore, to be a good reason for favoring the Ability over the Want Conception of Liberty.

Yet even if we endorse the Ability Conception of Liberty, problems of interpretation still remain. The major problem concerns what is to count as a constraint. On the one hand, libertarians would like to limit constraints to positive acts (that is, acts of commission) that prevent people from doing what they are otherwise able to do. On the other hand, welfare liberals interpret constraints to include, in addition, negative acts (that is, acts of omission) that prevent people from doing what they are otherwise able to do. In fact, this is one way to understand the debate between defenders of "negative liberty" and defenders of "positive liberty." For defenders of negative liberty would seem to interpret constraints to include only positive acts of others that prevent people from doing what they otherwise are able to do, while defenders of positive liberty would seem to interpret constraints to include both positive and negative acts of others that prevent people from doing what they are otherwise able to do.[9]

So in order not to beg the question against libertarians, suppose we interpret constraints in the manner favored by them to include only positive acts by others that prevent people from doing what they otherwise either want and are able to do, or are just able to do.[10]

Libertarians go on to characterize their political ideal as requiring that each person should have the greatest amount of liberty morally commensurate with the greatest amount of liberty for everyone else.[11] Interpreting their ideal in this way, libertarians claim to derive a number of more specific requirements, in particular, a right to life, a right to freedom of speech, press, and assembly, and a right to property.

Here it is important to observe that the libertarian's right to life is not a right to receive from others the goods and resources necessary for preserving one's life; it is simply a right not to have one's life interfered with or ended unjustly. Correspondingly, the libertarian's right to property is not a right to receive from others the goods and resources necessary for one's welfare, but rather typically a right not to be interfered with in regard to any goods and resources that one has legitimately acquired either by initial acquisition or by voluntary agreement.[12]

---

9 On this point, see Maurice Cranston, *Freedom* (New York: Basic Books, 1953), pp. 52–3; C. B. Macpherson, *Democratic Theory* (Oxford: Oxford University Press, 1973), p. 95; and Joel Feinberg, *Rights, Justice and the Bounds of Liberty* (Princeton: Princeton University Press, 1980), ch. 1.

10 I have earlier referred in a shorthand and somewhat imprecise way to "people doing what they want or are able to do" where I understood the first disjunct to include "and are able," as was clearly implied by the surrounding discussion.

11 Hospers, *Libertarianism*, ch. 7, and Tibor Machan, *Human Rights and Human Liberties* (Chicago: Nelson-Hall, 1975), pp. 231ff. We should think about the libertarian ideal of liberty as securing for each person the largest morally defensible bundle of liberties possible.

12 Property can also be legitimately acquired on the libertarian view by producing it out of what one already owns or legitimately possesses.

A partial defense

In support of their view, libertarians have advanced examples of the following sort. The first two are adapted from Milton Friedman, the last from Robert Nozick.[13]

In the first example, you are to suppose that you and three friends are walking along the street and you happen to notice and retrieve a $100 bill lying on the pavement. Suppose a rich fellow had passed by earlier throwing away $100 bills, and you have been lucky enough to find one of them. Now, according to Friedman, it would be nice of you to share your good fortune with your friends. Nevertheless, they have no right to demand that you do so, and, hence, they would not be justified in forcing you to share the $100 bill with them. Similarly, Friedman would have us believe that it would be nice of us to provide welfare to the less fortunate members of our society. Nevertheless, the less fortunate members have no right to welfare, and hence they would not be justified in forcing us to provide such.

The second example, which Friedman regards as analogous to the first, involves supposing that there are four Robinson Crusoes, each marooned on one of four uninhabited islands in the same neighborhood. One of these Crusoes happens to land on a large and fruitful island, which enables him to live easily and well. The others happen to land on tiny and rather barren islands from which they can barely scratch a living. Suppose one day they discover the existence of each other. Now, according to Friedman, it would be nice of the fortunate Robinson Crusoe to share the resources of his island with the other three Crusoes, but the other three Crusoes have no right to demand that he share those resources, and it would be wrong for them to force him to do so. Correspondingly, Friedman thinks it would be nice of us to provide the less fortunate in our society with welfare, but the less fortunate have no right to demand that we do so, and it would be wrong for them to force us to do so.

---

13 See Milton Friedman, *Capitalism and Freedom* (Chicago: University of Chicago Press, 1962), pp. 161–72; Nozick, *Anarchy, State, and Utopia*, pp. 160–4.

In the third example, Robert Nozick asks us to imagine that we are in a society that has just distributed income according to some ideal pattern, possibly a pattern of equality. We are further to imagine that in such a society someone with the talents of Wilt Chamberlain or Michael Jordan offers to play basketball for us provided that he receives, let us say, one dollar from every home-game ticket that is sold. Suppose we agree to these terms, and two million people attend the home games to see this new Wilt Chamberlain or Michael Jordan play, thereby securing for him an income of two million dollars. Since such an income would surely upset the initial pattern of income distribution whatever that happened to be, Nozick contends that this illustrates how an ideal of liberty upsets the patterns required by other conceptions of justice, and hence calls for their rejection.

Of course, libertarians allow that it would be nice of the rich to share their surplus goods and resources with the poor, just as Milton Friedman would allow that it would be nice of you to share the $100 you found with your friends, and nice of the rich-islanded Robinson Crusoe to share his resources with the poor-islanded Robinson Crusoes. Nevertheless, they deny that government has a duty to provide for such needs. Some good things, such as providing welfare to the poor, are requirements of charity rather than justice, libertarians claim. Accordingly, failure to make such provisions is neither blameworthy nor punishable. As a consequence, such acts of charity should not be coercively required. For this reason, libertarians are opposed to coercively supported welfare programs.

The ideal of liberty and the problem of conflict

Now in order to see why libertarians are mistaken about what their ideal requires, consider a conflict situation between the rich and the poor. In this conflict situation, the rich, of course, have more than enough resources to satisfy their basic needs.[14]

14 Basic needs, if not satisfied, lead to significant lacks or deficiencies with respect to a standard of mental and physical well-being. Thus, a person's needs for food, shelter, medical care, protection, companionship, and

In contrast, imagine that the poor lack the resources to meet their basic needs so as to secure a decent life for themselves, even though they have tried all the means available to them that libertarians regard as legitimate for acquiring such resources. Under circumstances like these, libertarians maintain that the rich should have the liberty to use their resources to satisfy their luxury needs if they so wish. Libertarians recognize that this liberty might well be enjoyed with the consequence that the satisfaction of the basic needs of the poor will not be met; they just think that liberty always has priority over other political ideals, and since they assume that the liberty of the poor is not at stake in such conflict situations, it is easy for them to conclude that the rich should not be required to sacrifice their liberty so that the basic needs of the poor may be met.

Of course, libertarians allow that it would be nice of the rich to share their surplus resources with the poor. Nevertheless, according to libertarians, such acts of charity are not required because the liberty of the poor is not thought to be at stake in such conflict situations.

In fact, however, the liberty of the poor is at stake in such conflict situations. What is at stake is the liberty of the poor not to be interfered with in taking from the surplus possessions of the rich what is necessary to satisfy their basic needs.

Needless to say, libertarians want to deny that the poor have this liberty. But how can they justify such a denial? As this liberty of the poor has been specified, it is not a positive liberty to receive something but a negative liberty of noninterference. Clearly, what libertarians must do is recognize the existence of such a liberty and then claim that it unjustifiably conflicts with other liberties of the rich. But when libertarians see that this is the case, they are often genuinely surprised, for they had not previously seen the conflict between the rich and the poor as a conflict of liberties. In responding to my work in recent years,

---

self-development are, at least in part, needs of this sort. For a discussion of basic needs, see my *How to Make People Just* (Lanham, MD: Rowman and Littlefield, 1988), pp. 45–8.

libertarians Tibor Machan, Eric Mack, and Jan Narveson, among others, have come grudgingly to recognize that this liberty of the poor, as I have specified it, is indeed a negative liberty, but then they want to go on to argue that this liberty is illegitimate.[15]

Now when the conflict between the rich and the poor is viewed as a conflict of liberties, we can either say that the rich should have the liberty not to be interfered with in using their surplus resources for luxury purposes, or we can say that the poor should have the liberty not to be interfered with in taking from the rich what they require to meet their basic needs. If we choose one liberty, we must reject the other. What needs to be determined, therefore, is which liberty is morally enforceable: the liberty of the rich or the liberty of the poor.[16]

The "ought" implies "can" principle

I submit that the liberty of the poor, which is the liberty not to be interfered with in taking from the surplus resources of others what is required to meet one's basic needs, is morally enforceable over the liberty of the rich, which is the liberty not to be interfered with in using one's surplus resources for luxury purposes. To see that this is the case, we need only appeal to one of the most fundamental principles of morality, one that is common to all moral and political perspectives, namely, the "ought" implies "can" principle. According to this principle, people are not morally required to do what they lack the power to do or what would involve so great a sacrifice or restriction that it is unreasonable to ask them, or in cases of severe conflict of interest, unreasonable to require them to abide by.

For example, suppose I promised to attend a departmental meeting on Friday, but on Thursday I am involved in a serious car accident that puts me into a coma. Surely it is no longer the

---

15 Tibor Machan, *Libertarianism Defended* (Burlington, VT: Ashgate, 2006), ch. 20; Eric Mack, "Libertarianism Untamed," *Journal of Social Philosophy* 22 (1991), pp. 64–72; and Jan Narveson, "Sterba's Program of Philosophical Reconciliation," *Journal of Social Philosophy* 30 (1999), pp. 401–10.

16 Libertarians have never rejected the need for enforcement when important liberties are at stake.

case that I ought to attend the meeting, now that I lack the power to do so. Or suppose instead that on Thursday I develop a severe case of pneumonia for which I am hospitalized. Surely I can legitimately claim that I cannot attend the meeting on the grounds that the risk to my health involved in attending is a sacrifice that is unreasonable to ask me to bear. Or suppose instead that the risk to my health from having pneumonia is not so serious, and it is reasonable to ask me to attend the meeting (a supererogatory request). However, it might still be serious enough to be unreasonable to require my attendance at the meeting (a demand that is backed up by blame and coercion).[17]

This "ought" implies "can" principle claims that reason and morality must be linked in an appropriate way, especially if we are going to be able to justifiably use blame or coercion to get people to abide by the requirements of morality. It should be noted, however, that although major figures in the history of philosophy, and most philosophers today, including virtually all libertarian philosophers, accept this linkage between reason and morality, this linkage is not usually conceived to be part of the "ought" implies "can" principle.[18] Nevertheless, I claim that

17 The reason for distinguishing between these two cases with respect to the "ought" implies "can" principle is that when interpersonal conflicts of interest are not severe, moral resolutions must still be reasonable to ask everyone affected to accept, but they need not be reasonable to *require* everyone affected to accept. This is because not all moral resolutions can be justifiably enforced; only moral resolutions of severe interpersonal conflicts of interest can and *should* be justifiably enforced. Furthermore, the reason why moral resolutions of severe interpersonal conflicts of interest should be enforced is that if the parties are simply asked but not required to abide by a moral resolution in such cases of conflict, then it is likely that the stronger party will violate the resolution and that would be unreasonable to ask or require the weaker party to accept.

18 This linkage between morality and reason is expressed in the belief that (true) morality and (right) reason cannot conflict. Some supporters of this linkage have developed separate theories of rationality and reasonableness, contending, for example, that, while egoists are rational, those who are committed to morality are both rational and reasonable. On this interpretation, morality is rationally permissible but not rationally required, since egoism is also rationally permissible. Other supporters of the linkage between reason and morality reject the idea of separate theories of rationality

there are good reasons for associating this linkage with the principle, namely, our use of the word "can" as in the example just given, and the natural progression from logical, physical, and psychological possibility found in the traditional "ought" implies "can" principle to the notion of moral possibility found in my formulation of the principle. In any case, the acceptability of my formulation of the "ought" implies "can" principle is determined by the virtually universal, and arguably necessary, acceptance of its components and not by the manner in which I have proposed to join those components together.[19]

Now applying the "ought" implies "can" principle to the case at hand, it seems clear that the poor have it within their power to relinquish such an important liberty as the liberty not to be interfered with in taking from the rich what they require to meet their basic needs. They could do this. Nevertheless, it is unreasonable in this context to require them to accept so great a restriction. In the extreme case, it involves requiring the poor to sit back and starve to death. Of course, the poor may have no real alternative to relinquishing this liberty. To do anything else may involve worse consequences for themselves and their loved ones and may invite a painful death. Accordingly, we may expect that the poor would acquiesce, albeit unwillingly, to a political system that denied them the right to welfare supported by such a

and reasonableness, contending that morality is not just rationally permissible but also rationally required and that egoism is rationally impermissible. But despite their disagreement over whether there is a separate theory of rationality distinct from a theory of reasonableness, most in both groups usually link morality with a notion of reasonableness that incorporates a certain degree of altruism. But for those who do not so link morality with a notion of reasonableness that incorporates a certain degree of altruism, and instead favor a self-interested-based Hobbesian perspective a nonquestion-begging argument for making that linkage in the last section of my essay in connection with my discussion of Jan Narveson's form of libertarianism, is absolutely necessary.

19 It should be pointed out that the "ought" implies "can" principle primarily ranges over that part of morality which we can justifiably enforce against others because we can reasonably expect that its requirements are accessible to those to whom they apply.

liberty, at the same time we recognize that such a system has imposed an unreasonable restriction upon the poor – a restriction that we could not morally blame the poor for trying to evade.[20] Analogously, we might expect that a woman whose life is threatened would submit to a rapist's demands, at the same time that we recognize the utter unreasonableness of those demands. By contrast, it is not unreasonable to require the rich in this context to sacrifice the liberty to meet some of their luxury needs so that the poor can have the liberty to meet their basic needs. Naturally, we might expect that the rich, for reasons of self-interest or past contribution, might be disinclined to make such a sacrifice. We might even suppose that the past contribution of the rich provides a good reason for not sacrificing their liberty to use their surplus for luxury purposes. Yet, the rich cannot claim that relinquishing such a liberty involves so great a sacrifice that it is unreasonable to require them to make it; unlike the poor, the rich are morally blameworthy and subject to coercion for failing to make such a sacrifice.

Consequently, if we assume that however else we specify the requirements of morality, they cannot violate the "ought" implies "can" principle, it follows that, despite what libertarians claim, the right to liberty endorsed by them actually favors the liberty of the poor over the liberty of the rich.[21]

This means that within the bundle of liberties allotted to each person by the basic principle of libertarianism, there must be the liberty not to be interfered with (when one is poor) in taking from the surplus possessions of the rich what is necessary to satisfy one's basic needs. This must be part of the bundle that constitutes the greatest amount of liberty for each person because this liberty is morally superior to the liberty with which it directly conflicts, that is, the liberty not to be interfered with

20 This is also a restriction that we could legitimately coercively stop.
21 Moreover, while application of the unreasonable standard of the "ought" implies "can" principle can be disputable in some contexts, I will argue that in the context where we have coercively to enforce either the liberty of the poor or the liberty of the rich, the standard does offer a clear resolution, one that favors the liberty of the poor over the liberty of the rich.

(when one is rich) in using one's surplus possessions to satisfy one's luxury needs. In this context, the "ought" implies "can" principle establishes the moral superiority and enforceability of the liberty of the poor over the liberty of the rich.[22]

Yet couldn't libertarians object to this conclusion, claiming that it would be unreasonable to require the rich to sacrifice the liberty to meet some of their luxury needs so that the poor can have the liberty to meet their basic needs? As I have pointed out, libertarians do not usually see the situation as a conflict of liberties, but suppose they did. How plausible would such an objection be? Not very plausible at all, I think.

For consider: what are libertarians going to say about the poor? Isn't it clearly unreasonable to require the poor to restrict their liberty to meet their basic needs so that the rich can have the liberty to meet their luxury needs? Isn't it clearly unreasonable to coercively require the poor to sit back and starve to death? If it is, then, there is no resolution of this conflict that is reasonable to coercively require both the rich and the poor to accept. But that would mean that libertarians could not be putting forth a moral resolution because a moral resolution, according to the "ought" implies "can" principle, resolves severe conflicts of interest in ways that it is reasonable to require everyone affected to accept,[23] where it is further understood that a moral resolution can sometimes require us to act in accord with altruistic reasons.[24] Therefore, as long as

---

22 Here again we should think about the libertarian ideal of liberty as securing for each person the largest morally defensible bundle of liberties possible.

23 This requirement "that moral resolutions must resolve conflicts of interest in ways that it is reasonable to require everyone affected to accept" is actually the contrapositive of the "ought" implies "can" principle, as I stated it in the text. While the "ought" implies "can" principle claims that if any action is not reasonable to ask or require a person to do, all things considered, that action is not morally required or a moral resolution for that person, all things considered [-R/C(A v Req) → -MReq/MRes], this requirement claims that if any action is morally required or a moral resolution for a person to do, all things considered, that action is reasonable to ask or require that person to do, all things considered [MReq/MRes → R/C(A v Re)].

24 As we shall see, the basis for this understanding is the priority of high-ranking altruistic reasons over conflicting low-ranking self-interested reasons that is

libertarians think of themselves as putting forth a moral resolution, they cannot allow that it is unreasonable in cases of severe conflict of interest both to require the rich to restrict their liberty to meet their luxury needs in order to benefit the poor and to require the poor to restrict their liberty to meet their basic needs in order to benefit the rich. But I submit that if one of these requirements is to be judged reasonable, then, by any neutral assessment, it must be the requirement that the rich restrict their liberty to meet their luxury needs so that the poor can have the liberty to meet their basic needs; there is no other plausible resolution, if libertarians intend to put forth a moral resolution.[25]

It should also be noted that this case for restricting the liberty of the rich depends upon the willingness of the poor to take advantage of whatever opportunities are available to them to engage in mutually beneficial work, so that failure of the poor to take advantage of such opportunities would normally cancel the obligation of the rich to restrict their own liberty for the benefit of the poor.[26] In addition, the case for favoring the liberty of the poor is also conditional on there being sufficient resources available to meet everyone's basic needs.

nonquestion-beggingly justified in Morality as Compromise combined with the further realization (following from our discussion of the libertarian ideal of liberty) that since we must coercively support one or the other of these reasons, we should support (require) the reason that has moral priority, in this case, the high-ranking altruistic reason that corresponds to the negative liberty of the poor not to be interfered with in taking from the surplus of the rich what they require to meet their basic needs.

25 By the liberty of the rich to meet their luxury needs, I continue to mean the liberty of the rich not to be interfered with when using their surplus possessions for luxury purposes. Similarly, by the liberty of the poor to meet their basic needs, I continue to mean the liberty of the poor not to be interfered with when taking what they require to meet their basic needs from the surplus possessions of the rich.

26 The employment opportunities offered to the poor must be honorable and supportive of self-respect. To do otherwise would be to offer the poor the opportunity to meet some of their basic needs at the cost of denying some of their other basic needs.

Of course, there will be cases where the poor fail to satisfy their basic needs, not because of any direct restriction of liberty on the part of the rich, but because the poor are in such dire need that they are unable even to attempt to take from the rich what they require to meet their basic nutritional needs. Accordingly, in such cases, the rich would not be performing any act of commission that prevents the poor from taking what they require. Yet, even in such cases, the rich would normally be performing acts of commission that prevent other persons from aiding the poor by taking from the surplus possessions of the rich. And when assessed from a moral point of view, restricting the liberty of these other persons would not be morally justified for the very same reason that restricting the liberty of the poor to meet their own basic needs would not be morally justified: it would not be reasonable to ask all of those affected to accept such a restriction of liberty.

Notice too that it is not the mere size of the sacrifice required of the poor that is objectionable about the possibility of favoring the liberty of the rich over the liberty of the poor because sometimes morality does require great sacrifices from us. For example, it requires us to refrain from intentionally killing innocent people even to save our lives.[27] Rather, what is objectionable about this possibility is the size of the sacrifice that the poor would be required to bear compared to the size of the benefit that would otherwise be secured for the rich. In the case of the prohibition against intentionally killing innocent people, the sacrifice that violating this prohibition would impose on (innocent) people is normally greater than the benefit we ourselves and others would realize from violating that prohibition; hence the reasonableness of the prohibition. Correspondingly, in the conflict between the rich and the poor, the sacrifice that would be imposed on the poor by denying them the satisfaction of their

---

27 Narveson raises the objection that it cannot just be the size of the sacrifice that is required because sometimes morality does require significant sacrifice. See his "A Critique of Sterba's Defense of the Welfare State," in *Political Philosophy*, ed. Louis Pojman (New York: McGraw-Hill, 2002), p. 231.

basic needs is clearly greater than the benefit the rich would obtain from satisfying their nonbasic or luxury needs; hence the unreasonableness of imposing such a sacrifice on the poor. In this case, it is more reasonable to require a certain degree of altruism from the rich than to require an even greater degree of altruism from the poor. In all such cases, the goal is to avoid imposing an unreasonable sacrifice on anyone, where the reasonableness of the sacrifice is judged by comparing the alternative possibilities.

It is sometimes thought that there is a different interpretation of libertarianism where rights, not liberties, are fundamental and where another argument is needed to establish the conclusion I have just established here.[28] Under this presumptively different interpretation, the rights taken as fundamental are a strong right to property and a weak right to life. Yet given that for libertarians such rights are also rights of noninterference, that is (negative) liberty rights, the question arises of why we should accept these particular rights of noninterference (liberties) and not others – which is just the question that arises when we consider the conflicting liberties to which an ideal of liberty gives rise. What this shows is that the "rights" interpretation of libertarianism is not really distinct from the "liberty" interpretation we have just been discussing.

One might think that once the rich realize that the poor should have the liberty not to be interfered with when taking from the surplus possessions of the rich what they require to satisfy their basic needs, it would be in the interest of the rich to stop producing any surplus whatsoever.

Suppose a producer who could produce a surplus did not want to do so even though she knew that others needed that surplus to meet their basic needs. Imagine that these others through no fault of their own could not produce enough to meet their own basic needs and that their basic needs would be met only if they took from the nonsurplus resources of the producer

---

28 For a time, I thought so myself. See my *Justice for Here and Now* (New York: Cambridge University Press, 1998), ch. 3.

or threatened to do so in order to motivate her to produce more. In these circumstances, I think that the producer could be legitimately interfered with by those seeking in the only way possible to meet their basic needs by appropriating or threatening to appropriate her nonsurplus resources.

Of course, the producer in this case would probably respond to the appropriations or threat to appropriate by producing more.[29] Nevertheless what the producer is morally required to do is not that, but rather not to interfere with the appropriation or the threat to appropriate her nonsurplus resources by others who are in need through no fault of their own and who cannot meet their own basic needs in any other way.

Of course, our producer could respond by doing nothing. The poor could then appropriate the nonsurplus resources of the producer, and then, by not producing more, the producer would just waste away because she is unwilling to be more productive. If that happens, then both the poor and the producer would lose out due to the inaction of the producer. Still, the producer is not obligated to respond to the negative welfare right of the poor by doing something productive, however self-destructive being unproductive would be for her. This is how the negative right to welfare differs from a positive right requiring the producer to do something. It falls short of what a positive right to welfare can do for the poor. Yet it only falls short when the producers of the world choose to act in a self-destructive way – a very unlikely possibility.

Nevertheless, libertarians might respond that even supposing welfare rights could be morally justified on the basis of the liberty of the poor not to be interfered with in taking from the rich in order to meet their basic nutritional needs and the liberty of third parties not to be interfered with in taking from the rich in order to provide for the basic nutritional rights of the poor, the poor still would be better off without the enforcement of such

---

29 Working for one's fellow citizens is somewhat analogous to fighting for them, but libertarians are unlikely to see it that way.

rights.[30] For example, it might be argued that when people are not forced through taxation to support a system of welfare rights, they are both more productive, since they are able to keep more of what they produce, and more charitable, since they tend to give more freely to those in need when they are not forced to do so. As a result, so the argument goes, the poor would benefit more from the increased charity of a libertarian society than they would from the guaranteed minimum of a welfare state. Yet surely it is difficult to comprehend how people who are so opposed to the enforcement of welfare rights would turn out to be so charitable to the poor in a libertarian society.

Moreover, in a libertarian society, the provision of welfare would involve an impossible coordination problem. For if the duty to provide welfare to the poor is at best supererogatory, as libertarians claim, then no one can legitimately force anyone who does not consent to provide such welfare. The will of the majority on this issue could not be legitimately imposed upon dissenters.[31] Assuming then that the provision of welfare requires coordinated action on a broad front, such coordination could not be achieved in a libertarian society because it would require a near unanimous agreement of all its members.[32]

There is also an interesting practical reason why coercive welfare systems are needed. For many people, coercive welfare systems provide them with the opportunity to be as morally

30 See John Hospers, "The Libertarian Manifesto," in *Morality in Practice*, ed. James P. Sterba, 7th edn (Belmont: Wadsworth Publishing Co., 2004), pp. 21–31, esp. p. 31.
31 Sometimes advocates of libertarianism inconsistently contend that the duty to help others is supererogatory but that a majority of a society could justifiably enforce such a duty on everyone. See Theodore Benditt, "The Demands of Justice," in *Economic Justice*, ed. Diana Meyers and Kenneth Kipnis (Lanham, MD: Rowman & Littlefield, 1985), pp. 108–20.
32 Sometimes advocates of libertarianism focus on the coordination problems that arise in welfare states concerning the provision of welfare, and ignore the far more serious coordination problems that would arise in a night watchman state. See Burton Leiser, "Vagrancy, Loitering and Economic Justice," in *Economic Justice*, ed. Meyers and Kipnis, pp. 149–60.

good as they can be. This is because many people are willing to help the poor but only when they can be assured that other people, similarly situated, are making comparable sacrifices, and a coercive welfare system does provide the assurance that comparable sacrifices will be made by all those with a surplus. Such people, and there appear to be many of them, would not give, or not give as much, to the poor, without this coercive requirement.[33]

Nevertheless, it might still be argued that the greater productivity of the more talented people in a libertarian society would increase employment opportunities and voluntary welfare assistance, which would benefit the poor more than a guaranteed minimum would in a welfare state. But this simply could not occur. For if the more talented members of a society were to provide sufficient employment opportunities and voluntary welfare assistance to enable the poor to meet their basic needs, then the conditions for invoking a right to a guaranteed minimum in a welfare state would not arise, since the poor are first required to take advantage of whatever employment opportunities and voluntary welfare assistance are available to them before they can legitimately invoke such a right. Consequently, when *sufficient* employment opportunities and voluntary welfare assistance obtain, there would be no practical difference in this regard between a libertarian society and a welfare state, since neither would justify invoking a right to a guaranteed minimum. Only when *insufficient* employment opportunities and voluntary welfare assistance obtain would there be a practical difference between a libertarian society and a welfare state, and then it would clearly benefit the poor to be able to invoke the right to a guaranteed minimum in a welfare state. Consequently, given the conditional nature of the right to welfare, and the practical possibility and, in most cases, the actuality, of insufficient employment opportunities and voluntary welfare assistance

---

33 This issue is taken up again in conjunction with regard to an objection raised by Tibor Machan. See *Libertarianism Defended*, p. 36.

obtaining, there is no reason to think that the poor would be better off without the enforcement of such a right.[34]

In brief, if a right to liberty is taken to be basic, then, contrary to what libertarians claim, not only would a right to welfare be morally required but also such a right would clearly benefit the poor.[35]

Now it might be objected that the right to welfare that this argument establishes from libertarian premises is not the same as the right to welfare endorsed by welfare liberals and socialists. This is correct. We could mark this difference by referring to the right that this argument establishes as "a negative welfare right" and by referring to the right endorsed by welfare liberals as "a positive welfare right." The significance of this difference is that a person's negative welfare right can be violated only when other people through acts of commission interfere with its exercise, whereas a person's positive welfare right can be violated not only by such acts of commission but by acts of omission as well. Nonetheless, this difference will have little practical import because in recognizing the legitimacy of negative welfare rights, libertarians will come to see that virtually any use of their surplus possessions is likely to violate the negative welfare rights of the poor by preventing

---

34 It is true, of course, that if the rich could retain the resources that are used in a welfare state for meeting the basic needs of the poor, they might have the option of using those resources to increase employment opportunities beyond what exists in any given welfare state, but this particular way of increasing employment opportunities does not seem to be the most effective way of meeting the basic needs of the poor, and it would not at all serve to meet the basic needs of those who cannot work.

35 What, you might ask, is my response to the defenses of libertarianism provided by the examples from Friedman and Nozick at the very beginning of my essay? My response to Friedman's defense should be obvious. When basic needs are at stake, the poor can have a claim of noninterference against the rich, and poor Robinson Crusoes can have a claim of noninterference against rich Robinson Crusoes. My response to Nozick's defense of libertarianism is that the inequalities of income generated in his example would be objectionable only if they deprived people of something to which they had a right, such as welfare. And whether people are so deprived depends on to what uses the Wilt Chamberlains or Michael Jordans of the world put their greater income. Thus, it is perfectly conceivable that those who have legitimately acquired greater income may use it in ways that do not violate the rights of others.

the poor from rightfully appropriating (some part of) their surplus goods and resources. So, in order to ensure that they will not be engaging in such wrongful actions, it will be incumbent on them to set up institutions guaranteeing adequate positive welfare rights for the poor. Only then will they be able to use legitimately any remaining surplus possessions to meet their own nonbasic needs. Furthermore, in the absence of adequate positive welfare rights, the poor, either acting by themselves or through their allies or agents, would have some discretion in determining when and how to exercise their negative welfare rights.[36] In order not to be subject to that discretion, libertarians will tend to favor the only morally legitimate way of preventing the exercise of such rights: they will set up institutions guaranteeing adequate positive welfare rights that will then take precedence over the exercise of negative welfare rights. For these reasons, recognizing the negative welfare rights of the poor will ultimately lead libertarians to endorse the same sort of welfare institutions favored by welfare liberals.[37]

---

36 When the poor are acting collectively in conjunction with their agents and allies to exercise their negative welfare rights, they will want, in turn, to institute adequate positive welfare rights to secure a proper distribution of the goods and resources they are acquiring.

37 It is important to see how moral and pragmatic considerations are combined in this argument from negative welfare rights to positive welfare rights, as this will become particularly relevant when we turn to a consideration of distant peoples and future generations. What needs to be seen is that the moral consideration is primary and the pragmatic consideration secondary. The moral consideration is that, until positive welfare rights for the poor are guaranteed, any use by the rich of their surplus possessions to meet their nonbasic needs is likely to violate the negative welfare rights of the poor by preventing them from appropriating (some part of) the surplus goods and resources of the rich. The pragmatic consideration is that, in the absence of positive welfare rights, the rich would have to put up with the discretion of the poor, either acting by themselves or through their allies or agents, in choosing when and how to exercise their negative welfare rights.

Now obviously peoples who are separated from the rich by significant distances will be able to exercise their negative welfare rights only either by negotiating the distances involved or by having allies or agents in the right place, willing to act on their behalf. And with respect to future generations, their rights can be exercised only if they too have allies and agents in the right place and time, willing to act on their behalf. So unless distant peoples

From welfare to equality

Now it is possible that libertarians, convinced to some extent by the above argument, might want to accept a right to welfare for members of their own society but deny that this right extends to distant peoples and future generations. Since it is only fairly recently that philosophers have begun to discuss the question of what rights distant peoples and future generations might legitimately claim against us, a generally acceptable way of discussing the question has yet to be developed. Some philosophers have even attempted to "answer" the question, or at least part of it, by arguing that talk about "the rights of future generations" is conceptually incoherent and thus analogous to talk about "square circles." Thus Richard DeGeorge writes:

> The argument in favor of the principle that only existing entities have rights is straightforward and simple: Nonexistent entities by definition do not exist. What does not exist cannot be subject or bearer of anything. Hence, it cannot be the subject or bearer of rights.[38]

Accordingly, the key question that must be answered first is this: can we meaningfully speak of distant peoples and future generations as having rights against us or of our having corresponding obligations to them?

Distant peoples

Answering this question with respect to distant peoples is much easier than answering it with respect to future generations. Few

are good at negotiating distances or unless distant peoples and future generations have ample allies and agents in the right place and time, the pragmatic consideration leading the rich to endorse positive welfare rights will diminish in importance in their regard. Fortunately, the moral consideration alone is sufficient to carry the argument here and elsewhere: libertarians should endorse positive welfare rights because it is the only way that they can be assured of not violating the negative welfare rights of the poor by preventing the poor from appropriating (some part of) the surplus goods and resources of the rich.

38 Richard DeGeorge, "Do We Owe the Future Anything?" *Law and the Ecological Challenge* 2 (1978), pp. 180–90.

philosophers have thought that the mere fact that people are at a distance from us precludes our having any obligations to them or their having any rights against us. Some philosophers, however, have argued that our ignorance of the specific membership of the class of distant peoples does rule out these moral relationships. Yet this cannot be right, given that in other contexts we recognize obligations to indeterminate classes of people, such as a police officer's obligation to help people in distress or the obligation of food producers not to harm those who consume their products.

Yet others have argued that, while there may be valid moral claims respecting the welfare of distant peoples, such claims cannot be rights, because they fail to hold against determinate individuals and groups.[39] But in what sense do such claims fail to hold against determinate individuals and groups? Surely all would agree that existing laws rarely specify the determinate individuals and groups against whom such claims hold. But morality is frequently determinate where existing laws are not. And at least there seems to be no conceptual impossibility to claiming that distant peoples have rights against us and that we have corresponding obligations to them.

Of course, before distant peoples can be said to have rights against us, we must be capable of acting across the distance that separates us. Yet as long as this condition is met – as it typically is for people living in most technologically advanced societies – it would certainly seem possible for distant peoples to have rights against us and we corresponding obligations to them.

Future generations

In contrast, answering the above question with respect to future generations is much more difficult and has been the subject of considerable debate among contemporary philosophers. One issue concerns the referent of the term "future generations." Most philosophers seem to agree that the class of future

---

39 Rex Martin, *Rawls and Rights* (Lawrence: University of Kansas Press, 1984), ch. 2.

generations is not "the class of all persons who simply *could* come into existence." But there is some disagreement about whether we should refer to the class of future generations as "the class of persons who will definitely come into existence, assuming that there are such" or as "the class of persons we can reasonably expect to come into existence." The first approach is more "existential," specifying the class of future generations in terms of what will exist; the second approach is more "epistemological," specifying the class of future generations in terms of our knowledge. Fortunately, there does not appear to be any practical moral significance to the choice of either approach.

Another issue relevant to whether we can meaningfully speak of future generations as having rights against us or our having obligations to them concerns whether it is logically coherent to speak of future generations as having rights now. Of course, no one who finds talk about rights to be generally meaningful should question whether we can coherently claim that future generations *will* have rights at some point in the future (specifically, when they come into existence and are no longer *future* generations). But what is questioned, since it is of considerable practical significance, is whether we can coherently claim that future generations have rights *now* when they do not yet exist.

Let us suppose, for example, that we continue to use up the earth's resources at present or even greater rates, and, as a result, it turns out that the most pessimistic forecasts for the twenty-second century are realized.[40] This means that future generations will face widespread famine, depleted resources, insufficient new technology to handle the crisis, and a drastic decline in the quality of life for nearly everyone. If this were to happen, could persons living in the twenty-second century legitimately claim that we in the twenty-first century violated their rights by not restraining our consumption of the world's resources? Surely

---

40 Anita Gordon and David Suzuki, *It's a Matter of Survival* (Cambridge, MA: Harvard University Press, 1990). See also Donella H. Meadows, Dennis L. Meadows, Jorgen Randers, and William W. Behrens III, *The Limits to Growth*, 2nd edn (New York: New American Library, 1974), chs. 3 and 4.

it would be odd to say that we violated their rights one hundred years before they existed. But what exactly is the oddness?

Is it that future generations generally have no way of claiming their rights against existing generations? While this does make the recognition and enforcement of rights much more difficult (future generations would need strong advocates in the existing generations), it does not make it impossible for there to be such rights. After all, it is quite obvious that the recognition and enforcement of the rights of distant peoples is also a difficult task.

Or is it that we do not believe rights can legitimately exercise their influence over long durations of time? But if we can foresee and control at least some of the effects our actions will have on the ability of future generations to satisfy their basic needs, why should we not be responsible for those same effects? And if we are responsible for them, why should not future generations have a right that we take them into account?

Perhaps what troubles us is that future generations are not yet in existence when their rights are said to demand action. But how else could persons have a right not to be harmed by the effects our actions will have in the distant future if they did not exist at the time those effects would be felt? Our contemporaries cannot legitimately make the same demand, for they will not be around to experience those effects. Only future generations can have a right that the effects our actions will have in the distant future not harm them. Nor need we assume that in order for persons to have rights they must exist when their rights demand action. Thus, in saying that future generations have rights against existing generations we can simply mean that there are enforceable requirements upon existing generations that will prevent harm to future generations.

A universal right to welfare

Once it is recognized that we can meaningfully speak of distant peoples and future generations as having rights against us and we corresponding obligations to them, there is no reason not to extend the argument for a right to welfare grounded on libertarian premises that I have defended in this essay to distant peoples

and future generations. This is because, for libertarians, fundamental rights are universal rights, that is, rights possessed by all
people, not just those who live in certain places or at certain
times. Of course, to claim that rights are universal does not mean
that they are universally recognized. Rather, to claim that rights
are universal, despite their spotty recognition, implies only that
they ought to be recognized because people at all times and
places have or could have had good reasons to recognize these
rights, not that they actually did or do so.[41] Nor need universal
rights be unconditional. This is particularly true in the case of the
right to welfare, which, I have argued, is conditional upon people
doing all that they legitimately can to provide for themselves.
In addition, this right is conditional upon there being sufficient
resources available so that everyone's welfare needs can be

41 Yet even though libertarians have claimed that the rights they defend are
universal rights in the manner I have just explained, it may be that they are
simply mistaken in this regard. Even when universal rights are stripped of
any claim to being universally recognized or unconditional, still it might be
argued that there are no such rights, that is, that there are no rights that all
people ought to recognize. But how does one argue for such a view? One
cannot argue from the failure of people to recognize such rights because we
have already said that such recognition is not necessary. Nor can one argue
that not everyone ought to recognize such rights because some lack the
capacity to do so. This is because "ought" implies "can" here, so that the
obligation to recognize certain rights only applies to those who actually have
or have had at some point the capacity to do so. Thus, the existence of
universal rights is not ruled out by the existence of individuals who have
never had the capacity to recognize such rights. It is only ruled out by the
existence of individuals who can recognize these rights but for whom it is
correct to say that it is at least permissible, all things considered, not to do so.
But we have just seen that even a minimal libertarian moral ideal supports a
universal right to welfare. And as I will argue later in this essay when
"ought" is understood both morally and self-interestedly, a nonquestion-
begging conception to rationality favors morality over self-interest when
they conflict. So for those capable of recognizing universal rights, it simply
is not possible to argue that they, all things considered, ought not to do so.
   It is also worth noting that the question of whether there are interpersonal
conflicts of interests, and, if so, how best to resolve them that seems to arise
in pre-Enlightenment philosophy parallels the more modern question of
whether there are interpersonal conflicts of liberty, and, if so, how best to
resolve them.

met.[42] So where people do not do all that they can to provide for themselves or where there are not sufficient resources available, people do not normally have a right to welfare. Given the universal and conditional character of this libertarian right to welfare, what then are the implications of this right for distant peoples and future generations?

Extending the right to welfare

At present, worldwide food production is sufficient to provide everyone in the world with at least 2,720 kilocalories per person per day.[43] To meet the nutritional and other basic needs of each and every person living today, however, would require a significant redistribution of goods and resources. To finance such redistribution, Thomas Pogge has proposed a 1 per cent tax on aggregate global income, netting $312 billion annually.[44] Peter Singer, as an alternative, has proposed a graduated tax on the incomes of the top 10 per cent of US families, netting $404 billion annually with an equal sum coming from the family incomes of people living in other industrialized countries.[45] Both Pogge and Singer are confident that their proposals would go a long way toward meeting basic human needs worldwide. In fact, Singer remarks that before coming up with his recent proposal, he never "fully understood how easy it would be for the world's rich to eliminate or virtually eliminate, global poverty."[46]

Yet while Pogge's and Singer's proposals would doubtless do much to secure a right to welfare for existing people, even in the current economic downturn, unfortunately they do not speak very well to the needs of future generations. How then do we

---

42 Actually, I only argued earlier that the poor must take advantage of whatever opportunities are available to them to engage in mutually beneficial work, but it is this broader claim that I am making here that is required.

43 www.worldhunger.org/articles/Learn/world%20hunger%20facts%202002

44 Thomas Pogge, *World Poverty and Human Rights* (Cambridge: Polity, 2002), pp. 204ff.

45 Peter Singer, "What Should a Billionaire Give – and What Should You?" *New York Times* (December 17, 2006).

46 *Ibid.*

best insure that future generations are not deprived of the goods and resources that they will need to meet their basic needs? In the USA, currently more than 1 million acres of arable land are lost from cultivation each year due to urbanization, multiplying transport networks, and industrial expansion.[47] In addition, another 2 million acres of farmland are lost each year due to erosion, salinization, and water logging.[48] The state of Iowa alone has lost one-half of its fertile topsoil from farming in the last hundred years. That loss is about thirty times faster than what is sustainable.[49] According to one estimate, only 0.6 of an acre of arable land per person will be available in the USA in 2050, whereas more than 1.2 acres per person are needed to provide a diverse diet (currently 1.6 acres of arable land are available).[50] Similar, or even more threatening, estimates of the loss of arable land have been made for other regions of the world.[51] How then are we going to preserve farmland and other food-related natural resources so that future generations are not deprived of what they require to meet their basic needs?

And what about other resources as well? It has been estimated that presently a North American uses seventy-five times more resources than a resident of India. This means that in terms of resource consumption the North American continent's population is the equivalent of 22.5 billion Indians.[52] So unless we assume that basic resources such as arable land, iron, coal, and oil are in unlimited supply, this unequal consumption will have to be radically altered if the basic needs of future generations are

---

47 www.balance.org/articles/factsheet2001.html
48 *Ibid.*
49 *Ibid.*
50 *Ibid.*
51 Lester Brown, *Plan B 2.0* (New York: W. W. Norton & Co., 2006), pp. 84–91. See also Lester Brown, *Outgrowing the Earth* (New York: W. W. Norton & Co., 2004), esp. ch. 5.
52 Linda Starke, ed., *State of the World 2004* (New York: W. W. Norton & Co., 2004), p. 9. For a lower comparative consumption comparison that still supports the same conclusion, see Jared Diamond, "What's Your Consumption Factor?" *International Herald Tribune*, January 3, 2008, p. 6.

to be met.[53] I submit, therefore, that recognizing a universal right to welfare applicable both to existing and future people requires us to use up no more resources than are necessary for meeting our own basic needs, thus securing for ourselves a decent life but no more.[54] For us to use up more resources than this, we would be guilty of depriving at least some future generations of the resources they would require to meet their own basic needs, thereby violating their libertarian-based right to welfare.[55] Obviously, this would impose a significant sacrifice on existing generations, particularly those in the developed world; clearly a far greater sacrifice than Pogge and Singer maintain is required for meeting the basic needs of existing generations. Nevertheless, these demands do follow from a libertarian-based right to welfare.[56] In effect, recognizing a right to welfare,

---

53 See Starke, *State of the World 2004*. There is no way that the resource consumption of the USA can be matched by developing and underdeveloped countries, and even if it could be matched, doing so would clearly lead to ecological disaster. See *Planet Under Stress*, ed. Constance Mungall and Digby McLaren (Oxford: Oxford University Press, 1990), and Frances Lappe and Joseph Collins, *World Hunger: Twelve Myths* (New York: Grove Press, 1986).

54 To say that future generations have rights against existing generations, we can simply mean that there are enforceable requirements against existing generations that would benefit or prevent harm to future generations.

55 Of course, there is always the problem of others not doing their fair share. Nevertheless, as long as your sacrifice would avoid some basic harm to others, either now or in the future, it would still seem reasonable to claim that you would remain under an obligation to make that sacrifice, regardless of what others are doing.

56 It could be argued that even if we continue our extravagant consumption of nonrenewable resources, future generations will be able to make up for the loss with some kind of a technological fix. We can even imagine that future generations will be able to make everything they need out of, say, sand and water. While surely this is possible, it would not be reasonable for us to risk the basic welfare of future generations on just such a possibility, anymore than it would be reasonable for persons starting out in the lowest paying jobs in the business world to start wildly borrowing and spending on themselves and their families, relying just on the possibility that in 15–20 years their incomes will rise astronomically so that they then could easily pay off the large debts they are now amassing. There are also many examples of human

applicable to all existing and future people, leads to an equal utilization of resources over place and time.[57]

Now it might be objected that if we fail to respect this welfare requirement for future generations, we would still not really be harming those future generations whom we would deprive of the resources they require for meeting their basic needs. This is because if we acted so as to appropriately reduce our consumption, those same future generations whom we would supposedly harm by our present course of action will not even exist.[58] This is because the changes we would make in our lives in order to live in a resource-conserving manner would so alter our social relations, now and in the future, that the membership of future generations would be radically altered as well. Yet to hold that we only harm those who would still exist if we acted appropriately is too strong a restriction on harming.

Consider an owner of an industrial plant arguing that she really did not harm your daughter who is suffering from leukemia due to the contaminants that leaked into the area surrounding the plant because only by operating the plant so that it leaked these contaminants was it economically feasible in this particular place and time. Hence, the plant would not have opened up, nor would you have moved nearby to work, nor would this daughter of yours even have been born, without its operating in this

---

civilizations that failed to find an appropriate technological fix. See, for example, Jared Diamond, *Collapse* (New York: Penguin, 2005), and Ronald Wright, *A Short History of Progress* (New York: Carroll & Graf, 2004).

57 What makes this an equal utilization of resources over place and time is that the utilization is limited to fulfilling people's basic needs. Of course, once basic needs are met among existing generations, renewable resources may be used for meeting nonbasic needs in ways that do not jeopardize the meeting of the basic needs of future generations. In addition, existing generations can also justifiably meet their nonbasic needs if this is a byproduct of efficiently meeting just their basic needs. Naturally, this holds equally for each subsequent generation as well.

58 Derek Parfit, *Persons and Reasons* (Oxford: Clarendon Press, 1984).

way.[59] In brief, the owner of the plant contends that your daughter was not really harmed at all because, if there had been no contamination, she would not even have been born. Assuming, however, that we reject the plant owner's counterfactual requirement for harming in favor of a direct causal one (the operation of the plant caused your daughter's leukemia), as we should, then we have to recognize that we too can be held responsible for harming future generations if, by the way we live our lives, we cause the harm from which they will suffer.

Now it might be further objected that if we did limit ourselves to simply meeting our basic needs – a decent life, but no more – we would still be harming future generations at some more distant point of time, leaving those generations without the resources required for meeting their basic needs. While our present non-conserving way of living would begin to harm future generations in, let us say, 200 years, our conserving way of living, should we adopt it, and should it be continued by subsequent generations, would, let us assume, lead to that same result in 2,000 years. So, either way, we would be harming future generations.

There is a difference, however. While both courses of action would ultimately harm future generations, if we do limit ourselves to simply meeting our basic needs, a decent life, but no more, and other generations do the same, then many generations of future people would benefit from this course of action that would not benefit from our alternative, nonconserving course of action. Even more importantly, for us to sacrifice further for the sake of future generations would require us to give up meeting our own basic needs, and this normally we cannot be morally required to do, as the "ought" implies "can" principle

---

59 A similar example was used by James Woodward in "The Non-Identity Problem," *Ethics* 96 (1986), pp. 804–31. Woodward also provides the example of Viktor Frankl, who suggests that his imprisonment in a Nazi concentration camp enabled him to develop "certain resources of character, insights into the human condition and capacities for appreciation" that he would not otherwise have had. At the same time, we clearly want to say that the Nazis unjustifiably violated Frankl's rights by so imprisoning him. Woodward, *ibid.*, p. 809. See also Norman Daniels, "Intergenerational Justice," *Stanford Encyclopedia* (2003).

makes clear. We can be required to give up the satisfaction of our nonbasic needs so that others can meet their basic needs, but, normally, without our consent, we cannot be required to sacrifice the satisfaction of our own basic needs so that others can meet their basic needs.[60] So while future generations may still be harmed in the distant future as a result of our behavior, no one can justifiably blame us, or take action against us, for using no more resources than we require for meeting our basic needs.

Of course, someone could ask: how do you distinguish basic from nonbasic needs? A person raising this question may not realize how widespread the use of this distinction is. While the distinction is surely important for global ethics, as my use of it attests, it is also used widely in moral, political, and environmental philosophy; it would really be impossible to do much philosophy in these areas, especially at the practical level, without a distinction between basic and nonbasic needs.

Another way that I would respond to the question is by pointing out that the fact that not every need can be clearly classified as either basic or nonbasic, as similarly holds for a whole range of dichotomous concepts like moral/immoral, legal/illegal, living/nonliving, human/nonhuman, should not immobilize us from acting at least with respect to clear cases. This puts our use of the distinction in a still broader context suggesting that if we cannot use the basic/nonbasic distinction in moral, political, and environmental philosophy, the widespread use of other dichotomous concepts is likewise threatened. It also suggests how our inability to clearly classify every conceivable need as basic or nonbasic should not keep us from using such a distinction at least with respect to clear cases.

There is also a further point to be made here. If we begin to respond to clear cases, for example stop aggressing against the clear basic needs of some humans for the sake of clear luxury needs of others, we will be in an even better position to know

---

60 Again, to appeal here to simply libertarian premises, giving up or sacrificing the satisfaction of basic or nonbasic needs can be taken to imply merely noninterference for the sake of the satisfaction of such needs.

what to do in the less clear cases. This is because sincerely attempting to live out one's practical moral commitments helps one to interpret them better, just as failing to live them out makes interpreting them all the more difficult. Consequently, I think we have every reason to act on the moral requirements that I have defended here, at least with respect to clear cases.

2   Other attempts to show that libertarians should accept welfare or equality

There have many other attempts to show that libertarians should accept a right to welfare or substantial equality. A few have even tried to show that libertarians should endorse welfare or substantial equality because their own libertarian view is impossible (Murphy and Nagel), self-contradictory (Okin), even absurd (Dworkin), but most have simply tried to show, as I have, that the libertarian ideal, properly interpreted, leads to welfare or equality. Let me now examine a number of these attempts.

Liam Murphy/Thomas Nagel and Henry Shue

In *The Myth of Ownership*, Liam Murphy and Thomas Nagel argue against libertarianism, or more specifically against a view they call "everyday libertarianism."[61] Murphy and Nagel not only think this libertarian view is mistaken; they think it is conceptually mistaken. They claim that there is no market without government and no government without taxes, and that the type of market there is depends on laws and policy decisions that governments must make. It follows that it is logically impossible for people to have any kind of entitlement to their pretax income. According to Murphy and Nagel, all people are entitled to is what they would be left with after taxes under a system that is supported by legitimate taxation. This shows, they claim, that we cannot evaluate the legitimacy of taxes by reference to pretax income. The logical order of priority between taxes and property

---

61 Liam Murphy and Thomas Nagel, *The Myth of Ownership* (New York: Oxford University Press, 2002).

rights, they say, is the reverse of that assumed by (everyday) libertarianism. This view about (everyday) libertarianism also accounts for the title of Murphy and Nagel's book: *The Myth of Ownership*. What is a myth, according to Murphy and Nagel – indeed, a conceptual impossibility – is the libertarian idea of pretax ownership.

However, the mistake that I have argued libertarians are making is not the sort of conceptual mistake that Murphy and Nagel have in mind here. This is because I believe that it is possible for us to conceive of persons with morally justified property rights in the absence of a governmental-supporting tax system. Indeed, isn't that what John Locke was asking us to envision in his *Second Treatise of Government* when he says of a person in the state of nature: "He that is nourished by the acorns he picked up under an oak or the apples he gathered from the trees in the woods has certainly appropriated them . . . and so they became his private right."[62] Surely, Locke's conception of persons with property rights in a state of nature is not a conceptual impossibility. So Murphy and Nagel's claim that we cannot even conceive of property rights absent a government and a tax system must be mistaken.

Yet maybe Locke's example is not really what Murphy and Nagel had in mind. Although they make a broader claim, they seem to be focused on the narrower claim of maintaining the logical impossibility of property rights arising from market transactions that are not supported by some kind of a governmental-enforced tax system. Locke's example of the acquisition of property rights I cited did not involve any market transactions. So examples of that sort do not count against the narrower claim that Murphy and Nagel may be intending to make.

Still, we can easily imagine a case that does count against even the narrower claim. Just imagine that there are two individuals in the state of nature, one collecting acorns, the other collecting apples, and that they later agree to exchange acorns and apples

---

62 John Locke, *Two Treatises of Government* (New York: Cambridge University Press, 1960), II, 5, 28.

between themselves. Wouldn't their market exchange give rise to moral property rights, absent any governmental-enforced tax system? It would seem that it would.

So rather than try to find a conceptual impossibility in the idea of pretax property rights either broadly or narrowly construed, under all conceivable conditions, wouldn't it be preferable to maintain its impossibility under the more typical conditions where property rights tend to arise. Surely libertarians would have to admit that property rights usually arise from market transactions that depend on some kind of a governmental-enforced tax system. In *Basic Rights*, Henry Shue similarly argued that negative rights typically require positive rights, that is, that they require a governmental-enforcement system supported by taxation which secures negative rights with protective positive rights.[63]

Nevertheless, libertarians can grant that negative rights require positive rights under certain conditions and still argue that what is crucial is not this requirement but rather which rights are basic. And the rights that are basic for libertarians are negative rights, that is, rights of noninterference. Moreover, at least since Robert Nozick's *Anarchy, State, and Utopia*, libertarians have had an account of how positive rights of protection could legitimately arise to secure property rights or rights of noninterference through the permissible evolution of mutual protection agencies into a minimal state. Moreover, these rights of noninterference, libertarians claim, do not require a right to welfare, even if they do typically require some positive rights of protection for property rights.

So interpreted, libertarianism still remains a formidable challenge to all tax schemes that seek to secure a right to welfare. While libertarians may grant the need for a governmental-enforced tax system to support the market and provide for general security, they would certainly reject the use of taxes to support a right to welfare. Since Murphy and Nagel favor tax

---

63 See Henry Shue, *Basic Rights*, 1st edn (Princeton: Princeton University Press, 1980).

schemes that support just such a right to welfare, they need an argument to overcome the libertarian view in this regard. Their argument that property rights cannot even be conceived without positive rights of protection is refuted by Locke himself, and the reformulated argument that I provided for them – that typically negative property rights entail, or require for their existence, some governmental-enforcement system of positive rights – works, but it does not, by itself, defeat the libertarian argument against welfare rights.

Fortunately, this weakness of Murphy and Nagel's (reformulated) argument against libertarianism – its inability to show that the libertarian's own ideal of liberty actually requires a right to welfare – is remedied by the main argument of my essay.[64] What my argument shows is that the libertarian's own ideal of negative liberty, specifically the libertarian's own conception of negative rights, requires a right to welfare under certain conditions. Notice I am not saying that it would require a right to welfare under all conditions. For example, it does not require a right to welfare for Locke's case where a person is all alone, gathering acorns in a forest. It could emerge, however, even where there are market transactions without a governmental-enforcement system, provided someone is in need and others have more than enough meet their basic needs.

In addition, it is important to note here that the right to welfare that is entailed by a person's rights of noninterference is not in itself a positive right to welfare. So, in this sense, I am agreeing with libertarians. The basic negative rights of the libertarian view do not entail a positive right to welfare. What they do entail under certain conditions, I claim, is a negative right to welfare, a right not to be interfered with in taking from the rich what they require to meet their basic needs. Then I further argued that this negative right to welfare can, and usually will,

---

64 Judging from the e-mail responses of the authors, it would seem that the authors would allow that the better way to critique libertarianism, as the view is usually conceived, is to object to its way of weighing competing liberties, as I have done in this essay.

give rise to a positive right to welfare. This is because libertarians will come to see that virtually any use of their surplus possessions is likely to violate the negative welfare rights of the poor by preventing the poor from rightfully appropriating (some part of) their surplus goods and resources. So in order to ensure that they will not be engaging in such wrongful actions, it will be incumbent on them to set up institutions guaranteeing adequate positive welfare rights for the poor. Only then will they be able to use legitimately any remaining surplus possessions to meet their own nonbasic needs. Furthermore, in the absence of adequate positive welfare rights, the poor, either acting by themselves or through their allies or agents, would have some discretion in determining when and how to exercise their negative welfare rights. In order not to be subject to that discretion, libertarians will tend to favor the only morally legitimate way of preventing the exercise of such rights: they will set up institutions guaranteeing adequate positive welfare rights that will then take precedence over the exercise of negative welfare rights. For these reasons, I claim that recognizing the negative welfare rights of the poor will ultimately lead libertarians to endorse the same sort of welfare institutions favored by welfare liberals.

John Harris

Another attempt to get libertarians to acknowledge welfare rights seeks to deny the moral relevance of the commission/omission distinction on which libertarians standardly rely to support their commitment to an ideal of negative liberty over ideals of positive liberty. According to this view, any attempt to invest such a distinction with moral significance is doomed to failure because a similar causality underlies both types of actions.[65] In particular, this view holds that we are just as much a cause of a person's death when we kill as when we let die. From this, John Harris claims, it follows that "in whatever sense we are morally responsible for our positive actions, in the same

65 John Harris, *Violence and Responsibility* (Boston: Routledge & Kegan Paul, 1980), p. 58.

sense we are morally responsible for our negative actions."[66] Hence, according to this view, there is little basis for the libertarian's prohibition of acts of commission but not of acts of omission when they both have the same consequences.

Yet while this view is correct in pointing out that there is a causal basis for moral responsibility in cases of acts of omission, the view is mistaken in identifying the standard causal role played by acts of omission with that played by acts of commission in the production of consequences for which people are morally responsible. For acts of omission causally contribute to the production of such consequences by failing to prevent a causal condition sufficient to produce those consequences, as in failing to save a person from drowning, while acts of commission causally contribute to the production of such consequences by creating a causal condition sufficient to produce those consequences, as in poisoning a person's food.[67] Thus to take only the fact that both acts of omission and acts of commission contribute to such consequences to be morally relevant and to ignore the different ways in which both types of acts causally contribute to such consequences is to beg the question against libertarians who want to morally distinguish between these two types of acts. Consequently, only by proceeding as I have, and basing a justification of welfare rights on an interpretation of constraints of liberty (and violations of rights) that involves acts of commission for which people are morally responsible, can we avoid begging the question against the libertarian view.

---

66 John Harris, "The Marxist Conception of Violence," *Philosophy and Public Affairs* 3 (1974), p. 211.

67 Of course, sometimes a person who performs an act of omission which contributes to the production of consequences for which the person is responsible may do so as part of a larger act of commission which is a sufficient causal condition for the production of those consequences. And sometimes a person who performs an act of commission which contributes to the production of consequences for which the person is responsible does so as part of a larger act of omission which simply fails to prevent those consequences. On this point, see O. H. Green, "Killing and Letting Die," *American Philosophical Quarterly* 20 (1980), pp. 195–204; Raziel Abelson, "To Do or Let Happen," *American Philosophical Quarterly* 22 (1982), pp. 219–27.

Allen Buchanan

Still another attempt to derive welfare rights from a libertarian foundation begins with the libertarian's assessment of various civil and political rights, like the rights of freedom of speech, press, assembly, due process, and equality before the law. It is then argued that because the effective exercise of these rights requires adequate social and economic resources, libertarians should be committed to guaranteeing such resources to each and every person. Allen Buchanan, for example, has defended just such a provision of resources on grounds of fairness.[68] Yet given the intimate connection between ideals of fairness and welfare rights, such a defense would appear to beg the question against the libertarian view.[69] Thus a better approach would be to argue that libertarians should be committed to the provision of resources necessary to secure an effective exercise of at least those civil and political rights, like due process and equality before the law, which relate to the imposition of significant burdens and penalties. For surely it would not be reasonable to ask people to accept the imposition of significant burdens and penalties unless they have been guaranteed an effective exercise of the rights of due process and equality before the law. Obviously this is to appeal to the "ought" implies "can" principle.

This argument, however, would not directly support the provision of resources to secure the effective exercise of other civil and political rights, such as the rights of freedom of speech, press, and assembly. This is because the exercise of these rights relates not so much to the imposition of burdens and penalties in society

68 Allen Buchanan, "Deriving Welfare Rights from Libertarian Rights," in *Income Support*, ed. Peter Brown *et al.* (Totowa, NJ: Rowman and Littlefield, 1981), pp. 233–46.

69 Of course, libertarians do need to provide some account of an ideal of fairness, but a well-grounded critique of libertarianism should not begin with such an ideal whose interpretation is widely contested. I made this mistake in "Neo-Libertarianism," *American Philosophical Quarterly* 18 (1978), pp. 115–21, but corrected it soon after. See the expanded version in *Justice: Alternative Political Perspectives*, ed. James P. Sterba (Belmont: Wadsworth Publishing Co., 1979), esp. pp. 185–6.

as to the distribution of benefits. Nevertheless, by directly focus-
ing on conflicts of negative liberty (noninterferences), as I have
done in this essay, and using the "ought" implies "can" principle
to provide a reasonable resolution of those conflicts, one that
ultimately leads to substantial equality, an effective exercise of
these other civil and political rights can thereby be secured.

Jeremy Waldron

Libertarians have long objected to the welfare state on the
grounds that it deadens people's charitable desires by coercing
them to help the poor. Jeremy Waldron tries to counter this
objection by showing that the provision of welfare is far less
coercive than it is usually thought.[70]

Waldron begins with the story of the Good Samaritan. In that
story, the Samaritan clearly put himself out to help a person who
has been set upon by thieves. In that case, there is no coercive
provision of welfare. By contrast, if people are forced by the state
to aid people in need then the provision of aid or welfare would
clearly be coercive. Yet Waldron wants us to focus on a different
sort of case.

Imagine a person caught in a blizzard in the mountains,
wandering about, poorly clothed, hungry, and in danger of per-
ishing from exposure to the elements. Imagine that this person
happens upon a log cabin with a light burning and the door
slightly ajar. She pushes into the cabin, warms herself by the
fire, and then serves herself from a large pot of soup that is
simmering on the stove. Just then the owner of the cabin, who
happens to be the Good Samaritan, comes in, sees what the
woman is doing – helping herself to his property – and does
nothing. In this case, Waldron claims, we also have the provision
of welfare without coercion.

Now imagine a similar case where our wanderer is not so
fortunate. She happens upon a similar cabin, enters, warms
herself, and begins eating some soup when a priest and a Levite,

70 Jeremy Waldron, *Liberal Rights* (Cambridge: Cambridge University Press,
    1987), ch. 10.

who are the owners of the cabin, burst into the room and begin to throw the wanderer out. Just then, imagine that the Good Samaritan appears, brandishing a tax bill equivalent to full accommodations for one night and threatening severe consequences for the priest and Levite if the bill is not paid immediately and in kind by providing food and shelter to the wanderer.[71] In this case, Waldron would allow that coercion is being used to secure the provision of welfare, but he would point out that here it is not an initial act of coercion but rather one that responds to the priest and the Levite who acted coercively first. What this shows, Waldron claims, is that as long as people in need are capable of appropriating the possessions of others, the provision of welfare to them can be accomplished either without any coercion at all, or with just second acts of coercion, done in response to initial acts of coercion by the property owners themselves.

Of course, although the wanderer is not coercing the Good Samaritan in the first cabin story, she is depriving him of a liberty – at least the liberty not to be interfered with respect to his cabin and pot of soup. And this restriction of liberty must be justified. Moreover, when the needy are incapable of appropriating the property of others themselves, others would have to act on their behalf to provide them with welfare. Waldron is particularly concerned about such cases because he thinks that they would require some people to make "unreciprocated sacrifices for the good of others" that are ruled out by a contractual view grounded in "reasonable cooperation."[72] At the same time, Waldron endorses a principle of need that maintains that "nobody should be permitted ever to use force to prevent another man from satisfying his very basic needs in circumstances where there seems to be no other way of satisfying them."[73] Yet, the

---

71 Waldron does not actually develop his story in this way, but I do not think he would reject my creative license since it is just another way of making the point that he wants to make.
72 Waldron, *Liberal Rights*, p. 247.
73 *Ibid.*, pp. 240–1.

forbearances required by this principle of need will sometimes also be "unreciprocated sacrifices for the good of others" ruled out by the form of contractarianism that Waldron accepts. So in the end, Waldron will just have to choose between his form of contractarianism with its mutual benefit requirement and his principle of need.[74]

Waldon also thinks that his argument for a provision of welfare says nothing about the transfer of resources between societies for meeting people's basic needs. "The victims of famine can hardly come here [the USA] and help themselves to our grain."[75] Yet prohibiting them from doing so would surely be in violation of Waldon's principle of need. Here Waldon favors his contractarian approach over his principle of need without providing an argument for doing so. So while Waldon does clearly succeed in showing that the provision of welfare is far less coercive than is usually thought, the grounds he actually provides for a right to welfare is both very limited within a society and absent beyond it. And, of course, an argument for substantial equality is nowhere to be found in his view.

Gillian Brock

In a number of articles, Gillian Brock has argued that libertarian property rights are constrained by a requirement that there always be enough left over for others so that they can meet their basic needs.[76] In this way, Brock also attempts to derive the equivalent of a right to welfare from libertarian premises. However, Brock's argument is directed primarily at Robert Nozick's defense of libertarianism. In fact, it is Nozick's use of a Lockean

---

74 In the next section of this essay, in discussing Jan Narveson's work, I put forward what I take to be a nonquestion-begging argument for rejecting this form of contractarianism.

75 Waldon, *Liberal Rights*, p. 248.

76 Gillian Brock, "Is Redistribution to Help the Needy Unjust?" *Analysis* 55 (1995), pp. 50–60; *eadem*, "Justice and Needs," *Dialogue* 35 (1996), pp. 81–6; *eadem*, "Morally Important Needs," *Philosophia* 26 (1998), pp. 165–7; *eadem*, "Just Deserts and Needs," *The Southern Journal of Philosophy* 37 (1999), pp. 165–88.

proviso in his interpretation of libertarianism that enables Brook to derive her welfare constraint on property rights. According to Nozick, the Lockean proviso rules out any appropriation that makes someone worse off "by no longer being able to use freely (without appropriation) what he previously could."[77] Nozick goes on to provide the following examples of where the proviso constrains property rights:

> Thus, a person may not appropriate the only water hold in a desert and charge what he will. Nor may he charge what he will if he possesses one, and unfortunately it happens that all the water holes in the desert dry up, except for his. This unfortunate circumstance, admittedly no fault of his, brings into operation the Lockean proviso and limits his property rights. Similarly, an owner's property right to the only island in an area does not allow him to order a castaway from a shipwreck off his island as a trespasser, for this would violate the Lockean proviso.[78]

In each of these cases, Brock points out that Nozick is allowing that it is the needs of others that places a welfare constraint on the rights of property owners, especially when other people are in need through no fault of their own. Brock further argues against Nozick's view that these cases do not generalize and that "the free operation of the market system will not run afoul of the Lockean Proviso."[79] Rather, she contends that Nozick "grossly underestimates the number and range of situations in which the free operation of a market system would actually run afoul of the Lockean proviso" by failing to allow others to meet their basic needs.[80]

It is interesting to note that the way that Nozick argues for his claim that the operation of the free market would not run afoul of his Lockean proviso is by pointing to the way that, on this view, a protection agency can legitimately become dominant

77 Nozick, *Anarchy, State, and Utopia*, p. 176.
78 *Ibid.*, p. 180.
79 *Ibid.*, p. 182.
80 Brock, "Is Redistribution to Help the Needy Unjust?" p. 54.

over everyone over whom it exercises its power.[81] However, the way this happens on Nozick's account is that the agency provides "free" protection services to those independents over whom it exercises its power without their consent. The analogy with respect to the legitimate dominance of the market would be that market activities are so constrained so that they secure the satisfaction of their basic needs, other things being equal.

Now I believe that the success of Brock's need-based argument against Nozick's libertarian view parallels the success of the use of my "ought" implies "can" principle against the libertarianism. However, I also believe that neither of these arguments alone is successful against Jan Narveson's Hobbesian interpretation of libertarianism. This is because in the same conflict cases where Nozick allowed that moral considerations required a constraint on property rights, Narveson will contend that no such constraint is required because it is not in the self-interest of the advantaged property owners to make such a concession. So, in order to defeat Narveson's view here, we will need a further argument for the imposition of moral constraints. In order words, we will need a rationality to morality argument that I will develop later against Narveson's version of libertarianism.

Richard Norman and Henry Shue

In his attempt to reconcile freedom and equality, Richard Norman regards freedom as the ability to make choices. He argues that this ability is closely connected with certain negative and positive conditions that facilitate our ability to make choices. The negative conditions are absence of constraints or interference – noninterference; the positive conditions are various political, social, and economic goods. If we are interested in promoting freedom in a society, Norman argues, we must then be concerned with securing both the negative and positive conditions that facilitate that freedom.[82] Another way of arguing for

---

81 Nozick, *Anarchy, State, and Utopia*, p. 182.
82 For a similar view, see Carol Gould, "Freedom and Women," *Journal of Social Philosophy* 15, 3 (1984), pp. 20–34, and Charles Taylor, "What is Wrong with

a similar conclusion is to point out that negative liberty or non-interference is not just sought for its own sake, but almost always as a means for attaining other goods. So why shouldn't the state not be concerned about the distribution of other goods too along with negative liberty?[83] Likewise, Henry Shue has argued that people can only begin to enjoy the negative liberties they have when their subsistence needs have been met. Shue claims that someone might even be willing to trade away her negative right (liberty) not to be tortured if she could not otherwise meet her subsistence needs.[84] So why then, Shue asks, should not the state be concerned with meeting at least the subsistence needs of its citizens along with securing for them rights of noninterference?

One way that libertarians have responded to this line of argument is by granting its premises but then denying its conclusion. They allow that there are social goods people would like to have in addition to negative liberties. The problem is the cost of providing social goods, other than negative liberties, to all those who would want them. While almost everyone would surely want such social goods for themselves, it does not follow that they all are willing to do what is necessary to secure those social goods for others who want them too. It is just here that libertarians claim that negative liberties are different from other social goods in that it is relatively easy to provide them for everyone. Securing negative liberties for everyone just requires, libertarians claim, that people not do certain things; it does not require that people actually do things for others, as is the case for the provision of other social goods. Moreover, libertarians claim that everyone can be provided with equal negative liberties without interfering with the liberty of anyone, whereas providing everyone with other social goods necessitates just such interference.

Negative Liberty," in *The Idea of Freedom*, ed. Alan Ryan (Oxford: Oxford University Press, 1979), pp. 175–93.

83 An argument of this sort is found in Elizabeth S. Anderson, "What is the Point of Equality?" *Ethics* 109 (1999), p. 315.

84 Shue, *Basic Rights*, pp. 184ff.

Opponents of libertarians, like Norman and Shue, similarly respond to this argument by granting its crucial premise – that securing negative liberties for everyone is easier and less costly to achieve than securing other social goods – but then deny its implicit conclusion – that we should just restrict ourselves to securing negative liberties for everyone. They just contend that the provision of these other social goods is worth the extra effort and cost it requires.

But there is a still better way to counter libertarians here – one that concedes less than the above response does. Instead of conceding that securing negative liberties for everyone is easier and less costly to achieve than securing other social goods, it can be argued that the provision of equal liberties to everyone involves the same kind of costs, including interferences, as does the provision of other social goods. To provide everyone with a bundle of certain negative liberties is to deny them other possible negative liberties that conflict with the liberties in that bundle. For example, if everyone has the negative liberty, when they are rich, not to be interfered with in using their surplus for luxury purposes, then they do not have the liberty, when they are poor, not to be interfered with in taking from the rich what they require to meet their basic needs. The provision of one of these liberties to everyone conflicts with the provision of the other. Further, we can show that for many social goods that appear not to be provided under the libertarian ideal, we can find a negative liberty the presence of which would be virtually equivalent to those social goods. For example, the social good of providing a basic needs minimum can be seen as nearly equivalent to the negative right not to be interfered with in taking from the surplus of the rich what is required for meeting one's basic needs.[85] This means that the choice between securing a certain bundle of negative liberties and securing other social goods can be approximately reformulated as simply the choice over which particular

---

85 I say nearly equivalent here because a negative right can never be truly equivalent to a positive right. But for a discussion of how the gap can be overcome in practice, see pp. 26–7.

negative liberties should be secured. So we do not have to concede that this debate with libertarians is over whether we should provide just negative liberties or whether we should provide other social goods as well. Rather, the whole debate can be recast as a debate over which negative liberties we should provide. The clear advantage of this approach is that it has the libertarian's full attention from start to finish, while, at the same time, as I argue in this essay, it still leads to substantial equality.

Susan Okin

Another argument against libertarianism, raised by Susan Okin, purports to show that the view leads to a contradiction.[86] Okin's argument is directed specifically at Robert Nozick's version of libertarianism, but Okin believes that it can be extended to other forms of libertarianism as well. According to Okin, the problem with Nozick's view stems from his failure to take women and their experience adequately into account. In particular, Okin claims, Nozick failed to take the facts of human reproduction adequately into account. Her argument begins with a basic premise of Nozick's libertarianism – self-ownership:

(1) I own myself.

She then adds a premise of human reproduction:

(2) My mother made me.

Here Okin assumes for the sake of argument that mothers have acquired freely and without obligation the male sperm needed for reproduction. She then draws on two other basic premises of Nozick's libertarian view:

(3) Making confers ownership, and
(4) No one has a right to something whose realization requires certain uses of things and activities that other people [already] have rights and entitlements over.[87]

---

86 Susan Okin, *Justice, Gender and the Family* (New York: Basic Books, 1989), ch. 4.
87 Nozick, *Anarchy, State, and Utopia*, p. 238.

From (2), (3), and (4), it then follows that:

(5) If I am (already) my mother's property, I cannot claim a conflicting right to own myself.

From which it then follows that:

(6) It is not the case that I own myself.

And that contradicts (1).

Philosophers trying to save Nozick's view from contradiction have interpreted (1) as an instantiation of a general liberty principle like:

Every person has a non-overridable right to such liberties as do not interfere with those of others.[88]

They then claim that (L) limits what one can own, even of those things one has clearly made. So interpreted, (L) would limit what anyone can own from reproductive labor, at least when what one makes is, or becomes, a person.

The difficulty with trying to save Nozick's view in this way is that it is not clear that Nozick is committed to a general liberty principle that limits what we can own through our labor. For example, Nozick does not think that a right to life, even understood negatively as a right of noninterference with one's life, would restrict what one can own through one's labor. Rather, he thinks that we need a theory of how property comes into existence first "before one can apply any supposed right to life."[89] Moreover, when Nozick talks about the relationship between liberty and property, it seems clear that for him it is the extent of justified property acquisition that determines what liberties one has.[90]

---

88 Duncan MacIntosh, "Who Owns Me: Me or My Mother?" in *Liberty, Games and Contracts*, ed. Malcolm Murray (Aldershot: Ashgate, 2007), pp. 157–71, and Jan Narveson, "Social Contract, Game Theory and Liberty," in *ibid.*, pp. 234–5.

89 Nozick, *Anarchy, State, and Utopia*, p. 179.

90 See, in particular, *ibid.*, pp. 238 and 262–3.

Of course, one could make a liberty principle like (L) basic in a libertarian theory, as Jan Narveson does, so that the theory's fundamental claim is that every person has an equal right to certain liberties or noninterferences. But then one faces yet another problem: why is it that only persons have a right to liberty or noninterference? Surely other living beings, rabbits, possums, etc., can also benefit from noninterference with their lives, especially by humans. So why should we not be committed to not interfering with them along with human persons? What we need here is a nonquestion-begging argument that only persons have such a right. Yet all that Narveson, in particular, tries to do here is justify excluding nonhuman living beings from such a right on grounds of human self-interest.[91] However, that is not good enough. What we need is a nonquestion-begging argument that determines what the relationship between human and nonhuman living beings should be.[92]

Ronald Dworkin

Against libertarianism, Ronald Dworkin has also defended an egalitarian view, specifically a view that requires equality of resources, an equal outlay of basic resources for each and every person, other things being equal.[93] He defends his view as required by a fundamental right of equal concern and respect.[94] He rejects the idea that people have a fundamental right to

---

91 Jan Narveson, "Animal Rights Revised," in *Ethics and Animals*, ed. Harlan Miller and William Williams (Clifton, NJ: Humana Press, 1983), pp. 45–59, and "On a Case for Animal Rights," *Monist* 70 (1987), pp. 31–49. He does a little more but not enough in *The Libertarian Idea* (Philadelphia: Temple University Press, 1988; republished at Peterborough, Ont.: Broadview Press, 2002), pp. 14–15.

92 For my attempt to provide such an argument, see *The Triumph of Practice Over Theory in Ethics* (New York: Oxford University Press, 2005), ch. 4.

93 Ronald Dworkin, *Sovereign Virtue: The Theory and Practice of Equality* (Cambridge, MA: Harvard University Press, 2002).

94 See Ronald Dworkin, *Taking Rights Seriously* (Cambridge, MA: Harvard University Press, 1977).

liberty, one that clashes with a fundamental right to equality, as absurd.[95] He writes,

> [I]t seems plain that there exists no general right to liberty as such. I have no political right to drive up Lexington Avenue. If the government chooses to make Lexington Avenue one-way downtown, it is sufficient justification that this would be in the general interest . . . It will not do [in this case] to say that although I have a right to drive up Lexington Ave, nevertheless the government for special reasons is justified in overriding that right. That seems silly because the government needs no special justification – but only *a* justification – for this sort of legislation. So I can have a political right to liberty, such that every act of constraint diminishes or infringes that right, only in such a weak sense of right that the so-called right to liberty is not competitive with strong rights, like the right to equality, at all. In any strong sense of right, which would be competitive with the right to equality, there exists no general right to liberty at all . . . [I]ndeed it seems to me absurd to suppose that men and women have any general right to liberty at all.[96]

If Dworkin were right about this, serious debate with libertarians would seem to be unnecessary.

But Dworkin is not right. His argument against a general right to liberty applies as well to a general right to equality. A general right to equality, like a general right to liberty, could be easily overridden in a multitude of ways by a legitimate government. Such a government can and should treat adults differently than children, senior citizens differently than nonsenior adult citizens, and advantaged citizens differently than disadvantaged citizens. And just consider all the exceptions there would be to a general right to be treated the same as everyone else on Lexington Ave. Surely, pedestrians should be treated differently than drivers and bicyclists differently than taxi drivers, and so on.

---

95 Ronald Dworkin, "We Do Not Have a Right to Liberty," in *Liberty and the Rule of Law*, ed. Robert L. Cunningham (College Station: Texas A&M Press, 1979), pp. 167–81.
96 *Ibid.*, pp. 171 and 168.

What Dworkin's argument really shows is that no one has a general right to liberty *unqualified*. But the same holds of a general right to equality. No one has a general right to equality *unqualified*. Even Dworkin's favored right to equality is not a general right to equality unqualified, but rather a qualified right to equal concern and respect. What this means is that Dworkin still needs to defend his egalitarian view against the way that libertarians have typically defended their view, not as a general right to liberty, but as a view that picks out certain liberties and defends each person's equal right to the very same or to a morally comparable bundle of liberties. In other words, Dworkin needs to show that the liberties that are picked out by his own right to equal concern and respect, assuming that right picks out a particular set of liberties, are preferable to the liberties favored by libertarians.[97] Yet, what this means is that in order for Dworkin to argue successfully against the libertarian view, he must proceed in much the same way I have in this essay. Just proclaiming the absurdity of a general right to liberty will not accomplish what needs to be done.

Some might think that Dworkin's main contention in regard to a right to liberty is that no such right can be defended "prior and independent of" a suitable normative standard.[98] But if this were Dworkin's main contention, the same would hold for a right to equality; it too could not be defended prior to and independent of a suitable normative standard. So this way of putting Dworkin's main contention would also undercut his view that there is a general right to equality – just what I had been previously claiming. In either case, the right in question would need to be grounded in a suitable normative standard.

Nor have Narveson or I failed to recognize the need to base our conclusions about what rights people have on a suitable

---

97 It is not clear that Dworkin's right to equal concern and respect does pick out a bundle of liberties that are distinct from those favored by libertarians. It is arguable that Dworkin's basic right to equality is relatively formal and can be satisfied by many different political views, including the libertarian view.

98 This objection to my discussion of Dworkin's view was raised by the anonymous author of the "clearance review" for our volume.

normative standard.[99] As we indicated in our joint introduction, the very purpose of our debate is to come up with nonquestion-begging argument – clearly a suitable normative standard – for our different interpretations of a political ideal of negative liberty, recognizing that we cannot both be successful in that quest.

To support my interpretation of a political ideal of negative liberty leading to a requirement of substantial equality, I have first appealed to the "ought" implies "can" principle, but then in order to win over those who may not accept a moral principle of this sort, I appealed directly to the standard of nonquestion-beggingness to support my conclusion. In this way, I claim to have provided a more securely grounded defense of a substantial ideal of equality and its compatibility with a defensible ideal of liberty than the one that Dworkin provides.

Left-libertarians

So-called left-libertarians also defend, to some degree, an egalitarian view, most of them maintaining that we all have an equal right to the earth's natural resources. What is also particularly attractive about their view is that they attempt to meet, at least half-way, traditional or right-libertarians who oppose them. They do this by endorsing a fundamental right of self-ownership – a right of noninterference by others with one's own person – a right that right-libertarians would surely also want to endorse. But then these left-libertarians go on to maintain that things are different with respect to the earth's natural resources, to which most of them claim we all have an equal right.[100]

This equal right to the earth's natural resources has been interpreted in different ways by different left-libertarians. It has

99 This is another issue raised by the author of the clearance review.
100 Unfortunately, the possibility that other nonhuman living beings might also have some moral claim to the earth's natural resources is never even considered by left-libertarians probably because they just assume that everything that is nonhuman on the earth is just a resource for humans. Of course, right-libertarians are no better in this regard. For a discussion of what conclusions we might reach when we go beyond such assumptions, see my *The Triumph of Practice Over Theory in Ethics*, ch. 4.

ranged minimally from endorsing Henry George's land tax on existing landowners to be distributed equally to all the citizens of each nation to maximally redistributive proposals that call for equal sharing of natural resources across nations, and, according to some proposals, across generations. Not surprisingly, the more demanding a view's requirements for the equal sharing of natural resources, the less demanding its requirements for self-ownership. For example, John Christman, Philippe Van Parijs, and Peter Vallentyne, who favor demanding requirements for the sharing of natural resources, see the requirements for self-ownership as fairly minimal and easy to satisfy.[101] Another way some left-libertarians have of rendering self-ownership compatible with high taxes for social welfare programs is by limiting what counts as "the fruits of one's labor," flowing from self-ownership. For example, Michael Otsuka offers as a paradigm of a product that is simply the fruit of one's labor and therefore not subject to taxation, the weaving of one's own hair into cloth.[102] Any dissimilar product for Otsuka would involve the use of natural resources and could thus be taxed for the general welfare. Still another way some left-libertarians have of achieving an egalitarian result is to employ a more expansive notion of a natural resource. For example, Hillel Steiner regards the germ-line genetic information in all living beings as a common natural resource to be used for the general welfare.[103]

The main problem with all of these left-libertarian views, however, is that their argumentative strategy *vis-à-vis* right-libertarianism is weaker than it should be. While left-libertarians are successful in showing that they too can embrace self-ownership under some interpretation or other, they forthrightly regard their equal natural resources requirement as an independent

---

101 John Christman, *The Myth of Property* (New York: Oxford University Press, 1994); Philippe Van Parijs, *Real Freedom for All* (Oxford: Oxford University Press, 1998); and Peter Vallentyne and Hillel Steiner, eds., *Left-Libertarianism and Its Critics* (Basingstoke: Palgrave, 2000).

102 Michael Otsuka, *Libertarianism Without Inequality* (Oxford: Oxford University Press, 2003), ch. 1.

103 Hillel Steiner, *An Essay on Rights* (Oxford: Blackwell, 1994), ch. 7.

principle, one that right-libertarians need not endorse. As Vallentyne, Steiner, and Otsuka put the point in a recent common defense of their view:

> [L]eft-libertarians do not hold that the egalitarian ownership of natural resources follows from their nonegalitarian libertarian commitments. We think it would, for example, be a mistake to hold that egalitarianism follows from universal full self-ownership, since the latter is compatible with a variety of nonegalitarian forms of ownership of natural resources as an independent principle.[104]

At best, then, their argument with right-libertarians has the following form: given that we have endorsed self-ownership, under some interpretation, a main thesis of your view, it really would be nice if you would return the favor and endorse an equality of natural resources principle, a main thesis of our view. Of course, this is not a very strong argument. Right-libertarians can easily, and consistently, refuse to endorse any such independent principle of equality of natural resources. Moreover, it seems that left-libertarians, like Vallentyne, Steiner, and Otsuka, are quite aware that they have no argument to convince right-libertarians to endorse their view. They just seem content to have carved out for themselves a view that shares some common ground with right-libertarianism, while sharing even more common ground with contemporary welfare liberals like John Rawls and Ronald Dworkin.

Yet more can be done than this to defend an egalitarian view, as I have shown in this essay. We need not introduce an egalitarian principle directly into our view in order to get egalitarian results. We can begin with the libertarian's own ideal of negative liberty, move to cases of conflict of liberty, and then argue on common ground acceptable to libertarians which liberties ultimately should be enforced. For the purposes of this discussion, the right to self-ownership and the right to natural resources are

---

104 Peter Vallentyne, Hillel Steiner, and Michael Otsuka, "Why Left-Libertarianism is Not Incoherent, Indeterminate, or Irrelevant," *Philosophy and Public Affairs* 24 (2005), pp. 201–15.

understood to be just negative liberties that need to be compared and evaluated along with other negative liberties to determine what particular bundle of negative liberties everyone should have. To make that determination, I appeal to the "ought" implies "can" principle, a principle common to all moral and political perspectives, but then I ultimately appeal to the principle of nonquestion-beggingness to convince even those who might be tempted to abandon morality to retain their preferred nonegalitarian conclusion.[105] I claim this is a preferable way of dealing with right-libertarians, like Robert Nozick and Jan Narveson, than the approach that is taken by left-libertarians.

So while these various attempts to get libertarians to endorse a right to welfare or substantial equality have certainly helped illuminate the libertarian view, they also have suffered from a number of deficiencies. Either they failed to show that the libertarian view should be abandoned in favor a welfare liberal or egalitarian view because it is impossible, self-contradictory or absurd, or they have failed adequately to show that libertarian premises, properly interpreted, lead to welfare liberal or egalitarian conclusions.

3 Objections from libertarians to my argument from liberty to equality

My debate with libertarians about what the ideal of liberty requires has been going on now for over twenty years. Libertarians have generally taken my argument for welfare and equality quite seriously because, unlike many other critiques of their view, I set out an argument from premises that libertarians themselves endorse. With some libertarians (Machan and Narveson) the debate has gone on over many years now, developing as it goes through public presentations and publications. With others (e.g., Rasmussen, Mack, Hospers, and Shapiro), there has been more of a one-time exchange. Yet all of these exchanges

---

105 See my response to Jan Narveson pp. 91ff.

have proved particularly helpful and illuminating and, in my judgment, have served to advance my argument from liberty to substantive equality. Here I will consider the most important of the exchanges that I have had with libertarians.

Tibor Machan

Tibor Machan and I have been discussing each other's work on this topic and debating the topic publicly for most of our careers as philosophers. In 1988, I discussed Machan's opposition to welfare rights for the poor on libertarian grounds in my book *How to Make People Just*. Machan returned the favor discussing my views in his 1989 book, *Individuals and Their Rights*. About a couple of years earlier, at a Meeting of the Society for the Advancement of American Philosophy, we had a memorable encounter. Machan and I were on a panel together with one other person (who shall remain nameless here). I had just presented a version of my argument that the libertarian ideal of liberty leads to an endorsement of welfare rights for the poor, and this third member of our panel began attacking my argument on the grounds that one can always formulate a political ideal in such a way as to get out of it whatever results one wants, and this is just what I had done with the libertarian ideal. What I had done, this person claimed, is skew the libertarian ideal in order to get welfare rights out of it. At that point, Machan spoke up claiming that he, as a libertarian, did not think that I had skewed or misstated the libertarian ideal, but that where he and I disagreed was not over the statement of the libertarian ideal but rather over the practical requirements that are derivable from it.[106] I always remember this as one of the high points in the philosophical dialogue about libertarianism that I have participated in over the years, and I have also always been grateful to Tibor Machan for saving me from the jaws of my critic on this occasion.

106 Machan recently endorsed my account of this exchange when I recounted it in "Author Meets Critics Session" on his book *A Passion for Liberty* (Lanham, MD: Rowman and Littlefield, 2003).

Such were the beginnings of the discussion that Machan and I have been having over the relationship between libertarianism and welfare rights, which for me ultimately lead to equality. Let me now recount more of its history.

Machan's "concession"[107]

In his 1989 book, *Individuals and their Rights*, Machan did criticize my argument that a libertarian ideal of liberty leads to a right to welfare, as I saw it, accepting its theoretical thrust but denying its practical significance, claiming that "if Sterba were right about Lockean libertarianism typically contradicting 'ought' implies 'can' then his argument would be decisive."[108] In so responding, I argued that Machan appreciated the force of the argument enough to grant that if the type of conflict cases that I described between the rich and the poor actually obtained, the poor would have a right to welfare. But Machan then denied that such cases – in which the poor had done all that they legitimately can to satisfy their basic needs in a libertarian society – actually obtain. "Normally," he wrote, "persons do not lack the opportunities and resources to satisfy their basic needs."[109]

But this response, as I interpreted it, virtually conceded everything that my argument intended to establish, for the poor's right to welfare is not claimed to be unconditional. Rather, it is said to be conditional principally upon the poor doing all that they legitimately can to meet their own basic needs. So it follows that only when the poor lack sufficient opportunity to satisfy their own basic needs would their right to welfare have any practical moral force. Accordingly, on libertarian grounds, I claimed that Machan had conceded the legitimacy of just the kind of right to welfare that the preceding argument hoped to establish.

---

107 In recent years, Machan has questioned whether he ever made any concession to me at all. But I have considerable difficulty interpreting the quoted sentence in the following paragraph as anything but a hypothetical concession.

108 Tibor Machan, *Individuals and Their Rights* (Chicago: Open Court, 1989), p. 103.

109 *Ibid.*, p. 107.

The only difference that remains, I claimed, is a practical one. Machan thinks that virtually all of the poor have sufficient opportunities and resources to satisfy their basic needs and, therefore, that a right to welfare has no practical moral force. In contrast, I think that many of the poor do not have sufficient opportunities and resources to satisfy their basic needs and, therefore, that a right to welfare has considerable practical moral force.

I also thought that this practical disagreement was resolvable. Who could deny that most of the 1.4 billion people who are currently living in conditions of absolute poverty "lack the opportunities and resources to satisfy their basic needs?"[110] And even in the USA, it is estimated that some 37 million Americans live below the official poverty index, and more than one-fifth of American children are growing up in poverty.[111] Surely it is impossible to deny that many of these Americans also "lack the opportunities and resources to satisfy their basic needs." Given the impossibility of reasonably denying these factual claims, I claimed that Machan would have to concede that the right to welfare, which he grants can be theoretically established on libertarian premises, also has practical moral force.

Actual verses nonactual conditions

Yet to my chagrin, Machan did not reach the same conclusion. In a later book, *Morality and Social Justice: Point/Counterpoint*, that Machan and I jointly authored with others, he claimed that the conclusion I drew here is a nonsequitur "because it speaks not to what may be expected in a country that functions within the framework of laws guided by Lockean libertarian principles – individual human negative rights, including the rights to life,

---

110 http://web.worldbank.org/WBSITE/EXTERNAL/TOPICS/EXTPOVERTY/
   0contentMDK:20153855~menuPK373757~pagePK:148956~piPK:216618~
   theSitePK:336992,00.html
111 http://en.wikipedia.org/wiki/Poverty_in_the_United_States

liberty and property – but is true of (a) the world at large and (b) the United States [under present conditions]."[112]

However, as I noted in my contribution to the same book, this response conceded that many of the poor lack the opportunities and resources to satisfy their basic needs but then contends that this lack is the result of political oppression in the absence of libertarian institutions. Now one might try to reconcile this response with Machan's earlier claim that "Normally, persons do not lack the opportunities and resources to satisfy their basic needs" by interpreting the claim as maintaining only that normally *in libertarian societies* the poor do not lack the opportunities and resources to satisfy their basic needs. The problem with this interpretation is that when Machan makes his "normally claim" he goes on to refer to typical conditions in actual societies. So this does raise the question of what sort of society Machan really intends his "normally claim" to refer.

Suppose, however, for the sake of argument, we take Machan to be referring to an idealized libertarian society. This interpretation, I argue, places the main responsibility for the fate of the poor on nonlibertarian political oppressors, but it also suggests that because of the existence of political oppressors, there is something the poor can do to meet their basic needs which they are not doing, namely, they can throw off their political oppressors and create libertarian societies. So according to this line of argument, the poor's lack of opportunities and resources to meet their basic needs is to some degree their own fault. They could conceivably throw off their political oppressors, but they have not yet done so.

But I have argued that this is to place responsibility for the fate of the poor where it normally does not belong. In actual societies, where the poor are oppressed, they usually have little or no political power to change the political system under which they live. Under conditions of oppression, virtually all of the responsibility for the failure to meet the basic needs of the poor must be placed on the political oppressors themselves and on those who benefit from such a system but fail to oppose it.

112 Tibor Machan, James Sterba, and Alison Jaggar *et al.*, *Morality and Social Justice* (Lanham, MD: Rowman & Littlefield, 1995).

Granting that this is the case, what then is the remedy? We can all agree that oppressive societies must be transformed into nonoppressive ones, but Machan contends that this involves transforming them into libertarian societies as well. I am on record as having no objection to this, provided that it is recognized that within a libertarian society the liberty of the poor takes precedence over the liberty of the rich to the extent required to secure welfare rights. Machan, of course, has resisted this interpretation of libertarianism, but to do so, I have argued, he needs to show how the denial of these rights to the poor is not itself a form of oppression that conflicts with the "ought" implies "can" principle, as I have interpreted it, and I do not see how he can do this.

There is a further question of how radical the transformations would have to be to change oppressive societies into libertarian societies. Machan has suggested that the changes that are necessary are fairly minimal, but a closer analysis suggests that only a radical transformation would do the job. This is because in oppressive societies wealth and resources have usually been concentrated in the hands of a few. To transform an oppressive into a nonoppressive society this inequality of wealth and resources would have to be eliminated. One way to do this would be to redistribute wealth and resources radically in favor of the poor. In fact, I argued that such a radical redistribution of wealth and resources is required by the libertarian's own ideal of liberty. But Machan does not want radically to redistribute wealth and resources in this way.[113] The kind of changes that

---

113 Why doesn't Machan want to go further and morally or legally resolve such conflicts? Part of his reason for not doing so is that he thinks of such situations as where for the rich to have any relevant obligations it would have to be an obligation to help the poor. This would put the rich under a positive obligation to help the poor and this is something he rejects. Yet if we interpret such conflicts as involving a negative obligation of the rich not to harm the poor, an obligation that the rich not interfere with the poor, then Machan would lose this objection. Still, Machan would object that the rich would have to give up part of themselves if they allow that the poor should not be interfered with in taking from their surplus. True, but if the rich stops the poor then they prevent them from meeting their basic needs.

Machan seems content with would not directly challenge the current unequal distribution of wealth and resources in existing oppressive societies, but only rule out certain oppressive or coercive ways of acquiring wealth and resources in the future. But this is like stopping a race in which some runners have been forced to wear heavy weights while others were left unencumbered, and then continuing the race after doing no more than letting the runners with weights remove them. Surely this would not suffice to make the results of the race fair. There is also a need for some kind of a corrective to compensate for the advantage enjoyed by those runners who have been running for so long unencumbered. Likewise, more needs to be done to transform oppressive societies into nonoppressive ones than Machan seems willing to do. After blaming oppressive structures for the plight of the poor, Machan seems reluctant to allow the poor and their allies to take the steps that are necessary for meeting of the basic needs of the poor.

How people fare under near-libertarian conditions

Machan elsewhere develops a different line of argument to try to undercut the practical force of my argument that the libertarian ideal leads to welfare rights. Rather than argue about what would obtain in an ideal libertarian society, Machan in this work seeks to defend libertarianism by comparing actual societies. Accordingly he contends that when we compare economic systems to determine which produce more poverty,

> No one can seriously dispute that the near-libertarian systems have fared much better than those going in the opposite direction, including the welfare state.[114]

Here one might think that Machan has the USA in mind as a "near-libertarian system," because earlier in the same paragraph he claims that "America is still the freest of societies, with many

---

Either the rich give up part of themselves, their luxury production, or the poor cannot meet their basic needs.

114 Tibor Machan, "The Nonexistence of Welfare Rights" (rev. version), in *Liberty for the 21st Century*, ed. Tibor Machan and Douglas Rasmussen (Lanham, MD: Rowman & Littlefield, 1995), pp. 218–20.

of its legal principles giving expression to classical liberal, near-libertarian ideas."[115] Yet apparently this is not what Machan thinks, since in a footnote to the same text he says:

> It is notable that the statistics that Sterba cites (mentioned above) are drawn from societies, including the United States of America, which are far from libertarian in their legal construction and are far closer to the welfare state, if not to outright socialism.[116]

Obviously, then, Machan is surprisingly unclear as to whether he wants to call the USA a near-libertarian state, a welfare state, or a socialist state. Yet whichever of these designations is most appropriate, what is clear is that the poor do less well in the USA than they do in the welfare liberal or socialist states of Western Europe such as Germany, Sweden, and Switzerland.[117] For example, 22.4 per cent of children live below the poverty line in the USA as compared to 4.9 per cent in Germany, 5 per cent in Sweden, and 7.8 per cent in Switzerland, and the USA shares with Italy the highest infant mortality rate of the major industrialized nations. The USA also ranks sixty-seventh among all nations in the percentage of national income received by the poorest 20 per cent of its population, ranking the absolute lowest among industrialized nations.[118] Accordingly the success that welfare liberal and socialist states have had, especially in Western Europe, in coming close to meeting the basic needs of their deserving poor should give us good

---

115 *Ibid.*

116 *Ibid.*

117 Richard Rose and Rei Shiratori, eds., *The Welfare State East and West* (Oxford: Oxford University Press, 1986). In fact, the living standards of poor children in Switzerland, Sweden, Finland, Denmark, Belgium, Norway, Luxembourg, Germany, the Netherlands, Austria, Canada, France, Italy, the United Kingdom, and Australia are all better than they are in the USA. See James Carville, *We're Right They're Wrong* (New York: Random House, 1996), pp. 31–2.

118 Michael Wolff, *Where We Stand* (New York: Bantam Books, 1992), pp. 23 and 115; George Kurian, *The New Book of Work Rankings*, 3rd edn (New York: Facts on File, 1990), p. 73; www.wsws.org/articles/2001/mar2001/pov-m14.shtml

reason to doubt what Machan proclaims is the superior practical effectiveness of "near-libertarian states" in dealing with poverty.

Machan challenges the statistical evidence on which I based my above claim that "the poor do less well in the US than they do in the welfare liberal or socialist states of Western Europe such as Germany, Sweden, and Switzerland."[119] Part of Machan's challenge consists of series of speculations as to how the statistical evidence I provide could be correct and still the conclusion I want to draw would not follow. Thus Machan considers how the USA could rank low (sixty-seventh) with respect to the percentage of national income received by the poorest 20 per cent of its population, and still the poor could be doing better off in the USA than in some country which ranks higher on the same scale. We are asked to imagine a relatively egalitarian Haiti (nothing like the real Haiti, which is actually very inegalitarian) in which the poorest 20 per cent of its population receive a higher percentage of national income, but are still worse off than the poor in the USA. But while this is certainly the case with respect to some of the sixty-six countries that rank higher than the USA in this comparison, it is not true of the welfare liberal or socialist countries of Western Europe, such as Germany, Sweden, and Switzerland, which rank significantly higher than the USA on this scale.

Machan also considers the possibility that the fact that the USA shares with Italy the highest infant mortality rate of the major industrialized nations may be explained in terms of our superior medical care which allows children to be born in the USA who would die at or before birth in other countries. But Machan makes no effort to see whether this does actually account for the difference, rather than the lack of prenatal care for the poor or the fact that roughly 40 million Americans have no health-care insurance, and so typically have poor health care.[120]

---

119 Tibor Machan, "Does Libertarianism Imply the Welfare State?" *Res Publica* 3, 2 (1997), pp. 131–48.
120 Wolff, *Where We Stand*, p. 110. For an interesting discussion of infant mortality as a useful international criterion of welfare, see Richard Rose,

Machan also cites the fact that the poor in America have a higher incidence of car ownership than any other country in the world other than Germany, and with 0.56 persons per room are less crowded "today" (the figures are from 1987) than the average West European household in 1980. But the lack of adequate public transportation in most places in the USA makes owning a car a necessity in a way that is not true in much of Western Europe, and Americans who live in places like New York City where adequate public transportation is available probably have similar person-per-room statistics to those in Western Europe.[121] Moreover, from an environmental perspective, Western Europe's lesser reliance on the automobile for transportation is clearly preferable.

Although Machan offers other speculations and bits of evidence, nowhere does he provide the kind of evidence that is needed to back up his original claim that "no one can seriously dispute that the near-libertarian systems have fared much better than those going in the opposite direction, including the welfare state." In fact, the more closely one looks at the relevant evidence, the clearer it seems that it better supports my claim that "the poor do less well in the US than they do in the welfare liberal or socialist states of Western Europe." Or, as sociologist Nathan Glazer puts the claim:

> The American welfare state came under attack long before it reached the levels of the European welfare states, whether measured in percentage of gross national product (GNP) taken for social purposes; in percentage of population in poverty, or by extensiveness of protection by public programs against unemployment, ill health or loss of wages in sickness, or of

"Making Progress and Catching Up: Comparative Analysis for Social Policy Making," in *UNESCO 1995* (Oxford: Blackwell Publishers, 1995), pp. 118–19.

121 It is also not clear how relevant such statistics are to judging overall welfare. Afghanistan, for example, before the US invasion ranked higher than the USA and, in fact, third in the world with respect to the number of rooms per dwelling. See George Kurian, *The Illustrated Book of World Rankings* (Amonk, NY: M. E. Sharpe, 1997), pp. 254–5.

child care services; or by degree of subsidization for housing. Indeed, possibly in only one respect, pensions for the aged, is the American welfare state comparable to the advanced European states. Without ever having reached European levels, the American welfare state has been in retreat since 1981.[122]

Institutional rights not needed for rare cases

Recently Machan has taken yet another tack on the liberty and welfare/equality debate.[123] Here he challenges my claim that, in his response to me, he has conceded even a theoretical legitimacy to welfare rights even when the poor really do not have any option for surviving unless they can exercise the liberty not to be interfered with in taking what they need from the surplus possessions of the rich. Rather what obtains in such situations, according to Machan, is that a person simply ought to disregard individual rights to property and take from another what he or she needs. In addition, Machan claims that such situations are quite rare.

But how does this differ from my account? In my account, in such situations a person should not be interfered with in taking from those who have a surplus (which is simply more than one requires to meet one's basic needs). Surprisingly, Machan appears to make an even stronger claim than I do here. Where I claim that those in need should not be interfered with in taking from those with a surplus, Machan claims that they ought to do so. This is because the underlying foundation for Machan's libertarian view is what he calls classical egoism, which holds each person ought to do what best serves his or her overall interest.[124] But while classical egoism does maintain that the needy ought to take from the rich in certain conflict situations, it also holds that in those same conflict situations the rich ought to stop the poor

---

122 Nathan Glazer, "Welfare and 'Welfare' in America," in *The Welfare Stat East and West*, ed. Rose and Shiratori, p. 44.

123 Tibor Machan, "Sterba on Machan's 'Concession'," *Journal of Social Philosophy* 32, 2 (Summer 2001), pp. 241–3.

124 Machan, *The Passion for Liberty*, p. 31.

from doing so. Eric Mack explicitly accepts this conclusion of classical egoism and, since Machan and Mack have endorsed each other's views on many occasions, I am assuming that Machan has the same position as Mack here.[125]

Assuming, then, that I am interpreting him correctly, Machan is not making a stronger claim than I am here because my claim that those in need ought not to be interfered with in taking from those with a surplus is stronger than an "egoistic" ought-claim. My claim implies that others ought not to interfere with the poor doing what is permitted here, whereas egoistic ought-claims have no such implication. As in competitive games, it can be the case that one person ought to do x at the same time that someone else ought to stop the person from doing it. However, this classical egoist solution is not a moral solution. It violates the "ought" implies "can" principle because it assumes that the poor cannot object to the results of a power struggle in which both the rich and the poor are at liberty to appropriate and use the surplus of the rich insofar as they are able to do so. Such a solution usually favors the rich who tend to be more powerful over the poor. The only resolution that would not violate the "ought" implies "can" principle here would be the one that guaranteed the poor a right to welfare.

Yet Machan is reluctant to speak of a right to welfare in such situations. Is it because he thinks that such situations are rare, whereas I do not? This again raises the question of whether we are talking about actual societies or about nonexistent ideal libertarian societies. If we are talking about actual societies, including our own, it should be obvious that such situations are not rare, even in the USA. Moreover, the fact that we might rightly blame oppressive governments or oppressive individuals for the number of people who are actually needy does not show that the needy in those societies do not have a negative welfare right – even against nonoppressive rich people – if that turns out to be the only way for them to meet their basic needs.

125 Mack, "Libertarianism Untamed."

Even if we are talking about nonexistent, ideal libertarian societies, it is also hard to see how we can say that it will be rare for people in such societies to be needy. In wealthy societies that surely depends on whether resources are appropriately distributed to meet the basic needs of all their members. Moreover, if we take into account the needs of distant peoples and future generations as well, it is hard to see how it would be rare for the poor to lack the opportunities to meet their basic needs. Not interfering with the liberty of the rich does not seem like a prescription for providing the poor with adequate opportunities to meet their basic needs, especially when not interfering with the liberty of the rich involves interfering with the liberty of the poor.

What if the rich did not exist?

More recently, Machan has offered two new considerations against my argument from liberty to welfare.[126] He argues that by denying the poor a right to welfare the rich would not be doing violence to them (that is, unjustly interfering with them), because the poor would still be in need if the rich did not exist. Now I wonder whether this claim is supposed to hold of both existing societies and of a not yet existing ideal libertarian society? In any case, I responded in the same book by arguing that what Machan claims here is clearly not true for just any particular group of rich people. A particular group of rich people's hoarding of resources may be exactly why other people are poor. Moreover, consider a group of people for whom the claim holds. Suppose you and I would still be very needy even if certain rich people did not exist. Does this show that we do not have a right not to be interfered with in taking from the surplus resources of those same rich people when they do exist? Suppose you and I are drowning in a pond. Even when others did not cause our plight, surely they may still be required not to interfere with our

126 Tibor Machan, "Libertarian Justice," in *Social and Political Philosophy: Contemporary Perspectives*, ed. James Sterba (London: Routledge, 2001), pp. 93–114.

attempts to save ourselves, even when these attempts involve using their own surplus resources. So I do not see how this objection of Machan undermines the case for welfare rights.

Machan also claims that there may be other ways to meet the needs of the poor, for example by obtaining wealth from the punishment of rich citizens or from resources not owned by anyone. My response is that it stands to reason that I am all in favor of utilizing these means for meeting the needs of the poor. I just do not see how these means will suffice to meet the basic needs of all those who are poor without also having recourse to a right to welfare.

Using a Kantian argument against using people

In *The Passion for Liberty*, Machan restates some of the lines of argument that he had previously used against the possibility of welfare rights on a libertarian foundation.[127] Yet there is at least one line of argument that he develops here for the first time: Machan opposes welfare rights on the grounds that "no one may be used by another without consent because each individual is important and valuable in his or her own right." Obviously, this ground that Machan provides against welfare rights has a Kantian favor to it. But Kant's restriction "never to use anyone as a means only" is a far weaker restriction than Machan's. Machan's restriction is absolute unless actual consent is secured. Kant's restriction allows for using people provided that they are treated as ends as well, and it can presumably be satisfied even when actual consent has not been secured. So the Kantian restriction appears to be consistent with welfare rights because taxing those who have surplus for the benefit of the deserving poor is consistent with wanting everyone to have the necessary resources for a decent, flourishing life and, therefore, with treating everyone as ends at least in this regard.

Moreover, it is possible to show that even Machan's more restrictive prohibition against using people is still consistent with

---

127 *The Passion for Liberty*, pp. 113ff.

welfare rights. In the type of conflict situation between the rich and the poor that we have been considering in order to determine who is using whom we need to know who has an enforceable right against whom. If the poor do have a right not to be interfered with in taking from the surplus possessions of the rich what they need to meet their basic needs, then the rich do not have the right not to be interfered with in using their surplus for meeting their luxury needs. If so, the poor would not be using the rich when they appropriate what they have a right to appropriate, and so would not be violating even Machan's more restrictive principle against using people. Who is using whom here all depends of whose liberty – that of the poor or that of the rich – has greater moral priority.

Now it might be objected that I am employing a moralized sense of using people whereas the sense that Machan employs is primarily descriptive. But this is not the case. Consider our practice of incarcerating prisoners against their will for serious crimes against persons such as murder, rape, and other forms of aggravated assault. Surely, in the descriptive sense of using people, we are usually using these prisoners against their will by imposing imprisonment upon them. But then in a moralized sense of using people that I am employing, and which Machan must certainly be employing as well to deal with such cases, we are not really using people because our actions are fully morally justified, and so we are still treating the prisoners as ends in themselves as is appropriate.

Rights determined by what would obtain in nonactual ideal libertarian societies

There is still another line of argument that makes its appearance in *The Passion of Liberty* as part of the case against the recognition of welfare rights on libertarian grounds.[128] While Machan has advanced it in his earlier work, I have not commented on it before. What Machan argues is that the most fully moral actions

128 *Ibid.*, pp. 117ff.

we perform are those we do freely. So if we are coerced to do something, as we would be if we are forced to pay taxes to help the poor, our helping the poor in this way would not be as moral as it could be. So if we want the highest level of morality possible, we should want only voluntary assistance of the poor – not assistance that comes by way of a coercive welfare system.

In response to this argument, I agree that if a system of voluntary helping the poor would do the job, that is, the job of caring for those who are in need, we would not require welfare rights. In fact, virtually all defenders of welfare rights maintain, as I do, that welfare rights are only justified when voluntary charity is insufficient. But when voluntary charity is insufficient, surely the poor would be better off with a welfare system.

Now it might be objected that some of those who were not moral enough to help the poor voluntarily would find ways to evade the costs of the welfare system or even take advantage of the system. No doubt this can happen, but those same individuals would probably cause trouble if there were no welfare system as well. There will always be ways for evil people to be evil. Moreover, for many others, a coercive welfare system would provide them with the opportunity to be as morally good as they can be. This is because they may be willing to help the poor but only when they can be assured that others are making comparable sacrifices, and a coercive welfare system does provide the assurance that comparable sacrifices will be made by all those with a surplus. So if many, possibly even most, people fall into this category of being willing to help if they can be assured that other similarly situated will do likewise, a coercive welfare system would provide just the right institutional setting for them. This also seems to be a dominant reason why most electorates vote for such systems. In addition, a welfare system would also provide the opportunity for the poor to develop themselves morally, now that they would have the resources required for a decent life.

Moreover, those who would have given generously to the poor even when they were not coercively required to do so would still have that virtuous disposition even if they cannot display it as clearly. Their disposition to greater virtue is still there, it is just not as visible for all to see. But this is hardly a great loss. Nor would much virtue otherwise have been displayed by those who would not have helped the poor voluntarily, and are only doing so under a welfare system because they are being coerced. Here too there are moral gains for the poor because they now would have the necessary resources to morally develop themselves.

In sum, voluntary charity is morally preferable only when it suffices to take care of the needs of the poor. When it does not suffice, a welfare system:

(1) Does not take away the virtue of the supremely generous who would display their supreme generosity more clearly in a society without welfare.
(2) Provides the right kind of help for many people to enable them to be as generous as they can.
(3) Provides the needed resources for the poor so that they can be as virtuous as they can.

In the summer of 2008, a number of issues in the debate between Machan and myself became clear. Most importantly, what became clear is that when Machan claims that normally people do not lack the opportunities and resources to satisfy their basic needs, he is simply referring to nonexistent ideal libertarian societies, not existing societies.[129]

Yet it is hard to see how Machan could claim that in such ideal societies it would be rare for people to lack the opportunities and resources to meet their basic needs. He cannot do so simply by stipulation. Surely it would depend on the availability and distribution of resources, and he cannot simply stipulate that

---

129 E-mail from Tibor Machan, May 16, 2008: "Since we have no fully free libertarian society, any more than some full blown welfare state or socialist polity – indeed virtually all but the most authoritarian systems (e.g., Saudi Arabia) are a political-economic smorgasbord – there is no way to resolve this purely empirically. Thought experiments are what we can use because we have no way to set up controlled ones. And that is what we do in political philosophy and theory."

resources will be plentiful and distributed widely. And if it is not rare for people to lack the opportunities and resources to satisfy their basic needs in such ideal libertarian societies, then Machan's reason for not having an established right (exceptional cases make bad law)[130] would not hold. It would then follow that the "ought" implies "can" principle would favor the liberty of the poor over the liberty of the rich and thus support at least a negative right to welfare for such ideal societies.[131] And the same would hold true for distant peoples and future generations under such ideal conditions, because it would be even more unlikely for all of them to have adequate opportunities and resources to meet their basic needs. Furthermore, under the nonideal conditions in which we currently live, where everyone's basic needs are clearly not being met, in any transition to greater justice either nationally, internationally, or intergenerationally, when sufficient resources for meeting people's basic needs obtain, there too would be grounds for supporting a negative right to welfare. In fact, in all circumstances except when it turns out that sufficient resources are being voluntarily made available for meeting people's basic needs nationally, internationally, and intergenerationally, normally a negative right to welfare would be normatively grounded. In this way, a negative right to welfare would almost always be supported by the libertarian premises that Machan endorses.

The utter unlikelihood of everyone having the opportunity to meet their basic needs both worldwide and into the future without a right to welfare in the ideal libertarian societies that Machan envisions is further demonstrated by how relatively easy Machan allows the transition to such societies to be.[132]

---

130 See Machan, "Sterba on Machan's 'Concession'," p. 241, and *Individuals and Their Rights*, pp. 100–11.

131 For how a negative right to welfare is distinct from a positive right, yet can practically lead to the latter, see pp. 97ff.

132 This became most evident in e-mail exchanges that I had with Machan from March 25–30, 2009, but it was also foreshadowed in earlier discussions about how to transition to an ideal libertarian society appropriately. For example, on March 29, Machan commented that the

Somewhat like the current Obama administration, which says it will not prosecute CIA interrogators for torturing detainees in the war against terror given that they were authorized to do so by higher officials in the Bush Administration, Tibor claims that in transitioning to an ideal libertarian society, there is no justification for going after the wealth amassed legally but in nonlibertarian ways by such corporations as Haliburton and Blackwater. Machan just expects such inequalities of wealth to "wash away" over time. He does not propose to correct them in the transition to ideal libertarian societies.

Yet surely allowing such inequalities of wealth amassed in the past by coercive but legal means to remain in place, while presumably putting an end to welfare institutions favoring the poor, would do little to decrease the likelihood that a significant number of people worldwide and into the future would regularly lack the opportunity to meet their basic needs. And if this is regularly the case, it follows from Machan's own libertarian theory that a right to welfare would be institutionally required.

Douglas Rasmussen (and Douglas Den Uyl)

Douglas Rasmussen has developed another challenge to my argument from libertarian premises that begins by conceding what Machan wanted to deny, at least for ideal societies – that the poor lack the opportunity to satisfy their basic needs.[133] Rasmussen distinguishes two ways that this can occur. In one case, only a few of the poor lack the opportunity to satisfy their basic needs. Here, Rasmussen contends that libertarian property rights still apply even though the poor who are in need morally ought to take from the surplus property of the rich what they need for survival and presumably the rich morally ought to help

effects of unjust-yet-legal past coercion that impacted on the distribution of property and human capital (education and developed skills) would be "washed away but not rectified" in transitioning to an ideal libertarian society.

133 Douglas Rasmussen, "Individual Rights and Human Flourishing," *Public Affairs Quarterly* 3 (1989), pp. 89–103. See also Douglas Rasmussen and Douglas Den Uyl, *Liberty and Nature* (La Salle: Open Court, 1991), chs. 2–4.

the poor. As libertarian property rights still do apply, however, Rasmussen contends that the poor who do take from the legal property of the rich can be arrested and tried for their actions, but their punishment, according to Rasmussen, should be simply left up to judges to decide.[134] Rasmussen also rejects the suggestion that the law should make an exception for the poor in such cases on the grounds that one can never have perfect symmetry between what is moral and what the law requires.[135]

But why should the question of punishment simply be left up to judges to decide? If the judicial proceedings determine what is assumed in this case – that the poor morally ought to take from the legal property of the rich what they need for survival and that the rich morally ought to help the poor – then it is difficult to see on what grounds a judge could inflict punishment.[136] Surely if it would be unreasonable to require the poor to do anything contrary to meeting their basic needs at minimal cost to the rich, it would be equally unreasonable to punish the poor for actually doing just that – meeting their basic needs at minimal cost to the rich.

Nor will it do to claim that we cannot expect symmetry between what morality requires and what the law requires in this case. Of course, there is no denying that sometimes the law can justifiably require us to do what is morally wrong. In such cases, opposing the law, even when what it requires is immoral, would do more harm than good. This can occur when there is a bona fide disagreement over whether what the law requires is morally wrong (for example, the Roe vs. Wade decision), with those in favor of the law justifiably thinking that it is morally right and those against the law justifiably thinking that it is morally wrong, When this occurs, failing to obey the law, even

134 Rasmussen, "Individual Rights and Human Flourishing," p. 98.
135 *Ibid.*, p. 99.
136 For this case, Rasmussen clearly seems to hold that the rich morally ought to help. He definitely grants that this is the case when many people are in need. In that context, Rasmussen allows that the rich refusing assistance would be acting immorally. See "Individual Rights and Human Flourishing," p. 100.

when what it requires is immoral, could, by undermining the legal system, do more harm than good. However, in our case of severe conflict of interest between the rich and the poor, nothing of the sort obtains. In our case, it is judged that the poor morally ought to take from the legal property of the rich and that no other moral imperative favoring the rich overrides this moral imperative favoring the poor. So it is clear in this case that there are no grounds for upholding any asymmetry between what morality and the law require. Accordingly, the law in this case should be understood to favor the poor.

However, Rasmussen distinguishes another case in which many of the poor lack the opportunity to satisfy their basic needs.[137] In this case, so many of the poor lack the opportunity to satisfy their basic needs that Rasmussen claims libertarian property rights no longer apply. Here he contends that morality requires that the poor should take what they need for survival from the legal property of the rich, and that the rich should not refuse assistance. Still he further contends that the poor have no negative or positive right to assistance in this case, or the rich presumably any corresponding obligation to help or not interfere with the poor because "the situation cannot be judged in social and political terms."[138]

But why cannot the situation be judged in social and political terms? If we know what the moral directives of the rich and the poor are in this case, as Rasmussen admits we do, why would we not be justified in setting up a legal system or altering an existing legal system so that the poor would have a guaranteed negative or positive right to welfare? Now it may be that Rasmussen is imagining a situation where it is not possible for the basic needs of everyone to be met. Such situations are truly lifeboat cases. But although such cases are difficult to resolve (maybe only a chance mechanism would offer a reasonable resolution), they surely do not represent the typical conflict situation between the rich and the poor. For in such situations, it is recognized that it is

137 Rasmussen, "Individual Rights and Human Flourishing," p. 100.
138 *Ibid.*, p. 101.

possible to meet everyone's basic needs, and what is at issue is whether the nonbasic or luxury needs of the rich should be sacrificed so that everyone's basic needs can be met.

More recently Rasmussen, in a book he co-authored with Douglas Den Uyl, offers an "ethical meta-normative" reason for not recognizing a right to welfare in such cases, a reason why these cases should not be judged in "social and political terms."[139] It is that, unlike "the prohibition against the initiatory use of physical force and coercion," welfare rights would benefit one group over others thus revealing a troubling bias. Now it is true that not everyone will benefit from a right to welfare and so it does favor some over others, but the same would have held true for an unconditional right to property. That right too favors some over others.

What is needed here, and what I provided in Section I of this essay, is a moral argument to determine whose interests we should favor. That is why I appealed to the "ought" implies "can" principle, and ultimately to the principle of nonquestion-beggingness, to provide such an argument.[140] So whether we are dealing with cases where only a few or many lack the opportunities to meet their basic needs, I have provided an argument for favoring a negative right to welfare over absolute property rights. Thus Rasmussen and Den Uyl's attempt to provide an ethical metanormative reason for not enforcing welfare rights in cases where the poor lack the opportunities to meet their basic needs clearly fails.

John Hospers

Quite different objections to my attempt to argue from libertarian premises to welfare liberal or egalitarian conclusions have been raised by John Hospers.[141] First, Hospers contends that I am

139 Douglas Rasmussen and Douglas Den Uyl, *Norms of Liberty* (University Park, PA: Pennsylvania State University Press, 2005), pp. 309–10.
140 For this ultimate appeal, see pp. 97ff.
141 John Hospers, "Some Unquestioned Assumptions," *The Journal of Social Philosophy* 22 (1991), pp. 42–51.

committed to distributing welfare too broadly, to the undeserving poor as well as to the deserving poor. Second, he contends that the taxes on the wealthy that I defend, in effect, commit me to killing the goose that lays the golden egg because the poor would be worse off under a tax-supported welfare system than they would be in a completely libertarian society.

In response to the first objection Hospers raises, I have in a number of places made it clear that I am defending a right to welfare only for the deserving poor, that is, the poor who have exhausted all their legitimate opportunities for meeting their basic needs. Hospers's second objection, however, questions whether even the deserving poor would be better off demanding welfare, even if they have a right to it. He cites the example of Ernst Mahler, an entrepreneurial genius who employed more than 100,000 and produced newsprint and tissue products that are now used by more than 2 billion people. Hospers suggests that requiring Mahler to contribute to a welfare system for the deserving poor would not only "decrease his own wealth but that of countless other people."[142]

In response to this objection, I contend that if the more talented members of a society provided sufficient employment opportunities and voluntary welfare assistance to enable the poor to meet their basic needs, then the conditions for invoking a right to welfare would not arise, since the poor are first required to take advantage of whatever employment opportunities and voluntary welfare assistance are available to them before they can legitimately invoke such a right. Consequently, if *sufficient* employment opportunities and voluntary welfare assistance obtained, there would be no practical difference in this regard between a libertarian society and a welfare or socialist state, as neither would justify invoking a right to welfare. Only when *insufficient* employment opportunities and voluntary welfare assistance obtained would there be a practical difference between a libertarian society and a welfare or socialist state,

142 *Ibid.*

and then it would clearly benefit the poor to be able to invoke the right to welfare. Consequently, given the practical possibility, and, in most cases, the actuality of insufficient employment opportunities and voluntary welfare assistance obtaining, there is no reason to think that the poor would be better off without the enforcement of such a right.

Now one might think that once the rich realized that the poor should have the liberty not to be interfered with when taking from the surplus possessions of the rich what they require to satisfy their basic needs, they would stop producing any surplus whatsoever. This appears to be what Hospers is suggesting by citing the example of Ernst Mahler. Suppose they all did. Wouldn't the poor be justified in appropriating, or threatening to appropriate, even the nonsurplus possessions of those who can produce more in order to get them to do so?[143] Surely this would not be an unreasonable imposition on those who can produce more because it would not be unreasonable to require them to be a bit more productive when the alternative is requiring the poor to forgo meeting their basic needs. Surely if we have no alternative, requiring those who can produce more to be a bit more productive is less of an imposition than requiring the poor to forgo meeting their basic needs.

This is an important conclusion in our assessment of the libertarian ideal, because it shows that ultimately the right of the poor to appropriate what they require to meet their basic needs does not depend, as many have thought, upon the talented having sufficient self-interested incentives to produce a surplus. All that is necessary is that the talented are able to produce a surplus and that the (deserving) poor not be able to meet their basic needs in any other way.

It might be objected, however, that if the talented can be required to produce a surplus so that the (deserving) poor can meet their basic needs, then why cannot the poor be required to sterilize themselves as a condition for receiving that surplus.

---

143 Actually, the possessions in question are not truly nonsurplus as those who have them could relatively easily produce a surplus.

What the objection rightly points to is the need for the poor, and everyone else as well, to take steps to control population growth. What the objection wrongly maintains is that the poor would have a greater obligation to limit their procreation than the rich would have to limit theirs. Surely population can be brought under control by a uniform policy that imposes the same requirements on both rich and poor. There is no need or justification for a population policy that comes down harder on the poor.

Eric Mack (and Murray Rothbard)

Eric Mack wants to characterize severe conflict situations between the rich and the poor as lifeboat situations. Murray Rothbard seeks to deal with these situations by distinguishing between a "political ethics," which supports unconditional property rights even in the face of dire need, and "a moral course of action," which may recommend the violation of such property rights.[144] By contrast, Mack seeks to deal with such situations by claiming that no one has any rights when such situations obtain; Mack thinks that in such situations all parties are at liberty to pursue their own interests.[145] Thus Mack would object to my derivation of welfare rights from a consideration of severe conflict-of-interest situations between the rich and the poor.

Yet Mack avoids endorsing welfare rights in such situations only by giving up rights altogether, and so his account cannot provide a satisfactory resolution, even from a libertarian point of view.[146] On the other hand, while Rothbard distinguishes between a political ethics which supports unconditional property rights and a moral course of action which may recommend the satisfaction of basic needs, he still claims that in cases of conflict it is always punishable and never excusable to follow a moral course of action. So Rothbard's alternative to following

---

144 Murray Rothbard, *The Ethics of Liberty* (New York: Collier Books, 1978), pp. 149–53.
145 Eric Mack, "Individualism, Rights and the Open Society," in *The Libertarian Reader* (Totowa, NJ: Rowman and Littlefield, 1982), pp. 9–11.
146 On this point, see Rothbard, *The Ethics of Liberty*, pp. 151–3.

unconditional property rights seems to be a "moral course of action" in name only. In any case, he clearly has failed to deal with the strong moral challenge to unconditional property rights contained in the "ought" implies "can" principle.

Mack raises still another objection to my libertarian argument for welfare.[147] Mack allows that my appeal to the "ought" implies "can" principle does show that in severe conflict-of-interest situations the rich do not have a right to their surplus. What Mack denies, however, is that I have shown that the poor in such situations have a right to the surplus of the rich. He contends that in these conflict situations neither the rich nor the poor have a right to the surplus of the rich. Instead, he thinks that both the rich and the poor are at liberty to appropriate and use the surplus if they can. Thus, what obtains in these conflict-of-interest situations, according to Mack, is a Hobbesian state of nature, a war of all against all.

There are two problems with Mack's analysis of these conflict situations between the rich and the poor. The first problem is that his analysis denies the existence of property rights to a surplus whenever severe conflicts of interest between the rich and the poor obtain, without recognizing any alternative (welfare) rights as applicable in those circumstances. This means that property rights to a surplus would be justified only in those rare cases in which they equally served the interest of both the rich and the poor. In all other cases, no property rights to a surplus would be justified. But surely this is not the real-world justification of property rights that libertarians had promised.

The second problem with Mack's analysis is even more serious. It is that while he accepts the "ought" implies "can" principle, his own proposed moral resolution of severe conflict-of-interest situations violates that very principle, because it requires the poor to accept the results of a power struggle in which both the rich and the poor are at liberty to appropriate and use the surplus resources of the rich insofar as they are able to

---

147 Mack, "Libertarianism Untamed."

do so. Obviously such a resolution favors the rich over the poor. Consequently, it would be no more reasonable to require the poor to accept this resolution than it would be to require them to accept the resolution that Mack concedes fails to satisfy the "ought" implies "can" principle – the resolution that secures for the rich property rights to their surplus. This implies that for severe conflict-of-interest situations only a resolution that guarantees the poor a right to welfare would satisfy the "ought" implies "can" principle.

Moreover, this is just the sort of resolution that the contrapositive of the "ought" implies "can" principle, which I call the conflict resolution principle, requires.[148] This principle requires that moral resolutions of severe conflicts of interest must be reasonable to require everyone affected to accept them. So in the severe conflict-of-interest situation we are considering, only a moral resolution that guaranteed the poor a right to welfare would be reasonable for both the rich and the poor to accept. Thus, for such conflict situations, only a moral resolution that guarantees the poor a right to welfare would satisfy both the "ought" implies "can" principle and its contrapositive, the conflict resolution principle.

Daniel Shapiro

Daniel Shapiro in his book *Is the Welfare State Justified?* also challenges my argument from libertarian premises.[149] He sees me as simply arguing from libertarian premises to the welfare liberal conclusions. But this is not exactly correct. What I have been arguing for, at least since 1987, when Doug Rasmussen and I produced a pro-and-con book in conjunction with a workshop at Bowling Green University, is that libertarianism leads not just to a right to welfare but to substantial equality. Or, as I would put it today, what we are entitled to is to use up no more resources

---

148 For an explanation of the conflict resolution principle, see n. 23.
149 Daniel Shapiro, *Is the Welfare State Justified?* (New York: Cambridge University Press, 2007).

than are necessary for meeting our own basic needs, thus securing for ourselves a decent life but no more.

My argument has been that once a right to welfare established on libertarian premises is extended to distant peoples and future generations, as it must be, then it leads to substantial equality over place and time. In my 1988 book, *How to Make People Just*, I further argued that the same holds for the welfare liberal, egalitarian, and communitarian views that Shapiro discusses. And in more recent work, I have presented similar arguments. That is why, from my perspective, choices between the particular policy initiatives that Shapiro discusses, such as the Cato Plan and the Brookings Plan, are only rightly made insofar as they serve to advance us toward the substantial equality that I claim all of these political perspectives, including libertarianism, require.

Of course, my argument from libertarian premises to a right to welfare may be mistaken, along with my further argument from a right to welfare to substantial equality. And Shapiro does raise a number of challenges that I will now address. Unfortunately, Shapiro does not take into account the formulation of my argument from libertarian premises that I give in my 2005 book, *The Triumph of Practice Over Theory in Ethics*. In the workshop that Doug Rasmussen and I participated in at Bowling Green back in 1987, I unwisely took the advice of a well-meaning libertarian, and thereafter divided the libertarian view into two forms: Spencerian libertarians who take a right to liberty as basic and then derive all other rights from this right to liberty, and Lockean libertarians who take a set of rights, typically a right to life and a right to property as basic and then interpret liberty as being unrestrained by other persons from doing what one has a right to do. It was only when working on the *Triumph* book that I realized that this distinction between two forms of libertarianism is bogus. Given that for libertarians the fundamental rights of the so-called Lockean perspective are also rights of noninterference, that is, (negative) liberty rights, the question arises of why we should accept these particular rights of noninterference (liberties) and not others – which is just the question that arises when we consider the conflicting liberties in the so-called Spencerian perspective. What this shows is that the "rights" of the Lockean perspective are not really distinct from the "liberties" in the Spencerian perspective. The central question is always which fundamental liberties people should have.

In his book, Shapiro primarily discusses my argument in its now superseded Lockean formulation. Since I use an example there in which the rich in preventing poor from taking what they require to meet their basic needs would cause the poor to starve to death, in effect, killing the poor, Shapiro thinks that, at best, what I have established is a negative right to subsistence of the poor against the rich. However, given that he also thinks that the rich will almost always, by the exercise of charity, meet the subsistence needs of the poor, he concludes that one of the conditions that I require for a negative right to welfare, namely, the inadequacy of charity, will not be met. So it would follow, on my account, that the poor would not even have a negative right to subsistence, let alone a positive right to subsistence, which, I allow, would require still further conditions to be met. In his discussion, Shapiro never takes up the question of whether the subsistence needs of the poor around the globe and into the future would also be met by the rich providing the necessary resources for those presently existing and saving resources for those who will come into existence in the future. I will return to this issue later.

Shapiro recognizes that I want to defend, on libertarian grounds, more than a right to subsistence. He recognizes that I want a right to welfare to be a conditional right to have one's basic needs met. As I define them, basic needs if not satisfied lead to significant lacks or deficiencies with respect to a standard of mental and physical well-being. Thus a person's need for food, shelter, medical care, protection, companionship, and self-development are, at least in part, needs of this sort. However, Shapiro tries to rule out any such more substantive right to welfare on the grounds that my argument could only work in the limited case where the rich in protecting their surplus from being used by the poor would, in effect, be killing the poor.

Yet recall what my project is here. It is to determine what bundle of fundamental liberty rights should be assigned to each and every person. Clearly, the liberty, when one is poor, not to be interfered with in taking from the surplus of the rich what one needs to prevent oneself from dying is a liberty that should be in everyone's bundle. Obviously, it conflicts with another liberty, the liberty, when one is rich, not to be interfered with when using one's surplus for luxury purposes. But here, even Shapiro grants that, if charity were insufficient and we really had to choose between these two liberties, this liberty of the poor would trump the liberty of the rich with which it conflicts.

This being the case, why would we not want other liberties favoring people when poor through no fault of their own in that bundle of fundamental liberties given to everyone? Why just have this one liberty that only prevents the poor from being killed by the rich? Consider the liberty of the poor not to be interfered with in taking from the surplus possessions of the rich what is necessary to satisfy their own basic needs, which I discuss in the publications that Shapiro cites. This liberty too would conflict with the liberty of the rich not to be interfered with in using their surplus resources for luxury purposes and have priority over it. Why then would we not favor the liberty of the poor not to be interfered with in taking from the surplus possessions of the rich what is necessary to satisfy their own basic needs over the liberty of the rich not to be interfered with in using their surplus resources for luxury purposes?

Moreover, we need an enforceable resolution here determining which of these liberties has priority. For libertarians, as we have seen, it must be a moral resolution, one that is reasonable and not contrary to reason to coercively require both the rich and the poor to accept. The issue is whether coercively to require the poor to sacrifice the liberty to meet some of their basic needs in order that the rich have the liberty to meet some of their luxury needs, or coercively to require the rich to sacrifice the liberty to meet some of their luxury needs so that the poor can have the liberty to meet their basic needs. Now I have argued that if one of these requirements is to be judged reasonable and not contrary to reason, then, by any neutral assessment, it must be the requirement that favors the liberty of the poor over the liberty of the rich. There is no other plausible resolution, I claim, if libertarians intend to be putting forth a moral resolution.

So that is how I get to a more substantive right to welfare and not just a right to subsistence – by considering more liberties of the poor than just the liberty of the poor not to be interfered with in taking from the surplus of the rich what they need to prevent themselves from dying. Once these other liberties are introduced into the discussion and morally weighed against the liberties of the rich with which they conflict, then, I claim, a more substantive right to welfare emerges as coercively enforceable, one that provides for basic needs. And once considerations of the interests of distant peoples and future generations are introduced, then a demand for substantial equality emerges as well.

Jan Narveson

While this book represents the first full-scale debate between Jan Narveson and myself, Narveson and I have been exchanging our views on the compatibility of liberty and equality for some time now. And I, at least, have found these exchanges to be extremely helpful for the purpose of getting clear about the points of agreement and disagreement between our views. Let me begin with the points of agreement.

Points of agreement

Responding to some of my earlier work, Narveson argues that there are not two forms of libertarianism, Spencerian libertarianism (which takes an ideal of liberty to be supreme) and Lockean libertarianism (which takes a particular set of rights to be supreme), as I had earlier claimed, but only one form of libertarianism.[150] I now agree with Narveson about this, as the way that I have set out the libertarian view in this essay indicates.

---

150 Jan Narveson, "Comments on Sterba's 'Ethics' Article" (circulated unpublished paper), November 9, 1994, p. 4.

The ideal of libertarianism coming in two forms was recommended to me a number of years ago as a useful way to think about the view by Jeffrey Paul, who is himself a libertarian. Recently, however, not as a result of reading Narveson's work unfortunately, but rather from responding to an objection from one of my colleagues, Alastair MacIntyre, I came to the conclusion that there are not really two forms of libertarianism after all, but only one form, which you can label either Spencerian or Lockean, and for which a right to liberty is fundamental.[151]

Yet after acknowledging this point of agreement between Narveson and myself, it becomes harder to find others. But there may be at least one more, an important point of agreement that is hidden beneath an apparent disagreement. The apparent disagreement is that Narveson says that there are no conflicts of liberty in the libertarian view, whereas I hold that there are conflicts of liberty in the view. Yet when I maintain that there are conflicts of liberty, I do not mean that there are conflicts among approved liberties – the liberties that people should have. And when Narveson says there are no conflicts of liberty, he seems to just mean that there are no conflicts among approved liberties – the liberties that people should have.

Consider the following passage where Narveson appears to support this interpretation:

> We should, of course, bear in mind that all rights restrict liberty. In saying that someone has a right to do something, what we are saying is that someone else may not do certain things, and if necessary may be compelled to refrain from them. The libertarian case is that the fundamental right is a right to liberty, but in being so it is automatically a prohibition of the liberty to do certain things: namely, acts that infringe liberty . . . [From t]he fact that it is the liberty of the poor [not to be interfered with when taking] from the rich that is being restricted, then, it does not follow that what we have is a clash of liberties in the relevant sense: namely, a clash of liberties that the theory protects. It is, instead, a clash between a

---

151 The argument for this conclusion is given on pp. 22, 88–9.

familiar kind of liberty that it is the very essence of the theory to forbid and another kind of liberty that it is the very essence of the theory to protect.[152]

Accordingly Narveson and I do not appear to be disagreeing about whether there are conflicts of liberty. We both seem to be claiming that at the approved level, there are no such conflicts, but then allowing that approved liberties can and do come into conflict with unapproved liberties.

Moreover, if I am right that the liberty of the poor not to be interfered with in taking from the rich what they require to meet their basic needs is an approved liberty then the rich would be unjustifiably interfering with the poor if they were to try to stop the poor from exercising that liberty. On the other hand, if Narveson is right that there is no such approved liberty then the poor would be unjustifiably interfering with the rich if they were to try to take from the surplus of the rich what they require to meet their basic needs. Or put another way, by determining what approved liberties there are, we would also be determining who is justified in interfering with whom.[153]

A standard for approved liberties

Now to determine what approved liberties there are, Narveson appeals to a standard that he suggests is identical with my "ought" implies "can" principle or its contrapositive, which

---

152 "Comments on Sterba's 'Ethics' Article," p. 7.
153 Narveson allows that what counts as interference is determined by the approved liberties. He writes: "So I deny that rich person R defending what he takes to be his property is interfering in any relevant sense with the liberty of the poor when he attempts to keep them from appropriating for themselves what he brought about. Not, that is, in any sense other than the familiar sense in which absolutely all rights interfere with 'liberty,' viz., entail that certain acts which it is possible for others to do are not to be done. You might prefer to leave the quotation marks off the last occurrence of the work 'liberty.' If so, though, we will have to reinstitute the distinction between legitimate and illegitimate 'liberties' . . ." (private correspondence, April 1, 1990).

I have called the conflict resolution principle.[154] Narveson himself variously formulates his standard as "premises acceptable to all," "what is reasonable for me to demand of others," and "principles every reasonable person subscribes to given the options of others," and he uses the following extended example to indicate what he thinks follows from his standard.[155]

> Let's go back to time T_0, at which there is the following state of affairs. Potential Starveling ('S') is over Here (on *This* island), while Potential Rich Person ('R') is over There (on *That* island). S proposes a deal to R: "Look, if either of us shouldn't make it on our own, and ends up facing starvation, then the other will agree to give him enough to keep him going. What do you say?"
>
> R thinks it over, and looks S over, and looks S's island over. He reasons as follows: "This guy probably isn't going to make it, and I probably am. If that happens, he's going to need Marginal Resources of amount X. I frankly hate agricultural activities, myself. To produce X, I have to spend a lot of extra hours at things I dislike doing. And what's in it for me? Having this guy's assurance that he would do likewise if I were in trouble isn't worth the soil he's ready to scratch it on frankly. No dice! But listen: any time you have a surplus of something I do like, just get in touch. I'm always ready to make a deal. No hard feelings, O.K.?"
>
> There are two ways of not making a deal about this. One of them is by running the Hobbesian State of Nature scenario. R knows that S will resort to force whenever it looks to him likely to be successful. So he decides to save himself a whole lot of trouble by getting S out of the way now – after all, he's a shrimp. S, on the other hand, realizes that it's in R's interest to

---

154 According to the conflict resolution principle, people are morally required to do what is reasonable to require everyone affected to accept. Narveson makes this comparison to my "ought" implies "can" principle in "Sterba on Reconciling Conceptions of Justice," a paper presented at the APA Symposium on Justice, Louisville, Kentucky, April 24, 1992, p. 6.

155 Jan Narveson, "Libertarianism: A Philosophical Introduction," pp. 41 and 53, www.againstpolitics.com/libertarian, and Jan Narveson, "A Critique of Sterba's Defense of the Welfare State," in *Political Philosophy*, ed. Louis Pojman (New York: McGraw-Hill, 2002), p. 232.

do this, and decides he'd better attack first. Both end up dead, or at least a lot worse off than if they had both been at liberty to use their own resources as best they can.

The ordering of these possibilities, then, is as follows: Welfare Rights for S, Welfare Duties for R gets S's top vote. But not R's. Warfare Rights for All looks better than that from R's point of view, though not from S's. *Full Property Rights for all, however, is better for both than full Warfare Rights.*

So that's the deal – best for both. Remember, we need the consent of both, not just S. And remember, too, that this is a real consent by real people, not the eviscerated consent available at bargain-basement conceptual prices in the fabulous Rawlsian World-Behind-The-Veil-Of-Ignorance. Thus, for example, don't try to argue for S on the basis of Rawls' Bleeding-Heart Principle: "maximize the lot of the bleeding." That principle is of no interest to R. Of course it might be of interest to "him" *if he were somebody else*, especially S. But then, he isn't. And we have supposed that S is a ne'er do well. For if he weren't, then he would make it on his own, in the sense that either he'd do well on his own island, or he'd make R a profitable offer to help, say with the agricultural work (which R would rather avoid).

Suppose that S and R actually agree on this principle – as they clearly will, since it dominates all alternatives. Now, 10 years later, S as predicted has got into trouble and he comes to R's door (or dock). And he says, "Help me, I'm starving!" (Behind him, in the bushes just out of sight, are his starving wife and kiddies.) And R, correctly, says: "Sorry: there isn't enough for you. Of course, I do have a fabulous set of wind-chimes over here, but that isn't what you want (and you can't have them anyway – why do you think I went to all this trouble to make them?). What you want is food, and I don't have any extra of that, since producing it is such a pain."

There is no reason for R to think that he *owes* S anything. No mutually reasonable principle calls upon him to give it to S, even if S is starving. R doesn't, remember, *care* whether S is starving.

If R had been worried about his own situation and thought S might actually be of some help, he might, of course, have made a different arrangement. But he didn't think that, so he didn't make the arrangement. Was this stupid on his part? Only if S might actually have been of some help. But R plausibly surmised that he would not . . .

Sterba thinks we can go *straight* from the "ought implies can" principle to his [welfare rights] principle. I have shown this to be wrong. It can be better for the potentially starving to accept a principle giving everyone full liberal property rights than to hold out for a Sterba-like principle which the competent, the strong, the able, the ambitious, etc., needn't accept.[156]

Clearly Narveson thinks that this example shows why I cannot go from my "ought" implies "can" principle to a right to welfare. But does it show this? Think of the situation of S. At one point in his description, Narveson says "we have supposed that S is a ne'er do well." But his earlier description does not suppose this at all, only that S is not a very talented person who probably will not be able to make it on his own with the resources at his disposal.[157] Of course, if S were a ne'er do well, then he would be responsible for his later destitute state and so, on my account, not entitled to a right to welfare. But then the conclusion that Narveson would draw from his example would not be incompatible with the conclusion that I would want to draw.

So let us drop the idea that S is a ne'er do well, and consider whether, as Narveson implies, it would still be reasonable for R and S to agree to a system of Full Property Rights with no right to welfare at T_0. Presumably both R and S are aware of the likelihood of S's becoming destitute and that is why S wants to negotiate a social security pack with R at T_0 and that is also why R, for self-interested reasons, wants to resist such a pact. Both R and S also know that war would be counterproductive for both of them. In S's case, we can imagine that war would bring death and starvation even sooner.

---

156 Jan Narveson, "Sterba on Reconciling Conceptions of Justice," paper presented at the APA Symposium on Justice, Louisville, Kentucky, April 24, 1992, pp. 8–9. Another version of this same example is found in "Comments on Sterba's 'Ethics' Article," pp. 7–8.

157 We learn that S is assumed to be male since he turns up ten years later with a wife and children.

Would it be reasonable, then, for both S and R to agree to a system of Full Property Rights with no right to welfare even though this has the consequence that S and his family will starve to death in ten years? Does the fact that S cannot do better for himself and his family because he will be unable to take from the surplus resources of R what he and his family in their time of need will require render his submission to that agreement reasonable? Not necessarily. The fact that a person has no better option but to agree to something does not, by itself, render that agreement reasonable. As we noted earlier, we would not want to say that the fact that a woman whose life was threatened had no better option but to submit to a rapist's demands would render those demands reasonable. So too with respect to Narveson's example, we have to ask about the reasonableness of the self-interested stance taken by R that effectively limits S's options. Is that stance reasonable for R to take?

A standard of nonquestion-beggingness

Suppose we interpret this question as asking whether there is a good argument supporting R's taking that stance. Given that good arguments are nonquestion-begging, what we are asking is whether there is an argument supporting R's stance that does not beg the question, that is, an argument that does not assume what it is trying to prove.

Let us assume that R is capable of entertaining and acting upon both self-interested and altruistic reasons and that the question we are seeking to answer is what sort of reasons for action it would be rational for R to accept.[158] This question is not

---

158 "Ought" presupposes "can" here. So unless people have the capacity to entertain and follow both self-interested and moral reasons for acting, it does not make any sense asking whether they ought or ought not to do so. Of course, this presupposes the falsity of psychological egoism. Moreover, moral reasons here are understood to necessarily include (some) altruistic reasons but not necessarily to exclude (all) self-interested reasons. So the question of whether it would be rational for us to follow self-interested reasons rather than moral reasons should be understood as the question of whether it would be rational for us to follow self-interested reasons exclusively rather than some appropriate set of self-interested reasons and altruistic reasons that constitutes the class of moral reasons.

about what sort of reasons R should simply publicly affirm, since people will sometimes publicly affirm reasons that are quite different from those they are prepared to act upon. Rather, it is a question about what reasons it would be rational for R to accept at the deepest level – in his heart of hearts – since we are trying to answer this question as far as possible without self-deception or hypocrisy.

Of course, there are people who are incapable of acting upon altruistic reasons. For such people, there is no question about their being required to act altruistically. Yet the interesting philosophical question is not about such people but about people, like ourselves, who are capable of acting altruistically as well as self-interestedly and are seeking a rational justification for following a particular course of action. So let us assume that R is such a person.

Now the question at issue here is what reasons R should take as supreme, and this question would be begged against egoism if we proposed to answer it simply by assuming from the start that altruistic reasons are the reasons that R should take as supreme. But the question would be begged against altruism as well if we proposed to answer the question simply by assuming from the start that self-interested reasons are the reasons that R should take as supreme. This means, of course, that we cannot answer the question of what reasons R should take as supreme simply by assuming the general principle of egoism:

> Each person ought to do what best serves his or her overall self-interest.

We can no more argue for egoism simply by denying the relevance of moral reasons to rational choice than we can argue for altruism simply by denying the relevance of self-interested reasons to rational choice and assuming the following general principle of altruism:

> Each person ought to do what best serves the overall interest of others.[159]

---

159 The altruist is here understood to be the mirror image of the egoist. Whereas the egoist thinks that the interests of others count for them but

Consequently, in order not to beg the question, we have no other alternative but to grant the prima facie relevance of both self-interested and altruistic reasons to rational choice and then try to determine which reasons R would be rationally required to act upon, all things considered. Notice that in order not to beg the question, it is necessary to back off both from the general principle of egoism and from the general principle of altruism, thus granting the prima facie relevance of both self-interested and altruistic reasons to rational choice. From this standpoint, it is still an open question, whether either egoism or altruism will be rationally preferable, all things considered.

In this regard, there are two kinds of cases that must be considered: cases in which there is a conflict between the relevant self-interested and moral reasons, and cases in which there is no such conflict.

It seems obvious that where there is no conflict and both reasons are conclusive reasons of their kind, both reasons should be acted upon. In such contexts, R should do what is favored both by altruism and by self-interest.

Now when we rationally assess the relevant reasons in conflict cases, three solutions are possible. First, we could say that self-interested reasons always have priority over conflicting altruistic reasons. Second, we could say just the opposite, that altruistic reasons always have priority over conflicting self-interested reasons. Third, we could say that some kind of compromise is rationally required. In this compromise, sometimes self-interested reasons would have priority over altruistic reasons, and sometimes altruistic reasons would have priority over self-interested reasons.

Once the conflict is described in this manner, the third solution can be seen to be the one that is rationally required. This is because the first and second solutions give exclusive priority to one class of relevant reasons over the other, and only a question-begging justification can be given for such an exclusive priority.

---

not for herself except instrumentally, the altruist thinks that her own interests count for others, but not for herself except instrumentally.

Only by employing the third solution, and sometimes giving priority to self-interested reasons, and sometimes giving priority to altruistic reasons, can we avoid a question-begging resolution.

Notice also that this standard of rationality will not support just any compromise between the relevant self-interested and altruistic reasons. The compromise must be a nonarbitrary one, for otherwise it would beg the question with respect to the opposing egoistic and altruistic perspectives.[160] Such a compromise would have to respect the rankings of self-interested and altruistic reasons imposed by the egoistic and altruistic perspectives, respectively. Since for R there is a separate ranking of his relevant self-interested and altruistic reasons, we can represent these rankings from the most important reasons to the least important reasons as follows:

Rich Person R	
Self-Interested Reasons	Altruistic Reasons
1	1
2	2
3	3
•	•
•	•
•	•
N	N

Accordingly, any nonarbitrary compromise among such reasons in seeking not to beg the question against either egoism or altruism will have to give priority to those reasons that rank highest in each category. Failure to give priority to the

---

160 Notice that by "egoistic perspective" here is meant the view that grants the prima facie relevance of both egoistic and altruistic reasons to rational choice and then tries to argue for the superiority of egoistic reasons. Similarly by "altruistic perspective" is meant the view that grants the prima facie relevance of both egoistic and altruistic reasons to rational choice and then tries to argue for the superiority of altruistic reasons.

highest-ranking altruistic or self-interested reasons would, other things being equal, be contrary to reason.

Of course, there will be cases in which high-ranking reasons conflict with high-ranking reasons. Some of these cases will be "lifeboat cases," as, for example, where you and someone else are stranded in a lifeboat that has only enough resources for one of you to survive. But although such cases are surely difficult to resolve (maybe only a chance mechanism, like flipping a coin, can offer a reasonable resolution), they surely do not reflect the typical conflict between R's relevant self-interested and altruistic reasons.[161] Typically, one or the other of the conflicting reasons will rank significantly higher on its respective scale, thus permitting a clear resolution.

Now we can see how morality can be viewed as just such a nonarbitrary compromise between self-interested and altruistic reasons. First, a certain amount of self-regard is morally required or at least morally acceptable. Where this is the case, high-ranking self-interested reasons have priority over low-ranking altruistic reasons. Second, morality obviously places limits on the extent to which people should pursue their own self-interest. Where this is the case, high-ranking altruistic reasons have priority over low-ranking self-interested reasons. In this way, morality can be seen to be a nonarbitrary compromise between self-interested and altruistic reasons, and the "moral reasons" that constitute that compromise can be seen as having an absolute priority over the self-interested or altruistic reasons that conflict with them.[162]

Interpreting morality as compromise

Of course, exactly how this compromise is to be worked out is a matter of considerable debate. So far developed, it is open to a number of different interpretations, and so it is anything but

---

161 A lifeboat conflict would be represented as a conflict between a high-ranking self-interested and a high-ranking altruistic reason of R.

162 For further discussion, see my *The Triumph of Practice Over Theory in Ethics*, ch. 2.

a decision procedure for solving practical moral problems. Accordingly, a Utilitarian approach seems to favor one sort of interpretation of the compromise, a Kantian approach another, and an Aristotelian approach yet another. Nevertheless, irrespective of how this debate is best resolved, it is clear that some sort of a compromise view, or moral solution, is rationally preferable to either egoism or altruism when judged from a nonquestion-begging standpoint. Surely that should suffice to show that the self-interested stance taken by R is not reasonable – that is, cannot be given a nonquestion-begging defense.

While Morality as Compromise can thus be seen as rationally preferable to both egoism and altruism, it is anything but a complete moral perspective.[163] In particular, it does not clearly specify when its requirements can be coercively enforced, and so its requirements seem to be open to a libertarian, or a welfare liberal, or even a socialist interpretation. Agreeing with libertarians, it would appear that we could hold that high-ranking altruistic reasons have priority over conflicting low-ranking self-interested reasons, and that acting upon them would provide comparably greater benefit, and still hold that we should not enforce that priority by means of a welfare state. Alternatively, it seems, we could agree with welfare liberals that we should coercively establish a right to welfare, or agree with socialists that we should go further and require substantial

---

163 Here is one way I like to think about the incompleteness or inadequacy of Morality as Compromise. Suppose that John Stuart Mill had given us a nonquestion-begging argument that utilitarianism is rationally preferable to egoism. I think that we would be happy to accept such an argument as useful in our defense of morality, but then we would still want to go on to indicate the ways that utilitarianism is an inadequate morality that needs to be improved upon or reinterpreted in various ways. That is the way I think about Morality as Compromise. It is a useful way to think about morality for the purpose of showing the rational superiority of morality over egoism, but it is not useful for other purposes. That is why to settle the question of which moral requirements should be enforced, I am now shifting the discussion to a comparative evaluation of the political-moral perspectives of libertarianism, welfare liberalism, and socialism.

equality. Morality as Compromise appears open to all three interpretations.[164] So while Morality as Compromise would have established that R's high-ranking altruistic reason to help S and his family trumps his low-ranking self-interested reason that conflicts with it, it does not establish that R can be justifiably forced to act on his altruistic reason. Morality as Compromise does establish that his professed egoism in this context is unreasonable, but not that he could be justifiably forced to act so as to benefit S and his family in their time of need. And so Morality as Compromise looks like it is compatible with a form of libertarianism that even Narveson could endorse that requires altruism in contexts like S's, but does not justify the enforcement of that requirement, and so would not support a right to welfare.

But appearances are deceiving here. This is because once we take into account my previous argument that conflicts between the rich, such as R, and the poor, such as S, can be understood to involve either restricting the liberty of the poor (S) to meet their basic needs or restricting the liberty of the rich (R) to meet their nonbasic needs, the need for an enforceable resolution becomes apparent.[165] In fact, Narveson was assuming just such an enforceable resolution. He was assuming that any attempt by S to secure from R's surplus what he and his family needed for survival would be met with forceful resistance by R and that resistance would leave S even worse off. Narveson further assumed that S knew that this would be the case and that this is why he "agreed" a system of Full Property Rights with no right to welfare. But the fact that R would effectively resist S's attempt to acquire the resources that he and his family require

---

164 It is important to note that the idealization that was introduced to show the superiority of Morality as Compromise over egoism and altruism renders the view not as useful as it appears to be for determining particular practical moral requirements. This is because the relatively precise rankings of self-interested and altruistic reasons were simply hypothesized to better illustrate the choice over egoism, altruism, and morality. Unfortunately, such relatively precise rankings are not likely to be found in real life.

165 Again, libertarians have never rejected the need for enforcement when important liberties are at stake.

for survival does not show that R would be rationally justified in so resisting.

We have seen that while Morality as Compromise establishes that R's high-ranking altruistic reason to help S and his family trumps his low-ranking self-interested reason that conflicts with it, it does not establish that R can be justifiably forced to act on that altruistic reason. In the context of Narveson's example, what does establish that R can be justifiably forced to act on that altruistic reason is that we either have to enforce R's low-ranking self-interested reason or to enforce his conflicting high-ranking altruistic reason. Having no alternative but to enforce one or the other of these conflicting reasons, it seems clear that we should enforce the high-ranking altruistic reason of R that corresponds to the negative liberty of the poor not to be interfered with in taking from the surplus of the rich what they require to meet their basic needs. Accordingly, justifying the enforcement of that high-ranking altruistic reason thereby secures a right to welfare and the rejection of Narveson's system of Full Property Rights in favor of a system of Conditional Property Rights.

Meeting Narveson's response

Now Narveson insists that the argument between R and S must start from their actual situation, not from some abstract, hypothetical position, like being behind a Rawlsian view of ignorance, and I agree. But there are at least two ways to do this. One way is to start with R's commitment to act in accord with his best self-interest. The other way is to start with R's commitment to act in a way that is supported by a good, that is, a nonquestion-begging argument.

As Narveson interprets his example, R starts with a commitment to act in accord with his best self-interest, as does S, and given that war would be counterproductive for both, they both conclude that libertarian Full Property Rights without a right to welfare would be in the best self-interest of each of them, even though it will lead to starvation and death for S and his family in ten years time.

But things could have been different. If R and S had both been talented, there could be a truly mutually beneficial exchange between them through which they both significantly benefited and secured a decent life for themselves. Or alternatively, let us say R had discovered a way to dominate S, such that R lives well by appropriating most of the product of S's labor while S just manages to scrape by with no viable alternative but to submit to R's domination – unfortunately a pattern of life that has a long history and still persists in many places.[166] While all of these arrangements meet Narveson's standard of mutual benefit from self-interested starting points, only one of them – the one where both R and S significantly benefit from their exchange, thereby both securing a decent life for themselves – also meets my standard of being supported by a good, that is, nonquestion-begging, argument. For the other two arrangements, my standard requires different resolutions, even when these resolutions are not realized in practice.

As I mentioned before, Narveson maintains that we should start the argument between R and S from their actual situation. He takes this to mean that we should assume that R and S are

166 This alternative is modeled by the game of chicken in rational choice theory. Peter Danielson raises the possibility of this choice situation as an objection to Narveson's preferred view of a prisoner's dilemma choice situation facing his rational contractors. See Peter Danielson, "The Rights of Chickens," in *For and Against the State*, ed. T. Sanders and J. Narveson (Lanham, MD: Rowman & Littlefield, 1996), pp. 171–93, and Peter Danielson, "Simple Games and Complex Ethics," in *Liberty, Games and Contracts*, ed. Murray, pp. 103–14. Surprisingly, Narveson's response to this challenge is to claim that his contractors will have moral reasons to transform Chicken choice situations into Prisoner Dilemma ones, thus making them more amenable to his libertarian solution. See Jan Narveson, "The Anarchist's Case," in *For and Against the State*, p. 207, and Jan Narveson, "Social Contract, Game Theory and Liberty: Responding to My Critics," in *Liberty, Games and Contracts*, pp. 325–7. But where do the moral reasons to make this transformation come from? Supposedly Narveson's goal was to derive moral reasons from self-interested ones, as Hobbes and Gauthier had attempted to do. If Narveson now wants to introduce more assumptions to get around the problem raised by Chicken choice situations, he need not introduce moral assumptions. As I have shown here, appealing to a standard of nonquestion-begginess would suffice.

each committed to self-interested reasons but not necessarily to altruistic ones. Relying on assumption, Narveson works through his example to the conclusion that R and S should agree to a system of Full Property Rights with no right to welfare on the grounds that this is the only option that is mutually beneficial, bringing about a Pareto improvement for both R and S.

Yet while rejecting any role for altruism in determining what R and S should do, Narveson admits that rival altruisms, even more than conflicts of self-interest, have had a significant impact on human affairs. Surely this is an odd way of starting from where people actually are.

My approach, as I have indicated, is to start from people's commitment to providing a good, that is, nonquestion-begging, argument for what they do. I also assume that I am talking about people who have the capacity to act upon both self-interested and altruistic reasons. But if we are not talking about such people who are we talking about?

Of course, if people are not committed to providing good, that is, nonquestion-begging, arguments for what they do, I do have a problem. In that case, I would probably want to adopt a different role, stop being a moral and political philosopher, and become a rhetorician trying to convince those who are not committed to providing good arguments for what they do, that given other commitments they have, they still should do such and such. This is in fact the approach that I think Narveson has taken upon himself. He is not trying to provide a good, that is, a nonquestion-begging, argument for what R and S should do, or he would have been led to my conclusion. Instead, he is addressing those who have at least implicitly renounced the goal of providing good arguments for what they do. By following out some of the commitments these people still seem to have (i.e., to their self-interest) he reaches an endorsement of Full Property Rights without a right to welfare. While both of these approaches are valuable, I think it is clear that moral and political philosophers should favor the approach I have taken, the one that is grounded in the principle of nonquestion-beggingness rather than in the principle of self-interest.

Narveson's more practical challenges to my argument

Now Narveson has also challenged my argument for welfare rights from libertarian premises in more practical ways. Noting that I allow that "the case for restricting the liberty of the rich depends upon the willingness of the poor to take advantage of whatever opportunities are available to them to engage in mutually beneficial work," Narveson contends, "We should . . . note that through this small door proceeds the entire argument de facto, concerning the contemporary welfare state," claiming that this requirement is not "fulfilled anywhere in the world."[167] This is truly an astonishing claim that the poor are everywhere themselves responsible for their fate! It is difficult to understand how Narveson could really believe that this is the case.

In the discussion from which Narveson is quoting I had included a further condition on restricting the liberty of the rich, namely, a willingness of the poor to take advantage of whatever charity is offered to them, and Narveson may be implicitly appealing to this condition as well as to his "astonishing claim" to alleviate the need for a welfare state. Nevertheless, he only sees charity as providing a subsistence minimum and then only in "contemporary front-line nations."[168] He does not claim that charity will suffice to meet even the subsistence needs of the poor "anywhere in the world."

In the end, much of the support for Narveson's Full Property Rights Libertarianism depends on whether he is correct in claiming that the poor are everywhere responsible for their fate. If he is wrong about this, as I think he surely is, then it is difficult to see how the poor would find his Full Property Rights Libertarianism to be acceptable? It is not because there is a good, that is, nonquestion-begging argument for his form of libertarianism. A good argument with respect to the conflict between the rich and the poor, as I have shown, favors the poor over the rich when the poor are truly in need through no fault of their own.

167 "Comments on Sterba's 'Ethics' Article," p. 6.
168 "Sterba on Reconciling Conceptions of Justice," p. 11.

Unable to provide a nonquestion-begging argument for his form of libertarianism, Narveson claims instead that it can be supported on the grounds that it is mutually beneficial to the rich and to the poor, or at least that it does not make either of them worse off.

Not surprisingly, even this claim depends on a question-begging specification of the starting point from which "mutual benefit" or "not being made worse off" is to be determined. For example, Narveson assumes that first acquisition, all by itself, establishes approved liberty rights from which starting point mutual benefit and not being made worse off is then to be specified, even when those who come, or will come, later would have no nonquestion-begging reasons to unconditionally recognize such liberties.

Of course, there is no denying that a resolution of the conflict between the rich and the poor based on a standard of nonquestion-beggingness can be quite demanding. For example, Narveson recognizes that the minimum that I derive from libertarian premises is not a subsistence minimum but one that provides the poor with the resources required to meet their basic needs so as to secure a decent life for themselves.[169] Narveson further objects that this more generous minimum is arbitrarily specified. For example, persons living below the poverty line in the USA have a monetary income several times the median income of people in India.[170] How could that be justified?

What Narveson fails to recognize here is that the costs of meeting basic needs can vary between different societies and within the same society at different times. Now a person's basic needs are those that must be satisfied in order not to seriously endanger a person's mental or physical well-being. Needs in general, if not satisfied, lead to lacks and deficiencies with respect to various standards. Basic needs, if not satisfied, lead to significant lacks and deficiencies with respect to a standard of mental

---

169 Jan Narveson, "Comment on 'Reconciling Liberty and Equality or Why Libertarians Should be Socialists'" (unpublished circulated paper), p. 2.
170 Jan Narveson, "Sterba's Program of Philosophical Reconciliation," p. 408.

and physical well-being. Thus a person's needs for food, shelter, medical care, protection, companionship, and self-development are, at least in part, needs of this sort.[171]

Actually, specifying a minimum of this sort seems to be the goal of the poverty index used in the USA since 1964.[172] This poverty index is based on the US Department of Agriculture's Economy Food Plan (for an adequate diet) and on evidence showing that low-income families spend about one-third of their income on food. The index is then adjusted from time to time to take changing prices into account. To accord with the goal of satisfying basic needs, the poverty index would have to be further adjusted to take into account (a) that the Economy Food Plan was developed for "temporary or emergency use" and is inadequate for a permanent diet, and (b) that recent evidence shows that low-income families spend one-quarter rather than one-third of their income of food.[173]

Of course, one might think that a minimum should be specified in terms of a purely conventional standard of living that varies over time and between societies. We could do this, for example, by specifying a minimum in terms of the income received by the middle-quintile household group in a society. For example, in the USA in 2004, the middle household income was between $34,738 and $55, 331.[174] Specifying a minimum in this way, however, leads to certain difficulties. Suppose that the middle-quintile household group in a society with the wealth of the USA fell within a $1,000–$1,499 income bracket in 2004

---

171 It also should be pointed out that at least some of the goods required for the satisfaction of people's basic needs are participatory in nature. These goods relate primarily to the satisfaction of people's basic needs for companionship and self-development. It also seems to be the case that a high level of participation in the institutions that control the distribution of goods in society is required to ensure that people's basic needs will be met. See Iris Young, "Self-Determination as a Principle of Justice," *The Philosophical Forum* 18 (1979), pp. 30–46.

172 John Iceland, *Poverty in America: A Handbook*, 2nd edn (Berkeley: University of California Press, 2006), ch. 3.

173 *Ibid*.

174 http://en.wikipedia.org/wiki/Household_income_in_the_United_States

dollars. Certainly, it would not thereby follow that a guarantee of $1,500 per household would constitute an acceptable minimum for such a society. Or suppose that the middle-quintile household group fell within the $95,000–$99,999 income bracket in 2004 dollars. Certainly, a minimum of $100,000 per household would not thereby be required. Moreover, there seem to be similar difficulties with any attempt to specify an acceptable minimum in a purely conventional manner.

Nevertheless, it still seems that an acceptable minimum should vary over time and between societies, at least to some degree. Fortunately a basic-needs approach to specifying an acceptable minimum can account for such variation without introducing any variation into the definition of the basic needs themselves. Instead, variation enters into the cost of satisfying these needs at different times and in different societies.[175] For in the same society at different times and in different societies at the same time, the normal costs of satisfying a person's basic needs can and do vary considerably. These variations are due in large part to the different ways in which the most readily available means for satisfying basic needs are produced. For example, in more affluent societies, the most readily available means for satisfying a person's basic needs are usually processed so as to satisfy nonbasic needs at the same time as they satisfy basic needs. This processing is carried out to make the means more attractive to persons in higher income brackets who can easily afford the extra cost. As a result, the most readily available means for satisfying basic needs are much more costly in more affluent societies than in less affluent societies. This occurs obviously with respect to the most readily available means for satisfying basic needs for food, shelter, and transportation, but it also occurs with respect to the most readily available means for satisfying basic needs for companionship, self-esteem, and self-development. For a person in more affluent societies cannot normally satisfy even these latter needs without participating in at least some

175 See Bernard Gendron, *Technology and the Human Condition* (New York: St. Martin's Press, 1977), pp. 222–7.

relatively costly educational and social development practices. Accordingly, there will be considerable variation in the normal costs of satisfying a person's basic needs as a society becomes more affluent over time, and considerable variation at the same time in societies at different levels of affluence. Over time, however, this can and should be changed, as more and more efficient ways of meeting people's basic needs worldwide are developed.

Citing data about how the American poor fare with respect to the number of persons per room (.56) and with respect to the number who lack indoor flush toilets (1.8 per cent), Narveson suggests that "the American poor are in fact better off in the usual 'material' terms as a group than the citizenry as a whole in (some) other . . . front-line countries, not to mention those in the Second and Third Worlds." Unfortunately, there are other data which I have cited earlier which suggest a less rosy picture.[176] For example, 22.4 per cent of children live below the poverty line in the USA as compared to 4.9 per cent in Germany, 5 per cent in Sweden, and 7.8 per cent in Switzerland, and the USA shares with Italy the highest infant mortality rate of the major industrialized nations. The USA also ranks sixty-seventh among all nations in the percentage of national income received by the poorest 20 per cent of its population, ranking it the absolute lowest among industrialized nations.[177]

Narveson also claims, citing Charles Murray, that the poor in the USA and Canada would have been better off if the welfare state had never existed. According to Murray,

> Basic indicators of well-being took a turn for the worse in the 1960s, most consistently and most drastically for the poor . . . We tried to provide more for the poor and produced more poor instead. We tried to remove the barriers to escape from poverty, and inadvertently built a trap.[178]

176 Rose and Shiratori, eds., *The Welfare State East and West*; Carville, *We're Right They're Wrong*.
177 Wolff, *Where We Stand*; Kurian, *The New Book of Work Rankings*.
178 Charles Murray, *Losing Ground* (New York: Basic Books, 1984), pp. 8–9.

Yet while Murray's work has been widely hailed in certain quarters, critics have argued that the relevant data do not support his argument.

For example, Michael Harrington points out that while black male labor-force participation did drop 7 per cent between 1969 and 1981 (thus fitting nicely with Murray's thesis that welfare programs are the villain) there was a drop of 7.4 per cent between 1955 and 1968.[179] So the drop in employment was actually greater before welfare programs came on line than it was after, just the opposite of what Murray's thesis would lead us to expect.

Or consider black women. Supposedly they are even more exposed than men to the supposed work disincentives of welfare programs, since as mothers they could have qualified for Aid to Families of Dependent Children during this period. But, as Harrington shows, their labor-force participation rate increased between 1955 and 1981 by 7.5 per cent, and more than half of that progress occurred after 1968.

And on the question of whether welfare programs did any good, Christopher Jencks claims that the relevant data tell a story that is quite different from the one Murray tells us in *Losing Ground*. He writes:

First, contrary to what Murray claims, "net" poverty declined almost as fast after 1965 as it had before. Second, the decline in poverty after 1965, unlike the decline before 1965, occurred despite unfavorable economic conditions, and depended to a great extent on government efforts to help the poor. Third, the groups that benefited from this "generous revolution," as Murray rightly calls it, were precisely the groups that legislators hoped would benefit, notably the aged and the disabled. The groups that did not benefit were the ones that legislators did not especially want to help. Fourth, these improvements took place despite demographic changes that would ordinarily have made things worse. Given the

---

179 Michael Harrington, "Crunched Numbers," *The New Republic*, 193 (28 January 1985), p. 8.

difficulties, legislators should, I think, look back on their efforts to improve the material conditions of poor people's lives with some pride.[180]

So much then for the claim that the poor, at least in the USA, would have been better off if the welfare state had never existed.

Narveson also cites Paul Krugman with respect to the benefits that international capitalism has brought to poor people in Third World countries like Indonesia and throughout the Pacific Rim. However, Krugman himself notes that for twenty years international capitalism did very little for these countries, keeping them as exporters of raw materials and importers of manufactures. Only recently, through a combination of factors, have industries been willing to take advantage of very low wages (sixty cents an hour), and, as a consequence, they have improved somewhat the situation of the poor in these countries.[181] Nevertheless, the situation of the poor would clearly be improved much more if Narveson and others were to recognize that what I have argued is the logical consequence of his own libertarian moral view – a basic needs minimum guaranteed to all those who are willing to take advantage of whatever opportunities are available to them to engage in mutually beneficial work.

Even so, a conflict can develop between providing normal and providing extraordinarily costly means for meeting people's basic needs, especially with respect to the means necessary for staying alive. This is particularly the case today as people in Western societies are now living longer and extraordinarily costly medical means, like dialysis and heart-and-lung machines, are now being used to extend lives. We can easily imagine the mounting costs of providing more and more people with such costly means for extending their lives at some point coming into conflict with the allocation of resources for meeting the normal costs of providing

---

180 Christopher Jencks, "How Poor are the Poor?" *New York Review of Books* 32 (9 May 1985), p. 44.
181 Paul Krugman, "In Praise of Cheap Labor," *Slate*, 20 March 2000 (http://slate.msn.com/Dismal/97-03-20/Dismal.asp).

other people with the means for meeting their basic needs. What is most important is that the provision of such resources for extraordinarily costly means for maintaining people's lives not be made unconditionally.[182] Just as the provision of even the ordinary means for meeting people's basic needs in a welfare system is conditional on people doing all that they can to meet their own basic needs, so likewise should the provision of extra-ordinarily costly means for meeting people's basic needs in an insured medical system be conditional upon people doing all that they can by incorporating preventive health-care practices into their lives so as not to have to rely on such costly means for meeting their needs. At the individual level, this would involve taking such preventive measures as maintaining a healthy diet and an adequate exercise program. At the social level, this would require greater restrictions on the workplace to minimize unhealthy and risky working conditions, and greater restrictions on the marketplace so as to better control environmental pollu-tants – those externalities of the free market, which, according to some estimates, are responsible for a large percentage of the cancers that now afflict us.[183] By introducing such measures, we should be able to discover a fair way for meeting both the normal and extraordinary costs of satisfying people's basic needs among existing generations.

Unfortunately the problem could arise again in a new and more pronounced form once future generations are taken into account. Here again, if some members of existing generations are using up nonrenewable resources to provide the extraordinarily costly means for satisfying their basic needs will not this in turn use up resources for meeting the normal costs of satisfying the basic needs of some members of future generations? Whose liberties should then have priority in such conflicts: the liberty

---

182 Daniel Shapiro discusses just such conflicts in his attempt to reconcile welfare liberal and libertarian views concerning medical insurance schemes, and I am happy to endorse the key element of his suggested solution. See his *Is the Welfare State Justified?*

183 See, for example, Kristin Shader-Frechette's *Taking Action, Saving Lives* (New York: Oxford University Press, 2007), esp. ch. 1.

of some existing people not to be interfered with in using nonrenewable resources to meet the extraordinary cost of satisfying their own basic needs or the liberty of a presumably greater number of future people not to be interfered with in using those same resources to meet the normal costs of satisfying their own basic needs? Suppose we imagine that the existing people who require the extraordinarily costly means for meeting their basic needs have done all that can be reasonably expected of them not to have to rely on such extraordinarily costly means. In that case, whose liberty should have priority?

It is important to note here that this question is not one of population policy. What we are imagining is that existing generations have already made procreative decisions that in the normal course of events will insure that the members of future generations with whom they are in conflict will come into existence and so now the question before them is: whose basic needs should have priority, or, put another way, whose liberty with respect to their basic needs should be respected?

I think that what we have to imagine here are morally constrained negotiations taking place between existing and future generations, something like the negotiations that John Rawls imagines taking place behind his veil of ignorance. In these negotiations, we can imagine existing generations committing themselves to doing all that they can to reduce those occasions when the costs of meeting their basic needs become extraordinary while at the same time imposing quality of life standards as to when such costs can be incurred that would be acceptable from the perspective of future generations. Obviously these negotiations would be difficult to carry out, yet no more difficult, in principle, than those of the Iroquois Indians when they asked themselves when facing major decisions: what would be the impact on the seventh generation?[184] Difficult though these deliberations would be, they are focused entirely on the appropriate means for meeting basic human needs. It is also important

---

184 Al Gore, *Earth in the Balance* (New York: Houghton Mifflin, 1992), p. 339.

to notice here that in this discussion what is taken as settled is that existing generations cannot use resources to meet their luxury or nonbasic needs in ways that interfere with the ability of future generations to meet their basic needs. So while some practical problems remain, the significance of that settled conclusion for global justice is hard to overestimate.

Narveson thinks that the ideals of liberty and equality are incompatible because the ideal of liberty is a negative ideal requiring that people not interfere in certain ways with one another, whereas the ideal of equality is a positive ideal requiring that people do certain things to bring about equality in society.[185] Yet even accepting this way of understanding the two ideals,[186] what the argument of this essay shows is that the ideals of liberty and equality can still be reconciled in practice. This is because the pattern of commissions or interferences that the ideal of equality requires can be approximated by the omissions or noninterferences that the libertarian ideal requires and because other permitted actions taken by the rich and the poor will render the practical gap between these two ideals virtually nonexistent.[187]

In this section, I have addressed the most detailed and important objections to my argument from liberty to equality, developed by libertarians themselves, who obviously have the greatest interest in defeating it. I believe that I have adequately responded to their objections and on grounds that they themselves either accept or should accept.

---

185 Narveson, *The Libertarian Idea*, pp. 61, 266–7, and "Liberty, Equality, and Distributive Justice."

186 Liberty can be characterized as a positive ideal, just as equality can be characterized as a negative ideal, as it is in those interpretations of equal opportunity where the ideal is understood to require that certain unfair constraints not be imposed on candidates for various positions.

187 Some of the permissible actions I have in mind here are the actions of the rich to set up positive welfare rights in order justifiably to prevent the poor and their agents from exercising the poor's negative welfare rights and the actions of the agents of the poor (in some cases "Robin Hoods") assisting the poor in their exercise of their negative welfare rights.

4   My argument again and its future prospects

To defend an ideal of substantial equality, one that provides everyone with the resources for a decent life but no more, I have taken the unusual step of starting with the premises of my libertarian opponents who defend an ideal of negative liberty and reject an ideal of substantial equality. My defense has simply been that libertarians are wrong about what their ideal requires. When properly interpreted, I claim, an ideal of negative liberty does lead to substantial equality. The first step of my argument involves seeing that there are conflicts of negative liberty between the rich and the poor. In particular, there is a conflict between the liberty of the rich not to be interfered with in using their surplus resources for luxury purposes, and the liberty of the poor not to be interfered with in taking from the rich what they require to meet their basic needs. To give priority to one of these liberties, as we must, we have to reject the other. I then argue in two ways that the liberty of the poor has priority over the liberty of the rich. First, I contend that the "ought" implies "can" principle, which is common to all moral and political perspectives, favors the liberty of the poor over the liberty of the rich. Second, I contend that for anyone who might be tempted to reject morality because it is too demanding in favor of rational egoism, the principle of nonquestion-beggingness favors morality over egoism, and thereby the liberty of the poor over the liberty of the rich. In this way, I provide the moral and rational grounding for a negative right to welfare.[188] Extending this right to welfare to distant peoples and future generations, as we must, I argue that the right requires that we use no more resources than we need for a decent life so that distant peoples and future generations will also, as much as possible, have the resources they will need for a decent life. And this, I claim, will lead to an equality in the use of resources over space and time. In this way,

---

188 Recall how I argue that a negative right to welfare leads to a positive right to welfare.

I conclude that an ideal of negative liberty leads to the practical requirements of an ideal of substantial equality.

Yet my debate with libertarians and others is far from over. Even if my argument from libertarian premises to substantial equality is successful, as I think it is, I do not expect that will suffice to win over large numbers of libertarians to my conclusions, at least not just yet. It will take some time for libertarians and nonlibertarians alike to come to terms with my full argument with its comparison to other others arguments directed at similar conclusions and with its responses to libertarian objections. My argument will also have to be evaluated in conjunction with that of my co-author Jan Narveson. While I think I have adequately responded to Narveson's attempts in the past to undercut my argument from liberty to equality, it may be that in his contribution to this volume, he has come up with a new truly devastating objection to my attempt to reconcile negative liberty and substantial equality. That is certainly a possibility that I will have to consider.

So you can expect that libertarians will be eying my argument warily, poking here and there, trying to come up with an objection that could plausibly undermine it. Of course, they cannot fairly do this forever. At some point, unless they can come up with an objection that plausibly works, they will have to endorse the conclusion that I derived from the premises they endorse. I am just hoping that the process of assessment does not take too long.

Where the success of my argument from liberty to equality is likely to have more of an immediate impact is among the relatively large group of people who are "fence sitters" with respect to this debate, particularly those who are attracted to an ideal of negative liberty but also would like to endorse an ideal of equality. Among this group of people, the success of my argument should lead to new adherents. There will be a problem, however, among those who want to endorse an ideal of equality, but not one, like mine, that requires substantive equality. These people would be happy enough with my argument from an ideal of negative liberty to a negative right to welfare. What bothers them is the move I make from that right to substantial equality. They may look for some way to avoid this step of my argument, relying as it does on the welfare rights of distant peoples and future generations. I myself do not see how the endorsement of this step of my argument can be avoided. Yet even if it could be, I actually have another argument that supports the same egalitarian conclusion. That argument is based on the moral status of nonhuman living beings rather than on the moral status of future (human) generations. Of course, I have not developed that argument here.[189] It is waiting in the wings, so to speak, just in case it turns out to be needed.

189 For a sketch of this argument, see my *The Triumph of Practice Over Theory in Ethics*, ch. 4.

Part II

3   The right to liberty is incompatible with the right to equality

Jan Narveson

1 The issue framed

Introduction

PROBABLY the two most popular notions in normative social theory have been those of liberty and equality. But can we have them both? Or must we take our choice between them? That is our question – but it is not really a clear formulation. Might not someone in a position to promote equality be quite at liberty to choose either way, and choose equality? Of course. Might we be equally at liberty, and might that constitute equality in the relevant sense? Maybe. So long as we leave liberty and equality simply as ideas, it seems quite clear that the idea that we must "choose" between them does not have much plausibility. In many recent books, authors have urged the point that equality and liberty are compatible.[1] But that is not what is at issue here. What is at issue is liberty or equality as possible requirements. Our subject is political principles, and politics is concerned, specifically, with the wielding of a certain kind of power. When someone has political power over someone else, the first is in a position to cause the other to be *coerced* into doing something, and coercion certainly cuts short the liberty of the coerced person, on the face of it. Governments produce laws, and laws

---

1 For example, Kai Nielsen, *Equality and Liberty* (Totowa, NJ: Rowman & Allanheld, 1985), and Richard Norman, *Free and Equal* (Oxford: Oxford University Press, 1987).

aim to induce everyone, or a great many, to do something or other, under threat – they involve, then, coercion of those people. On the face of it, that undercuts the liberty of those people, or, at least, of all those who would have wanted to do the things now forbidden. If, now, the purpose of a given law is to compel people to become equal in some way in which they would not otherwise have been, that appears to manifest incompatibility: equality seems, then, to be achieved at the price of liberty.

But are we sure of that? Might that be only an appearance, with something important having been overlooked? A clearer and deeper analysis is needed. I hope to provide that in the ensuing essay. But our question is very much narrower than what is suggested by these opening words, for my co-author, James Sterba, and I proceed from a premise shared by both of us: that we are to understand social morality in general as based, somehow, on a "social contract." Our question is whether we would agree to a general *right* of liberty, or to a general *right* of equality, or somehow to both. Moreover, what we will be concerned with is not equality generally, but rather, the idea of a social safety net, guaranteed by government.

To anticipate, I shall be arguing that the rights in question, taken as general rights, are indeed incompatible – and that the right to liberty is more fundamental, equality being limited to contexts such that we would need to reject a general right to it by comparison. I shall argue for this view on the basis of social contract ideas. In the senses relevant to our question, we *do* have to take our choice between liberty and equality, and I will support the preference for liberty. The preference for liberty is not a popular thesis these days, and so mine is, comparatively, the uphill effort in this matter.

To begin, then, we will need to become clearer about our major component notions: liberty, equality, their roles in political institutions, the sense in which "reconciliation" is relevantly possible, and the theory of social contract as it bears on this issue.

Liberty

Or should we say "freedom"? I shall use the terms interchangeably for the most part, but we might well begin by noting the very wide range of meanings for this term. There are, for example, the famous "four freedoms" of Franklin Delano Roosevelt: of speech and expression, of religion, from want, and from fear. Notably, two of these are said to be freedoms "of" something (speech, religion) and two freedoms "from" something (want and fear). The list looks rather odd, for plainly there are many more things we might want to do besides speak and practice a religion, and whether freedom "from" want and fear are exhaustive depends entirely on just which kinds of things are feared or wanted. In any case, however, such a list raises crucially the question of how these are supposed to relate to human actions and ref-rainings. With speech and religion, its relation is pretty clear: we want others not to prevent us from speaking, or from believing and practicing the religion of our choice, or lack of same. But with want and fear, there are problems: we can want all sorts of things, and to be "free from" those wants is presum-ably to have them satisfied. But who is to satisfy them, and why should that person provide whatever is needed to do so? In the case of fear, there are innumerable things we can fear, some rationally, and some irrationally. We can be paranoid, for example, but we could be in the neighborhood of a terrorist. We surely want that others not endanger us, but it is not clearly reasonable to expect others to allay any and all of our fears, and some fears are downright healthy in various circumstances: the bear circling our tent is definitely something to be concerned about. But who has to do something about this, if anyone besides the tent's occupants, and why?

Again, there is much talk of political freedom. A good deal of it is focused on *national independence*: the people in some areas will say that they are free if their government is not controlled by some foreign party. Yet the government they have might, for all that, be amply oppressive – it might be an out-and-out dictator-ship, for that matter. And then there is the subject of freedom from oppression, about which much is also said. But different people find different things oppressive, and which of these might we have a right to be free from? And again, who is to do what in order to avoid the oppression in question?

These questions help to bring into focus the subject of this book. That subject belongs to normative social theory. We want to know what we ought to do in society – what we ought to do in the way of conducting our interactions with others. My predilection is toward a classic thesis: that what we ought to do in general is to respect the liberty of our fellows. Liberty generally is being unimpeded in action: you want to do something, and nothing stops you from doing it; or if you do not want to do it, nothing compels you to. That is what it is to be free. Whether you do the thing is up to you – you are not compelled, one way or the other. But many different things can compel or impede us: lack of strength, lack of means, presence of mountains or germs, and so on. However, none of those is directly relevant here. For our present purposes, liberty is a matter of noninterference from *other people*, and especially from their intentional actions, rather than from other aspects of the world around us. (Though the "means" lacking are often obtainable for a monetary price, and lack of funds is a frequent problem for almost all of us, no doubt. And since money is a socially created resource, one which many egalitarians think ought in principle to be equal, it may be relevant.)

This general account needs a good deal of further explaining. First, while some of the interfering actions in question are *intended* to be interfering, many others are not, but manage to interfere anyway. If there is a principle calling upon Me not to interfere with You, does that extend to any and all of my actions whose further effects might conceivably prevent you from doing something you want to do? The short answer is no. At least, actions of mine which could have been reasonably foreseen to have such an effect are the main subject of concern here. We say, Don't kill!, but we know that accidents do happen, including fatal ones. If I fail to exercise due care and cross over the median on a rainy night, colliding with your vehicle and killing You, I am still not a murderer – my action is not directly of the kind we mean to proscribe in the no-killing principle. But still, it might well be criticized under the heading of negligence. There might have been driving competence at a level below what anyone piloting a vehicle can reasonably be expected to have at his command.

A more serious point about rules of the "Don't kill!" variety is that on some occasions killing is justified. Especially, we may sometimes be justified in killing in self-defense, or defense of others at risk and wanting protection from potential killers. When killings are executions, there is a serious question of whether they are justified – but we rarely suppose that the state's hired executioners are guilty of murder, for example.

Moral philosophy cannot achieve extreme precision, and we should not try. But still, a principle of general liberty, calling upon all to respect the liberty of others – to leave them in peace – is for the most part manageably clear and meaningful, despite rough edges.

Liberty: values and rights

Liberty is not properly viewed as "a value" on a par with real values such as good music, a hard day's work well done, and no end of other things. Indeed, it is fair to say that Liberty, taken by itself, has no value at all. That is because liberty is the absence of hindrance or impediment to the actions that are what we really do value, or whose results we value. And for purposes of social philosophy, it is specifically the absence of just one source of impediment, namely, the *actions of other people*, and more especially those among their actions that are specifically intended to disenable someone from his pursuits. What makes liberty important is that without it, we cannot, *by definition*, do the things whose hindrance is in question. If we do x, then it follows that we must have been free to do it.

Now what if the things in question are ones we do not care about anyway? It remains that we might be, or not be, *at* liberty to do them. But the absence of that particular liberty, that is, the presence of those particular impediments to doing those particular things, will then be of no interest to us, so far as it goes. However, and of course, it also does not go very far, for people change. If I know that I will never be able to do x, even if I should come to develop a passion for doing x, I will of course be concerned. It is imprudent to be careless of or indifferent to such things, though not only for that reason. It is, however, a very good reason, and there is no interesting objection to the standard definition of liberty that, when conjoined with a liberal view of values, it has this implication. If I were not allowed ever to eat broccoli, that would not, in my present condition, bother me in the least. But if ten years hence my doctor tells me that my life depends on it, or if I somehow conceive a gourmet's appetite for that bit of greenery, then the prohibition would indeed matter, and if I can presently do something, at sufficiently low cost, to ensure that I will not be deprived of the liberty of eating the stuff in that unlikely eventuality, I should do it. Moreover, of course, tastes and interests differ, and if I am uninterested, others may well be interested. We shall then have the question of what my attitude should be toward *their* being allowed to do the things in question. That points us down the road toward moral and political principles, which we will take up presently.

A much more important question concerns impediments to doing what we *cannot* do, even if we do very much want to do it. I would like to play the Tchaikovsky Violin Concerto, say – but I am quite sure I lack the ability to do so, now or ever, even with no end of instruction. Nevertheless, no one is impeding me from doing so. Should we say that I am "at liberty" to do so? I think we should, in the relevantly social sense of that term. Again, one with terminal cancer will be unable to live much longer, though he would very much like to. Still, if he dies from it, no one has prevented him from living.

Suppose I actually *could* play that concerto, if I were given good and sufficient instruction, and let us suppose that at present, one gets such instruction only by hiring someone to supply it – but I cannot afford it. Should we now say that the people who could teach me this but do not are "impeding" me? Are they infringing my liberty by not doing this? No. It is a serious confusion to claim that they are. Concerns about liberty are concerns about actions of others that *prevent* my doing something, not about the nondoing of actions which, if performed, might *help* me do something, even *enable* me to do it.

What others can do along that line is, certainly, an important subject but it is not the subject of liberty, as such. There are many who seem to want to make it out to be so, but if they are to make that out, it should not be by appropriating a vocabulary that is centrally devoted to something else.

Valuing liberty

One's own liberty does not have "value," though it is essential to activity and so important as to take priority over all else. We value our liberty when it is lacking, especially: if someone is preventing me from doing something I very much want to do, I shall be concerned to undo this impediment if I can. When I have it, on the other hand, I do not notice it: I simply do the interesting things I want to do – play tennis, read a book, what-ever. I devote effort to them, and try to improve my ability to do them, and to overcome various other obstacles to better performance.

We can also come to value other people's liberty, and here liberty can indeed become a value – with some people, a passion. I can think it very important that others not be prevented from doing various things. I can sympathize with them, even when I do not share their interests.

But also, one might not have this interest. When someone cannot achieve his ends, and those ends are inherently legitimate even if one does not share them, I might think, "Well, tough for him!" – but not be disposed to do anything about it. If we try to argue from the "value" of my own liberty to that of others, the result might be pretty pallid. An argument for general liberty is going to have to do better than that. Hopefully, that argument will be supplied in the ensuing pages.

Liberty and harm

The language above is misleading in one important respect. You curtail my liberty if you impede or prevent me from doing something. But suppose instead you inflict pain on me. Is this objectionable only because and if doing so prevents me from acting in certain ways? It is, of course, very likely to have that effect; at the least it will make my performance of desired actions more difficult, and insofar as it does that, it impedes me, even if it does not totally stop me from doing those things. However, pain is something that the person who experiences it does not like. One wants to be free of pain. An outsider who inflicts pain is, then, certainly putting someone into a condition that he does not want to be in. This too is the sort of thing that a concern for liberty includes. A right to liberty, as understood here, includes a right to personal security, and the absence of imposed pains or harms of all sorts. (As will be a major concern of this essay to emphasize and try to clarify, such rights are subject to universalizability conditions. We are all entitled to maximum compatible liberty, and therefore not entitled to the liberty to interfere with the liberties of yet others.)

We can be more general about this. Any given person at any given time can identify changes from his current condition that would be for the better or for the worse. Some of those alterations will be due to things happening to other persons with whom he may have relations of affection or some kind of interest. Others will be alterations in, recognizably, his own condition, independently of the existence of others. It is the imposition of worsenings by others, especially in respect of conditions of the latter kind, definable independently of others, that we may identify as "reductions of basic liberty," though not all of those would normally be so called. We are at liberty in relation to others when they do not impose on us for the worse.

This analysis makes it obvious, I hope, that there is no reason to think that some liberties are important, and others not, just as such. What makes liberty valuable is that without it you cannot accomplish your ends, and these are multifarious. No doubt some of our ends are more important to us than others, and so the liberty to accomplish those is going to be more valuable than the liberty to accomplish others. But almost anything might matter a lot to a given person, and then the liberty to do those things will be important. There is a reason for holding, as a matter of social-philosophical principle, to the importance of, simply, liberty, rather than itemizing some favored sorts and ignoring others. In so saying, I dissent from, for example, Rawls and Dworkin. Rawls moves from the general to the particular:

> no priority is assigned to liberty as such, as if the exercise of something called "liberty" had a preeminent value and were the main, if not the sole, end of political and social justice.[2]

And Dworkin notoriously tells us that

> it seems plain that there exists no general right to liberty as such. I have no political right to drive up Lexington Avenue ... if, as Bentham supposes, each of these laws diminishes my liberty, they nevertheless do not take away from me any thing that I have a right to have ... So I can have a political right to liberty ... only in such a weak sense of right that the so called right to liberty is not competitive with strong rights, like the right to equality, at all. In any strong sense of right, which would be competitive with the right to equality, there exists no general right to liberty at all.[3]

We will return to that when we discuss the thesis that there is or should be a right to general liberty. As an initial observation, however, it seems likely that both Rawls and Dworkin either overlook or at least greatly underappreciate the fundamental idea of the libertarian project. Proposing to make liberty a right means that we are turning the liberty of each into a constraint on the liberty of others. Only "compossible" liberty will be supported: liberty that is compatible with the "like liberty of all" – to use Rawls's earlier words, or, in Kant's terms, "such that it can coexist along with the freedom of the will of each and all in action, according to a universal law."[4] Or again, in Hobbes's version, "That every man be contented with so much liberty against other men, as he would allow other men against himself..."[5] Obviously

---

2 John Rawls, *Justice as Fairness: A Restatement*, ed. Kevin Kelly (Cambridge, MA: Harvard University Press, 2001), p. 44.

3 Ronald Dworkin, *Taking Rights Seriously* (Cambridge, MA: Harvard University Press, 1977), p. 269.

4 Kant, *Rechtslehre* (Doctrine of Right), Part I, Introduction, Section C. (Hastie's translation.)

5 Thomas Hobbes, *Leviathan* (New York: Dutton & Co., 1950), ch. 14.

this changes the picture completely from what Hobbes depicts as the "state of nature" in which no such restrictions are in place. And, also obviously, it means that to cite any particular example without context is simply irrelevant. The real question is whether we have the right to do all sorts of odd little things, provided doing so does not undermine the freedom of anyone else. Why should we have to make a list of particular freedoms and insist that it is only those that men are entitled to? People really are different, and the point of liberty is to declare that they are entitled to those differences – that others may not steamroller them on the ground that they are in those ways different.

Suffice to say for the present that in the view developed here, there is a general right to liberty, and, on the other hand, no general right to equality.[6] To be sure, Dworkin and Rawls are concerned especially with rights in relation to governments. Governments will, certainly, be better able to try to protect some of our liberties than others, and differences among them for that reason may well be recognized in the law. For example, the entitlement to defense counsel when arrested raises different problems than the entitlement not to be assaulted by private persons; the right to speak freely raises different problems than the right to walk the streets. Further, many things we do are comparatively trivial: we could as well do something else or do it slightly differently, and so on. We dislike in general to be inter-fered with, but often such interferences are by no means momentous. All that said, it remains that the basic point is that interferences with anything an individual intends to do require justification, specifically of the general kind that if allowed to do it, he would be, in his turn, in some way harming or endangering some other person. We do not want to add, at this fundamental level, that he is entitled not to be harmed "in respect of his rights" for the libertarian's thesis is that we have a general right not to be harmed, period, provided that what we do does not in

---

6 I develop this in Jan Narveson, "Liberty and Equality: A Question of Bal-ance?" in *Liberty and Equality*, ed. Tibor Machan (Stanford: Hoover Institution Press, 2002), pp. 35–60.

its turn harm still others. The concept of "harm" – of imposition, attack, injury, and worsening of condition – are prior to, not contingent on, independent notions of rights. What gets us from those non-normative ideas to rights has to be a normatively plausible metaethic. This is provided, in my view, by the basic contractarian idea, which proceeds from the independent, non-moral values of each to a general canon for all via an appeal to agreement.

Property

Very frequently, of course, the only harm that the individual might do in the case in question is to harm someone's property. If I take a certain car, and it is yours, then I have harmed you; if instead it is Jones's, then I have harmed Jones. But doesn't this make the notion of "harm" controversial in the way that critics of this idea claim? Consider again Dworkin's case of Lexington Avenue. By driving or walking on that bit of land, just as such, I need not be harming anyone in any way. But if Lexington Avenue belongs to someone, I may be harming him. If it belongs, in some sense, to the City of New York, which decrees that traffic proceed in such-and-such ways and not others on that street, then I in a sense "harm" it. But a decent political philosophy will accede no personhood and no rights to such an entity. Instead, it will view the agents of the city's government as agents of the people whose actions are intended to be directed or controlled by its rules of that kind. The rules issued by such a body should be coordination rules, and, if they are, then in going against the rules I would possibly, and often actually, be harming somebody (including, most often, myself). Now, the general right of liberty is a right: it has, so the libertarian intends, a normative status, the effect of which, necessarily, is to overrule certain behaviors that people really might want to engage in, and, therefore, to restrict their general liberty in those respects.

In the case of property, which is itself a normative notion, there are prior ideas that generate this notion. We must distinguish between possession, which I shall take to be descriptive, and property, which is moral or legal as the case may be. Property is certified or certifiable possession: rightful possession. And when is possession rightful? The libertarian holds that it is rightful when it is not gained at the expense of anyone else. Thus, notionally, first occupancy has always been a prominent consideration, for if one is first, it means that one has not gained the possession by dispossessing others. And liberty is, after all, precisely the condition of not being dispossessed – that is, not having one's ways forcibly altered at the hands of someone else. Once peaceable possession obtains, the possessor is then free to make exchanges with others of what are now his rights over those things – and modern civilization can get under way.

There is a thesis, promoted considerably by Robert Nozick's treatment[7] that property is historically traceable, century after century, in such a way that a break in the chain of legitimate transfers of it undoes everything ever after. If A is operating with what turns out to be stolen property, even if the theft took place twenty generations back, then A must restore it all to someone who was entitled to it. This idea is almost always completely unworkable in practice, of course, for a variety of reasons which may be summed up in the phrase "the sands of time," whose general operation makes it impossible any longer to apply those ideas. We will trace entitlements back only so far as they are really and clearly traceable. In the intervening periods, values will have changed enormously; a piece of land worth essentially nothing at time t is now worth hundreds of millions, and the case for claiming that the nth generation descendants of someone who was in legitimate possession of the original all but worthless plot are now entitled to it is overwhelmed by the obvious fact that to do so would be to enslave intervening generations of users to those supposed claimants. How to patch up residual claims of that kind is of course an interesting question, but the idea that the

---

7 Robert Nozick, *Anarchy, State, and Utopia* (New York: Basic Books, 1974), ch. 6.

whole concept of property is undone by it is without merit. Property, unsurprisingly, plays a major role in virtually all lives, and its underlying theory is liberty.[8]

Interference and failure to help

A crucial subject in this essay will be the difference, and the relation, between *interference* and *nonhelpfulness*. Shortly below we will define, and address, the distinction of negative and positive rights. We could make an analogous distinction of negative and positive liberty: negative liberty is where nothing prevents us from doing as we want, while positive liberty would be where you are not only unprevented, but have the power and resources necessary to do it.[9] And it might be that somebody else enabled you to do it, namely, by providing some of the needed resources, or the training, or whatever; also that this somebody else *could* have so enabled you, but *did not*. The latter person, in the circumstances, was *unhelpful* – he did not provide assistance, which would have enabled someone else to accomplish one or more of his ends, when he could have. Does such a person "interfere" in the sense in which liberty is the absence of interference?

Our normative question is: is there a duty to respect people's liberty – to allow them to make their own decisions rather than compelling them to do or not do? Some, including both this author and Sterba, think there is. If there is, does it follow that there is a duty to *provide* people with resources so that they can act – in short, to *help* – and this in the name of respecting liberty? On the face of it, at least, that looks to be a different thing. To see how different, consider that my respecting your liberty in the negative sense normally requires no transfer of resources at all

---

8 Jan Narveson, "Present Payments, Past Wrongs: Correcting Loose Talk about Nozick and Rectification," *Libertarian Papers* 1, 1 (2009): www.libertarianpapers. org

9 Possibly the modern originator of the terminology of "negative" and "positive" was Isaiah Berlin; see his *Four Essays on Liberty* (Oxford: Oxford University Press, 1969). "Two Concepts of Liberty" was the seminal paper, originally published in 1958.

from me to you. But my respecting your "positive liberty" depends on what you want and what you need in order to do it and what my resources are on which I can draw to help you out. In innumerable cases, clearly, I would be able to render some help, and so my "respecting your liberty" in *this* way would mean that *I do not have liberty to ignore you.*

The defender of positive freedom says: in order to do good thing x, individual A requires resources R1, R2. . .; lacking those, A cannot choose to do x, since A cannot do x at all without them. Therefore, in order to defend A's freedom to do x, the rest of us are required to supply A with R1 and R2. But the conclusion of that train of reasoning is that other people's freedom of action is *decreased.* Yet freedom of action is liberty, on any ordinary understanding of the term. Consider, for example, that with "negative" liberty, Robinson Crusoe is completely free (in the social respect). But with "positive" liberty, he is not. To be free in this notion of it is not to be independent of one's fellows in respect of their actions, but, on the contrary, it is to be able to command whatever one needs in order to do what one wants from others, who have not the liberty to refuse. Obviously these are two entirely different ideas. When we investigate the question whether liberty and equality are compatible, it is "negative" liberty that we have in mind. If we are to argue for a duty to promote positive liberty, it will have to be somehow generated from premises which do not presuppose it, but which do include respect for liberty in the negative sense.

Equality

There are two essentials to talking about equality.

Comparativeness

In contrast to liberty, the idea of equality is intrinsically relational and comparative: to be equal or unequal is to have the same, or more, or less, *than someone else.* (To be sure, we may speak intelligibly of what is more, or less, than what one had previously. Still, we usually ask, about our own situations, whether we are "doing well" or not, and sometimes whether we are doing better or not – but rarely do we have a special concern that we should be doing *equally* as well as yesterday or last month.) The relevant point here is that when we ask whether Jones is "at liberty" to do x, we are not thereby comparing Jones's situation with anyone else's; but when we ask whether he is equal, we are asking whether he has a certain relation to someone else. (Or some*thing* else, but for our present purposes such comparisons are not of direct concern. They would be of indirect concern, of course, since one's level of health or income, say, is a function of relations to various more or less measurable things, and those are what go into the data that constitute the basis of comparison among persons.)

Commensurability

The second essential is that the relation of equality or inequality be in a very broad sense *commensurable*. Not just any difference between one person and another is an inequality. Person A may be different, say, in skin color or in avocation from person B, but those are not inequalities – they are simply differences.

Differences in kind may of course be correlated with differences of degree. An obvious example is that persons of one color might be treated in some ways better or worse than persons of some other color. But that does not mean that differences in color are, as such, differences in degree (though some are such: for example, from white to black is a spectrum and people may be farther from one end than the other).[10] Roman Catholics might be treated better, or worse, than, say, Jews. But it is not that Catholics differ from Jews in their degree or amount of something; it is that an "amount of something" – respect, say, or public financial support – is given in greater measure to the one than to the other. Differences of kind, in short, are typical of differences on which inequalities of treatment have

10 And science tells us that light is a physical vibration, fundamentally, so that colors differ in wave-length. This correlates differences in perceivable kind with differences in degree, indeed. But I do not see that it makes color, *as such*, a matter of degree. Colors are phenomenal; physical light is not.

often been grounded. But it is the treatment itself that is unequal or equal, in those contexts, and that difference is what has to be commensurable if we are to characterize it as equal or unequal.

The notion of equality, in short, is at home when the difference is one of *degree* of something or other. The sense of degree may be vague and the means of measuring or estimating it imprecise, but unless there is at least some sort of difference or similarity of amount or degree or size, we cannot usefully speak of equality and inequality, or suppose that it is a matter of moral concern that the equalities in question be reduced or eliminated.

The differences in which the moral philosopher is interested are also understood to be in some way evaluatively significant. The unequal treatment we are worried about (if we are) has to be such that people would prefer more, or less, of whatever it is that is being given to various people: food, money, health, or health care are things people would rather have more of or better. The position of one's name in an alphabetical listing, or one's distance from the South Pole, on the other hand, is not usually of concern. But even when differences are significant to individuals, it does not follow that the social philosopher must take it to be morally significant, and especially to be a sign of injustice, that person A shows a different index of some desirable thing than person B. Issues of that kind, of course, are central to this investigation.

Equality and identity

Equality is not identity, though we use the "=" sign for both. Equality is indeed one kind of identity: identity of the amount or degree of whatever is relevant; if susceptible of a numerical measure, then equality would be identity of the number measuring each of the two quantities in question. It is to be noted that we can speak, sometimes usefully, of identity in the absence of notions of equality. The claim that x is identical with y need not involve quantitative comparison. We can recognize, for example, that A is the "twin" of B without having any idea how we would determine how much different they were, if they were different. For applying identity, it is enough that there are, or are not, discernible differences, of whatever kind, commensurable or not. That applies to identity in kind. For the more fundamental category of identity in case, comparisons are not between different things at all, since there is just one thing. If the jilted lover is the murderer, the point is that there is just one person of whom both descriptions are true: what we compare is the spatiotemporal track of the murderer and of the lover to see whether they are just one track, the life history of just one person, or of two or more, and we conclude that they are tracks of just one such person. Thus the morning star is identical with the evening star, so that there is just one star showing both manifestations. The relation of identity holds between a thing and itself. It is thus not comparative in the way that equality is.

Identity is not by any means useless in normative philosophy. It is important that we are all assessed in the light of the same principles. But as we have noted, those same principles for all need not be egalitarian; identity of principle, then, is a different matter from equality in the narrower sense with which we are concerned about it here. We are all – if we are not skeptics – "egalitarians" if what is meant by that is that morals extends to all, on the same fundamental terms. In that sense, but only in that sense, we may agree with Ronald Dworkin, that "No theory that respects the basic assumptions which define [our political] culture could subordinate equality to liberty, conceived as normative ideals, to any degree."[11] For of course any respectable political theory is one that declares something or other to be right for everyone – the same "something" in each case. But from this it does not follow that, as he goes on to say, "Any genuine contest between liberty and equality is a contest liberty must lose."[12] My point is that there is a much more specific sense of the word "equal" in which equalities as such may not be required or imposed. The same rule that we apply to all may call for Jones being treated very differently, even very unequally, with Smith

---

11 Ronald Dworkin, "The Place of Liberty," in *Sovereign Virtue* (Cambridge, MA: Harvard University Press, 2000), p. 128.
12 *Ibid.*

in some important way. For example, it may call for Jones getting twice the salary of Smith. Both may have been correctly dealt with by the same rule, which proportions salary to some kind of contribution, and Jones has contributed twice as much. Thus, in a genuine contest – one in which we attach reasonable significations to these terms, instead of collapsing the essential distinctions I have been concerned with here – liberty, I believe, will win, hands down. That Jones should be "leveled down" simply because he has more than Smith is a thesis that it is impossible to rationalize for the real, particular people that we all are. (Dworkin develops a theory of "equality of resources," which I regard as at base completely incoherent. But in the present work, we will be unable to pursue this further.)

Isms: libertarian and egalitarian

Libertarianism

Libertarianism is sometimes loosely identified with the view that liberty is a good thing, or an "ideal." But that is too loose. Liberty is the absence of restrictions on what one wants to do, what one is interested in doing, and as such it cannot help but be desired by the person wanting to do that thing, since, by definition, in the absence of it, he will not be able to do it. Our present question is a moral and political one. It concerns a certain political idea or program: that people have a *right* to liberty – not just that liberty might be a nice thing to have. The libertarian claim is that imposed restrictions on liberty are, insofar, prima facie[13]

---

13 Some readers may possibly not be familiar with the term "prima facie," which has become standard terminology among moral philosophers ever since its introduction by W. D. Ross (in *The Right and The Good* [Oxford: Oxford University Press, 1936]). The force of this term is that something is "prima facie" right or wrong if the thing, as described, is thereby right, or wrong, *unless* some other aspect of it outweighs the original attribution. When we make an all-things-considered judgment, we express it, simply, as right, or wrong, since the idea of an all-up judgment is that everything relevant has been taken into account. Libertarians hold that the right to liberty can only be overturned by the thing in question's being, in turn, such as to negatively affect some other person's liberty.

wrong. They require justifying. Many good things are such that A's not providing them to B is by no means wrong. But liberty, properly so called, is not of that kind. We need a justification for imposing on someone's liberty. Not "supplying" it is not like not supplying chocolate. Such, at any rate, is the libertarian's claim.

We can up the ante on this. Libertarians not only claim that interferences with people's freedom or liberty are wrong, but also that the *only* thing that can justify them is that what is interfered with is itself wrong – not just wrong in any old way, but wrong specifically in that it is in turn an interference with someone else, someone who is *not* in turn guilty of such interference with others. Thus, to take a reasonably current example, libertarians object to restrictions on various nonstandard sexual relations among consenting adults. What someone might think of, say, homosexuality, the libertarian claims that if it occurs between persons both of whom are willing participants, then the rest of us *must* allow this. John Stuart Mill puts it thus:

> the only purpose for which power can be rightfully exercised over any member of a civilized community, against his will, is to prevent harm to others. His own good, either physical or moral, is not a sufficient warrant. He cannot rightfully be compelled to do or forbear because it will be better for him to do so, because it will make him happier, because in the opinions of others to do so would be wise or even right. These are good reasons for remonstrating with him, or reasoning with him, or persuading him, or entreating him, but not for compelling him or visiting him with any evil in case he do otherwise.[14]

This is a very strong claim. At the time Mill wrote it, it was strikingly controversial, and, in terms of the political practice of today, it still is. The claim, in fact, is that nothing justifies restrictions on persons' liberty except the fact of their using their liberty to impose on the liberty of others. Government proceeds by law, and thus by compulsion: laws require us to do or forbear in this or that respect, with

14 John Stuart Mill, *An Essay on Liberty* (London: J. M. Dent, 1968), ch. 1, Introduction.

punishments or other required makings of compensation in store for those who disobey. On the libertarian view, then, there would appear to be only one general type of justification for any political action: that this action is necessary in order to reduce or eliminate or control some person or persons' impositions on relatively "innocent" others. In effect, this means that there is just one basic right, the right to liberty, that is, to do whatever is compatible with all having the same right: force may be used only to prevent (or, possibly, to punish) individuals from using force against those who are, in the relevant sense, innocent, that is, who are not themselves employing force against still others. Or as many libertarians efficiently express it, libertarianism asserts the wrongness of *initiating* force (or fraud – which raises important issues, some of which may be relevant here; I shall address that special question below, when I draw on the work of Hobbes).

The question at issue in this book is whether equality is like that as well: that is, whether actions that might have the effect of rendering two people, say, less equal than they already were before the action takes place, is something we may be "rightly compelled to forbear"; and further, whether doing something that would reduce an inequality or (if there is any other way to do so) promote equality, is something we may properly be compelled to do. Egalitarians think we may; libertarians, on the face of it at least, deny this. For purposes of present discussion, the ball, as it were, is taken to be in the egalitarian's court. Sterba and I both agree that there is a fundamental and general right to liberty. Our issue is whether this is compatible with a further right to (a measure of) equality.

Egalitarianism

A right to liberty requires others to allow the individual in question to do as he wants, just because he wants it, provided only that what he proposes to do is compatible with the like right of others. By contrast, *egalitarianism* is the thesis that we are (or may be) *required* to provide people with *equal amounts of* something or other, to be specified by the proponent. It is, then, the view that people have a general and fundamental right to equality of that something. And therefore it denies that people who are in a position to affect other persons' relative amounts of that something are at liberty regarding how they may so affect them. They are to "distribute" the thing equally rather than unequally, and are required so to do, and are therefore not at liberty in that respect. Indeed, their liberty to distribute the thing in some other way is denied, and may be taken away from them by law.

Thus I argue in this essay that libertarian*ism* is not compatible with egalitarian*ism* – but not that liberty simply as such is incompatible with equality as such. The latter is, so far as I can see, either a malformed question, or a nonissue. Compatibility and incompatibility obtain between sentences or statements, not between concepts. But if the claim is that to be equal is ipso facto not to be at liberty, or vice versa, then neither of those is true, and whether they are is, as I put it, a nonissue. But the former is very far from being a nonissue. It is, on the contrary, about as fundamental an issue as they come.

Reconciliation?

Are liberty and equality "reconcilable"? Of course they can be "reconciled," if by that is meant that people who are at liberty *could* choose to treat various people equally in whatever sense that might be possible and intended. But that is not our question here. The argument here is not that persons who are at liberty necessarily refrain from treating people equally in the respects in question, but only that they are not as such required to do so. Some will, and some will not; some will on some occasions and not on others; and so on. Egalitarianism demands a uniformity that libertarianism denies to be legitimately imposed.

For any given person, A, and B, is there anything such that A and B ought to have the same amount of it, and, further, that they ought to be given it, by *anybody* who has enough to be able to give it to them, if they do not already have it? More precisely yet, is there anything such that if A and B have different amounts, then the one with more not only ought to transfer some or all of his excess to the one with less, but may even be *compelled* to do so if he is disinclined to do it voluntarily? And in the latter case, at least, is the principle calling for *that* compatible with liberty? On the face of it, the answer to this last question is in the negative, and necessarily so.

Of course, we cannot discuss these questions intelligibly without further clarification. We need to know what the "things" and "amounts" are to which any principle calling for equalization would be referring. We need to have some idea of *how much* of these various "amounts" is in question. And we need to know what the principle of liberty does and does not entail. And we certainly need to know what would count as a "reconciliation." Initial discussions of each of these notions is, then, essential. We need, especially, to distinguish among the notions of equality, universality, and impartiality, the latter of which are often assimilated to, or just confused with, the first.

Equality, universality, and impartiality

Here are three notions playing major roles in the present discussion. They are distinct, and their distinctness needs to be clearly recognized. Let us try to get at their distinctive character here.

Universality

One of the defining properties of a moral principle is that it is to be *universal*, over the particular sets of persons whose morality we are concerned with.[15] Typically philosophers mean their principles to be universal in the sense of applying to everybody

---

15 To be sure, this has been denied, notably by Jonathan Dancy in a number of books and articles. He espouses "particularism," which I take to be a misleading name for what he really seems to be proposing. He does not, after all, think that two genuinely identical cases, in all respects, might call for entirely different moral assessments; but he does, I think, hold that we never find two such genuinely identical cases. He does think that we cannot assemble bulletproof generalizations in ethics, and appears to profess that generalization is – perhaps in consequence – useless. It is impossible to do justice to his views here, of course. Whether the rest of us really disagree with Dancy's main thesis is something not easy to fathom. But his attacks on universality do nothing to change my mind on this major point. For a delightfully named sample of his writings on the matter, see *Ethics Without Principles* (Oxford: Clarendon Press, 2004), p. 229.

there is (or rather, everyone capable of moral behavior, which may not be everyone). Over this universe, the principle affirms that all these agents are to act in some way(s), or to refrain from acting in some way(s). It says the *same* thing to all of them: murder no one! – for example. No one is left out.

It is easy to employ the term "equality" for this purpose: to apply to all is to say the same to all, and thus, it is supposed, to treat all "equally." But we should refrain from this assimilation. Equality is narrower than this. Equal treatment is not addressing the same, hence an equal number of, words to all! The equality in question here is an equality of some substantial aspects of the world. It is those aspects which are to be, somehow, equalized. Thus, for example, many egalitarians hold that incomes, in principle at least, should be the same for all. Others, like Dworkin, hold that "resources" should be the same for all.[16] Nowadays nearly all seem to think that we are entitled to "equal opportunity." And still others hold to yet further values of the variable to be equalized. What makes the theorist an egalitarian is not the choice of value but the advocacy that it be, as a matter of right, equalized among all.

To be sure, equality in the favored respect might be impossible; at the least, and typically, it might be highly impractical. The egalitarian might then refine his thesis, saying only that we should attempt where possible to reduce inequalities, or even, perhaps, that we should contain the permissible inequalities within certain limits. Thus John Rawls famously proposes his "difference principle" which permits inequalities provided that they maximally improve the prospects of the worst-off.[17]

16 Ronald Dworkin, "Equality of Resources," in *Sovereign Virtue* (Cambridge, MA: Harvard University Press, 2000), pp. 65–119; but further chapters are relevant, see esp. chs. 1, 3, 4, 6, and 7.

17 John Rawls, *A Theory of Justice* (Cambridge, MA: Harvard University Press, 1971), presentation of the "second principle of justice," p. 60; restated and extensively refined, p. 302. I have criticized Rawls's formulation, holding that it is in the end contentless. See Jan Narveson, "A Puzzle about Economic Inequality in Rawls' Theory," in *Respecting Persons in Theory and Practice* (Lanham, MD: Rowman & Littlefield, 2002), pp. 13–34 (originally published in *Social Theory and Practice*, 4, 1 [1976], pp. 1–27).

Finally, I reiterate that Sterba does not espouse general egalitarianism in this book. Rather, he holds that people have *welfare rights* of a "positive" kind (see below, "Negative and positive rights"). However, his thesis is nevertheless essentially comparative: the poor, he claims, have the rights that the rich provide them, if need be, with what will satisfy their basic needs. He thus places himself broadly in, as we might put it, the "egalitarian camp." Further discussion, of course, occupied the rest of this essay.

Impartiality

Another notion we need to distinguish from equality is *impartiality*. Most philosophers would take it as obvious that morality cannot be *partial*: it cannot single out some people or some subgroup of people for more, or less, favorable treatment than others at the level of basic principle, simply as such. Thus John Rawls lays it down as a "formal constraint of the concept of right" that a moral principle not contain proper names or what amounts to such.[18] Why we should want our moral system to be impartial is an important and interesting question, but that it should be such is, even so, fairly obvious. One feels that there is something seriously wrong with a "morality" that fails on this condition – so wrong that we are inclined to look on such a system as perhaps not really a morality itself, but a set of arbitrary dictates by some perhaps powerful group. Even so, though, impartiality is, again, not the same as equality. A moral principle can say, impartially to all, that they may treat some or all others in various quite unequal ways.

So far, then: a principle calls upon all to treat all in some way or ways. But if it calls upon all to treat all "equally" it does more than merely to tell all of them *the same thing* about how they are to treat others, just as it tells them more than only that some of them are to be especially favored or disfavored. What, then, does it do?

Egalitarianism contrasted

Equality is frequently just made synonymous, by one means or another, with one of the previous two; but that is pointless.

18 Rawls, *A Theory of Justice*, pp. 130–5.

There is a clear and meaningful understanding of the notion that makes it do some serious work. In the narrower and more useful sense in which it is a distinctive feature of some moral theories, to apply the notions of equality and inequality requires some sort of *commensuration*. The employed notions must be such that we can meaningfully say that this amount is less, or more, than that. Height, for example, is clearly a variable of the relevant kind. We can say that Martha is taller or shorter than Hilda; we can even say by how much. A moral principle calling for *equality* of something or other comes out in favor of everyone exemplifying the *same degree* of the variable in question, whatever it is. People are, say, to have equal opportunity or equal well-being or equal incomes or whatever, and in all these cases the theorist has to have some idea when people exemplify or counterexemplify the notion in question. When does A have "more" opportunity than B? If we cannot answer that, at least roughly, a principle calling for equal opportunity cannot get off the ground.

Equal opportunity is an interesting case, not least because it is widely regarded as a very important right. Many think that it is one thing that A has not succeeded as well as B at something, say, but that if this is because A did not even have the opportunity to do it whereas B did, then there has been some kind of injustice. For this purpose, without having any very good method of measuring opportunity in the abstract, it looks as though we could get by with simple difference of situation: B had the opportunity and A did not. But when someone can be said to "have" an opportunity is not so easy to say. If Smith is born brilliant and Jones is born with quite ordinary intelligence, should we say that Jones cannot have equal opportunity with Smith? Or do we say only that Jones will be unable to take advantage of opportunities that Smith would? So, for example, if Jones's parents can afford to pay for a fine education for Jones, but Jones simply cannot cut it in the institutions they would like to send him to, what does the egalitarian say about this? Some, of course, go so far as to deny that there are any genetic differences in ability, which would raise issues beyond the scope of this essay. (Where pertinent, we will simply assume the common-sense view, that there are such differences, the question being how or why they are significant, rather than whether they exist at all.)

The thesis that we are *entitled* to equal opportunity, that we *have a right* to it, lends itself readily to analysis for present purposes, because *opportunities* are normally *extended* by some persons to others. Insofar as they are extended by individuals acting on their own, here is a case where the incompatibility of liberty and equality is conspicuous, indeed stark. If I have it within my power to extend a certain opportunity to someone, and I am *free* to extend it to whomever I wish, then I am *not* under an obligation to extend it equally to all. And if it is denied that I may do this, then my liberty in that respect is, by definition, being denied.

In general, it seems, *prima facie* at least, perfectly clear that we can tell *everyone* that they are welcome to have or make differential amounts of, say, money; that they may go ahead and extend different and "more" opportunities to some than to others; and in either case that they may even be *partial* to some groups, or not, in the provision of such things.

This may surprise, or even shock, the modern reader who is used to being told that any sort of partiality for one group over another is somehow wrong. But the permitted partiality is entirely compatible with the required impartiality of morals. Morality requires that *the rules* treat no selected subset of persons better or worse than others. But those rules may permit *everyone* alike the *same right to be partial*. Mothers – any and all of them – *may* prefer *their own* children to other people's when it comes to dispensing love, care, attention, and material means of well-being. If this is true of Martha, then it is also true of Gabriella in Spain or Nafiza over in New Delhi. Despite being necessarily universal and essentially impartial, morality does not necessarily, just as a matter of logic, *require* us to provide equal amounts of anything to our fellows if it is to qualify as morality at all. The point here is only that this is a logically open question. Whether it actually *does* require this is a subject of our investigation here. If I am right that liberty is our basic right, then of course morality does indeed permit the skewed distributions of various things we can bestow on others – money, love, opportunities, and so on – that we are likely to see when individuals act as they wish. But the principle of liberty itself is, of course, totally impartial. Liberty for some – say, the white folks – but not others – say, the black folks – is, of course, completely antithetical to the notion of morals.

Equal and unequal liberty

Talk of "equal liberty" is familiar in social philosophy, and such talk is conducive to egalitarianism. But just what does this expression mean? On the face of it, person A would be equally at liberty with person B if the obstacles facing each were equal. How one could possibly measure such quantities is difficult to say, other than in very specific cases: A, for instance, has a broken leg while B's is normal, and both would like to win a race between them. Yet A's leg may not have been broken *by* anyone else, and thus as far as social liberty is concerned, there is no difference. Slavery, on the other hand, is clearly unequal in this relevant sense: the people who are enslaved have obstacles imposed on them by their masters, who by comparison have, therefore, more liberty. And more generally, when A has power over B that B has not voluntarily agreed to, we may say that they are unequal in respect of liberty.

But there is a natural lower limit to impositions: none. If A is, simply, *not* imposing any obstacles to B's pursuit of his interests, apart from the usual restrictions on B's using violence or fraud against others, then A is fully respecting B's liberty. Now, in principle everyone could do this. We could say about such a situation that we are equally at liberty – but then, that would be equivalent to saying that we were, simply, *at liberty*. The libertarian is not independently interested in seeing to it that the *amount* of imposition on some of us is about equal to that imposed on others. In whatever way that can be measured, libertarianism does not call for equalizing the amount of evil visited on different people – unless we count *zero* as the "amount" in question.

There are many cases in which people are entitled to equal amounts of something from someone – equal pay for what is counted as equal work, for example, in a business relation in which all who perform such work are specified to be entitled to a payment of a given amount per unit. In such cases, one who gets less has a relevant complaint. But the imposition he suffers is that of fraud, or broken agreements: he is not getting what he was promised. It is not a case of "unequal liberty" but of violation of a fairly precisely defined right. Two workers could easily not be entitled to equal pay, and in such cases, where they have nevertheless accepted their respective contractual arrangements, the inequality of pay would not be an inequality of relevant liberty. The relative imposition would be zero, because it is zero in both cases, despite the differential of payment.

I conclude that there would seem to be not very much point in talking about a right to "equal liberty," since the only independent meaning that can be attached to the expression yields a principle that liberty clearly rejects. We can instead – and should – be talking about a general, universal right *to liberty*. This would be much more accurate and much less misleading.

"Moral equality"

Another frequently employed expression is "moral equality." And again, it has a ring of self-evidence about it. People are unequal in innumerable respects, but the idea is that insofar as they are moral beings, they are "equal." But again, it is not very clear just what this refers to, and especially whether equality in the fairly specific sense in which we need, as I have argued above, to distinguish it from several other concepts, is really at stake.

Thus, consider the convicted serial rape-murderer-torturer with his thirty-seven victims, in comparison with Mr. or Ms. Ordinary Person, who may have cut a corner here or there but by and large has lived a perfectly decent life and done no significant harm to anyone. If they are to be said to be "morally equal," is there any significant sense to that? We have to scratch our heads a bit. Both, we might say, are entitled to a lawyer if needed, and to have the penalties imposed on them assessed on the basis of the same laws and in due proportion: viz., life imprisonment or perhaps execution in the first case, and no penalties of any kind for the second. But the significance of "equal" is, again, that of sameness of the basic rules governing their conduct: both are looked at in light of the same principles and rules. But the resulting treatment of each by the forces of the law is, entirely justly, greatly unequal.

Much of the background for this kind of talk no doubt stems from the European heritage that many of us have directly, and against the background of which our legal and political system was formed, considerably in hopes of significant improvement. That background was class-ridden in various ways, and that members of different classes were significantly "unequal" is hard to deny. That can be cashed out in terms of various specific kinds of bad treatment to which one could expect to be exposed in one class but not in some other. Many Europeans emigrated to America precisely in hopes of avoiding such differential treatment, especially at the hands of governments, and to a very considerable, and laudable, extent they succeeded in that hope. It is reasonable to say that the two large countries in northern North America are, near enough, "classless societies." Yet European philosophers invoked the sort of equality intended by the term "moral equality" quite some time ago – one thinks of Kant and Rousseau, for example. The general idea was that there are certain very general moral principles by which all persons, of whatever class or sex or color, are to be judged in terms of their conduct in relation to each other, and those principles are not dictated by class situation but simply by virtue of being a more or less normal human being. The sense of there being a commensurable quantity of something or other to which all are entitled is quite muted. In the end, what it really comes down to is still mainly, and perhaps entirely, the liberty principle, and that principle, as we have seen, is not helpfully expressed in terms of equality in any sense in which it is a distinctive concept.

"Luck" egalitarianism

We all live in environments that impact differently on us, independently of any moral properties we may have. The rain, as the proverb has it, falls on the just and the unjust alike. It also falls very differently on persons equally just, and sometimes falls much better on the unjust than the just. There is tough luck and there is good luck, deserved and undeserved luck. Nature is not an egalitarian.

It has become popular of late for moral philosophers to make a distinction between the sort of luck that might be nevertheless deserved, by virtue of being a consequence of some chosen action, and the sort of luck that is in no way deserved. Thus when we gamble, or knowingly neglect our brake linings, the good or bad things that may befall us can be claimed to have been deserved. By contrast, there is the sort of luck that is not deserved, which goes by the name of "brute" luck. Many egalitarian philosophers hold that morals calls upon us to equalize, if and so far as possible, the bad (or good?) effects of brute luck on us all. If Jones gets cancer through no fault of his own, while Smith is spared, then Smith has to help pay Jones for cancer treatment, say. And some, following Henry George, hold that insofar as what we acquire is a product strictly of our own labor (or investment ingenuity, or whatever), we are indeed entitled to that, however different in amount from one person to the next; but they hold that the natural resources, or in George's case the land, on which we work to bring about these desirable improvements by our own effort, does not belong to me or you or anyone individually; and they infer that society may tax us for our use of these uncreated resources.[19] We have, then, according to this view, entitlement to equal shares of unmodified nature,

19 See the well-known two-part paper by Ronald Dworkin, "What is Equality? Part II, Equality of Resources," *Philosophy and Public Affairs* 10 (1981), pp. 283–345. See also several essays in Peter Vallentyne and Hillel Steiner, eds., *The Origins of Left-Libertarianism* and *Left-Libertarianism and its Critics* (Basingstoke: Palgrave, 2000), especially those of Henry George in vol. I, pp. 1–22, and Vallentyne himself, in vol. II, pp. 193–216.

whatever we may have done to find those resources, or to discover new uses for, those things.

We cannot discuss this idea at length here, but it does, as we will see, have a possible application in the present subject, for it can be argued that some, at least, of "the poor" are so due to no fault of their own. Thus we can describe those persons as being victims of bad brute luck. So a brief comment is essential: on the face of it, the "Luck" egalitarian has made a fallacious assimilation of two very different things. When the rain falls on the just and the unjust alike, has an injustice occurred? We are unhappy about this eventuality, to be sure. But the trouble is, *nobody has committed* the "injustices" in question. When there is an unequal incidence of some good or bad thing, it does not follow that anyone did it, and therefore that anyone is responsible for it. So if the Luck Egalitarian proposes to take it out on the fortunate to benefit the less fortunate, he is, on the face of it, meting out undeserved punishment to the former. Holding people responsible for the inequities of nature is not obviously *just*: on the contrary, it is punishing the innocent. If inequality were morally wrong to begin with – which I deny – and if some persons get greatly unequal amounts of something the egalitarian thinks they are entitled to, but gets those amounts at the hands of Mother Nature, then in fairness the egalitarian should try to exact compensation from the lady in question – not from some one of us, who did nothing to deserve the exaction to which the egalitarian proposes to subject us.

If we are at general liberty, as called for by libertarianism, then how do we stand in relation to luck and its alleviation? Again on the face of it, nowhere in particular: that is to say, the fact that Jones has had a run of very tough luck while Smith has, owing to various deficiencies of character, got into a similarly bad way, does not require us to help out Jones any more than Smith. The libertarian can, and in my view should, agree that it would indeed be virtuous to help out Jones in this case, and to do so more than, or before, Smith. But his view entails that there is no actual *requirement* to do this, as it stands. The egalitarian is going to have to provide a special argument for this, and it is not clear how that is to be managed. (We will survey some efforts in that direction in later pages.)

Rights

Rights are *interpersonal duty-generators*. That is: to say that some individual has a *right* to some kind of treatment is to say that

(1) there is something about the right holder such that
(2) some relevant group of persons (possibly one-membered) is such that this individual's right is held "against" the members of this group – meaning that entailments of *normative requirements* on action fall upon members of that group in particular, in virtue of the rightholder's having the right in question; and
(3) that those persons are *required* to see to it, or to contribute in some reasonable way and in some degree – needing to be specified – toward seeing to it, insofar as they are able, that the rightholder in question gets that sort of treatment. Moreover, the person who fails to do what someone's rights require him to do is liable for some kind of reinforcement of a possibly forcible kind: some measure of compulsion may be used on him – he is not free to do as he likes in that respect.

Rights to do vs. rights to things

Often we will be discussing "things" that people should "get." This has perplexed some. But a conceptual economy is readily to hand, for the vocabulary of rights in terms of actions covers all such cases. A person's "having a right" to the "thing" in question is a matter of that person's being in a normative position to use the item in question (indefinitely, in the case of out-and-out ownership, or for some specified term or on some specified condition, if not), if he wishes to and is otherwise able to, and in particular to have *authority* over it in the sense that if anyone else might wish to utilize the item, that further person must obtain permission to do so from the rightholder proper (or be reasonably assured that it would be forthcoming if sought).

The libertarian basic right is often expounded as a matter of "self-ownership," which would, prima facie, make the right to act less basic than the right to a certain thing, viz., our selves. But this is a mistake. To "own oneself" is simply to be the person who gets to use the self in question, while others, if they wish to use it, must clear it with the owner. Self-ownership is not another thing, prior to and the foundation of, the right to do things; it is instead just another way of stating the general right of liberty.[20]

Negative and positive rights

The difference of negative and positive rights may now be explicated as follows:

A's right to do x is *negative* if those upon whom the normative entailments fall are required to *refrain* from actions that would prevent or impede A's doing of x at will. (In terms of the general definition just supplied, A is responsible for seeing to it that A does *not* do any of those things. A "brings it about that they don't happen" by, simply, not doing those things, or in the special case where efforts would be required to prevent himself doing them, to make (some relevant degree of) those efforts.)

A's right is *positive* if those upon whom the normative entailments fall are required to *supply* to A some or all (to be specified, but prima facie all, if possible and not otherwise qualified) of what A needs in order to do x, if A is unable to do x without assistance or by voluntarily proffered assistance only.

A major and essential refinement in all of the above concerns the *voluntariness* of the requirements in question. Especially in political and legal contexts, claims about rights are generally understood to be *enforceable*. The law, for example, may threaten punishments or other invasions of those who do not comply with the requirements in question. In the present discussions, this refinement will be generally assumed unless explicitly qualified. What is in question, then, is the moral acceptability of forcibly imposing on persons to fulfill the normative requirements in question. The issue, in short, is compulsion.

Egalitarians typically claim that persons who are well below the average level in respect of the variable they think society

20 See Jan Narveson, "Property and Rights," *Social Philosophy and Policy* 27, 1 (2009).

should be concerned with have what is now called a *positive right* to be supplied, by all and sundry among those who have the means, with whatever will bring them up to some level reasonably close to the average. (Imputing to them the view that they are entitled to *exactly* the average level would, I take it, be uncharitable. We all accept Aristotle's dictum, that one does not expect great precision in these matters. Still, as discussed above, egalitarianism requires commensurability: we must be able to make at least rough quantitative comparisons among diverse persons, and these comparisons must be commensurable, at risk of losing all impact from the general view. If we cannot tell who has more and at least roughly how much more, we are in no position to apply a principle calling for equalization.) Since the concept of a right, and also that of a "positive" versus a "negative" right, are crucially important in these discussions, we had best begin by defining these notions here.

Criticisms of the distinction

Some have challenged the distinction of "positive" and "negative" along lines that might be thought relevant here.[21] They point out that an *institutional enforcement* of any right, positive or negative, will have costs, and those costs will be imposed on the public in question. Every holder of a negative right will be required to provide some positive support, say in the way of taxation, for the provision of enforcement made by the state, and the same is true if our rights are positive. What, then, is the big deal? – they ask.

This could lead to a protracted discussion, to be sure. But by way of heading off at least some of that discussion, two points need to be made. First: the argument depends on assimilating two very different things. The distinction of negative and positive rights essentially lies in the *content* of the requirements imposed

---

21 Perhaps the first was Henry Shue, in "The Bogus Distinction – 'Negative' and 'Positive' rights," in *Making Ethical Decisions*, ed. Norman E. Bowie (New York: McGraw-Hill, 1985), pp. 223–31. Latterly, Cass Sunnstein with Stephen Holmes, *The Cost of Rights* (London and New York: W. W. Norton, 1999).

on people, *not* in the *methods of enforcement* to be used. And those distinctions of content are, at least typically, quite clear. For example, if people have only a negative right to life, that imposes a duty *to refrain from killing* those rightholders. All the citizen needs to do to comply with this is to avoid killing people. In a very few cases, which ingenious philosophers are adept at dreaming up, it might be rather difficult to decide precisely what actions are to be avoided – whether, for example, in some special cases it might require positive actions on the part of person B to avoid what would otherwise have the effect of killing person A. (These are the cases in which nonaction can somewhat plausibly be held to be a "kind of action" in a more robust sense than that in which action/inaction is simply what follows from an agent's decision about what to do.) In a court of law, it might be extremely important to identify those with some precision, and to inquire just how much "doing" might be required in order to accomplish what is fundamentally an avoidance, a "non-doing" in that case. Whether the sort of requirements that we are centrally concerned with in this inquiry will sometimes exemplify this difficulty is not obvious, but we should concede that it is quite possible.

But still, that will then leave the enormously huge class of cases in which there is simply no problem at all. The reader, for example, is in all likelihood right now, and probably for the whole of his or her life, in full compliance with the requirement to murder no one, and this is so easily accomplished that we literally think nothing of it. On the other hand, however, if we believe that there are *positive* rights to life, then we will almost certainly not be able to fulfill whatever normative requirements are entailed by such a right *by* doing nothing at all or nothing out of the ordinary. We shall have to contribute to aid agencies, for example, or part with taxes supporting efforts by officials, and so on. The fact that tracking down, convicting, and punishing murderers is expensive and normally done by way of involuntary taxation on the part of citizens does nothing to cast any doubt on the distinction in question.

The other point is of a quite different order and mentioned for purposes, mainly, of setting it aside in the rest of this essay. This other point is that those who argue for there being no significant difference between negative and positive rights because of the costs of enforcement assume that it is exclusively the duty of the state to do the enforcing in question. And that can be denied. Even though we accept that enforcement is called for and may, in a given case, be justified, we need not accept that the *state* is required for providing the enforcement in question. Philosophical anarchists believe that such enforcement not only can be but ought to be by means that in turn are voluntary.

Of course, it remains that whoever voluntarily incurs such costs does incur them, and so does more than the "nothing" that he is required to do by virtue of being in the requirement-set of some negative rights. But while that is true, it remains that the enforcement of rights need not be something to which others have a positive right, *in addition to* their negative right not to have the things done to them in the first place. If they have only a negative right to the item in question, they have also, prima facie, only a negative right to such enforcement as may, if needed, be forthcoming. Those who fail to help with the enforcement will *not* have violated anyone's rights thereby, though they will not, no doubt, have been very good citizens. What they would have is a status such that, if suitable other persons assisted in enforcing their rights, they would be doing what they are *morally permitted to do*; but the requirements imposed on them by whatever positive rights other persons have in relation to them are not, as such, requirements *to enforce*, but rather, requirements to *provide whatever it is that those persons have positive rights to*.

This familiar attack on the distinction is, then, entirely mistaken. The distinction is clear, and while the moral weight attached to it by some theorists (including myself) is no doubt contested and contestable, the argument that there simply is no distinction or that the one (negative) entails the other (positive) must be rejected.

So we do have a real distinction here. It matters, and matters a lot, whether people in general are required merely to refrain from killing, stealing from, or otherwise damaging other persons generally, or whether they *also* have a moral duty to provide those persons with such things as food, shelter, and medical attention – *plus* help in enforcing whatever rights people have. If they do have the latter duties, then the imposition of taxes and perhaps other participations in the systems aimed at providing people with what they have this positive right to would be just. If they do not, however, they would not – even if we accept that they have the duty to provide financial and perhaps some other sorts of support to help enforce the laws against murder, rape, assault, and theft. In short, addressing critics such as Shue and Sunnstein, *if* people have negative rights *and* we accept the legitimacy of the state, then what the state may and should do is to impose such taxes as it needs to achieve reasonable levels of security in respect of those rights; while *if* they have positive rights, then it may *also* impose taxes to administer the many further programs that would then be legitimate for it to pursue for *that* purpose. But you cannot infer the legitimacy of the latter purposes from the sheer fact that there are costs entailed by the enforcement of whatever rights there are. The path from negative rights to positive ones using only logic is paved with fallacy.

That this is a very big difference in practice is obvious. Consider the typical person's tax bill nowadays. How much of it goes toward sheer enforcement of the criminal law? And how much of it goes to support an immense panoply of public services (as they are now generally thought to be) – especially concerning health, education, and welfare support? The difference, in the case of the G8 countries at any rate, is probably on the order of 50:1 in favor of the latter (not counting support for foreign wars, which is entirely asymptotic to the present discussion). To assert that there is no difference between the one and the other is to fly in the face of fact.

The issue: framed by liberalism

Sterba and I agree on enough to make the issue between us a rather narrow and sharply defined one. Both of us think that the principles of justice are founded on a sort of "social contract," though differences on how we understand that could, certainly, be responsible for serious differences further down the line.

What we also agree about, I believe, is that the general shape of this conceptual agreement is such that *the chosen principles are those that enable each of us to do the best we can with our life, in our own understanding of what makes that life go well, compatibly with all the rest being enabled to do so as well.* This I take to be definitive of philosophical *liberalism.* For the liberal, there is no second-guessing of the individual: the citizen-consumer is king. If that individual seriously prefers x to y, then society is to take it that so far as he is concerned, x is to be chosen over y.

We will all, then, be looking at principles in light of the "bottom line." But, of course, that means that it is inadequate to look at it only from my point of view, or yours, or the Chinese People's, or any other proper subset of humankind. Always the question must be whether we all have adequate motivation to "sign" the proposal in question: if we know that some do not – be those persons ourselves or somebody else – then the deal is off and we go back to the drawing board.

Thus we cannot go from "Jones likes it" to "Smith ought to supply it to Jones." For Smith may *not* "like it" and the fact that Jones does cannot be assumed to matter to him. There is no cardinalizing of utility for purposes of interpersonal comparisons, for the liberal: you have your values, I have mine, and neither of us need attach any particular value to the other, or to that other person's values. Each is assumed to act on his or her *own* values, whose relation to others is entirely empirical. Liberalism leads, I think, to the social contract approach. In that approach, we each are presumed to act on our own values, and to attend to others' only insofar as they in turn, or the actions to which their possessor is impelled, affect ourselves. That may indeed be considerably, and often is, in various particular cases. But it is variable and not to be blithely assumed. Individuals are protected by the apparatus of the social contract, for our results need to be confirmed by everyone, from within their own standpoints.

Of course, there is the fundamental question whether social contract is the right idea, and in particular whether it can really be used to account for the normative force of moral ideas. But that most basic question will be skirted over lightly here; it is what Sterba and I do both, rightly or wrongly, agree on, and it is our differences that are the subject of this investigation.

Classical liberalism

My general point of view on this matter is that of the classical liberal, as I understand him: that is, a prohibition against violence, or, more generally, *aggression*, understanding this to mean the attempt to promote one's own interests at the *net* cost of someone else; that is to say, to use it against persons who are not themselves, in turn, doing any such thing to any others (which is what most people have in mind by the word "innocent," except that "innocent" typically carries further baggage; what is meant here is only that the person in question is peaceable in relation to his fellows). And I suggest that this prohibition on aggression is the only thing that all persons would agree on in the way of socially imposed requirements, and the *only* thing we can *all* agree on – if anything at all.

The word "net" has to be taken seriously here. The gangster pursues his interests at net cost to his victims: they were minding their own business, and the gangster deprives them of money, or perhaps life, with no compensation and no claim that they were anything but peaceable themselves. Most of us most of the time operate in an environment of voluntary cooperation with those around us. With the great majority, the cooperation in question consists of doing nothing to visit any sort of harm on them, nor they on us. With some others, we work together, agreeing on who does what and what the individual in question is to be paid for it, if anything, or what he or she is to get in return. Sometimes what we get in return is a payment, sometimes a thankyou or perhaps a kiss, or some pleasant company, and so on; or perhaps, nothing but continued peace and cooperation of whatever kind may be appropriate. And sometimes we engage in competitions, to be sure: but we do so voluntarily, and we stick by the rules mutually accepted, so that, win or lose, we do better than if we do not play at all. But in the main, indeed overwhelmingly, such peaceable, voluntary, cooperative interaction is what characterizes our social existence.

If we take Hobbes's First Law of Nature seriously, then the above is just how it should be, always and with everyone. His "Law" says: we are always to seek peace, and *only* if we cannot get it are we permitted to use the "helps and advantages of war."[22] Hobbes holds that this first "Law" is the foundation of all the others he sets forth. That is a very strong claim, and I am among a rather small number who think he is right about this. But for present purposes, I take it that among the further Laws that Hobbes claims to be derived from the first, only a few need concern us here.

The Second Law says that nobody is to insist on a liberty for himself which he[23] is unwilling to allow for all others. This is the classic statement of what later came to be known as the "equal liberty" principle. But Hobbes is clear what he means by liberty: it is the absence of restraints imposed by the actions of others. (This is social and political liberty; we are not here concerned, directly, with the lack of liberty you may be said to have by virtue of the fact that you are quite unable to run the mile in two minutes flat.) So a diminution of A's liberty by B is a "restraint imposed by others" – which is what the warlike activity proscribed in his first principle consists in. Death, destruction, imposition of barriers, destruction or removal of property, and the rest of it, are impositions against their victims, and are just what Hobbes believes to be the crucial obstacles to the good life for all insofar as politics and morals can provide that. But the lack of impositions cannot of itself, one must quickly add, be expected to provide any number of substantive goods, such as the ability to compose Mozart's String Quintet in C Major. What they can do is to create a social framework within which Mozart and all

---

22 Hobbes, *Leviathan*, ch. 14.

23 I assume that readers will automatically, as of old, take it that the words "he" and "his" and so forth in general are gender indifferent here. The practice of either writing "he or she" or of randomizing over gender is awkward and irritating, and I think in the end self-defeating. In this essay, I shall use the feminine gender when that is what I mean; or, when I need two different pronouns, I will use "she" and "he" as an easy way of distinguishing the persons in question, if "A" and "B" seem too formal.

the others, happily for the rest of us, are able to do that, because free of molestation as they go about it; and, of course, similarly for all the others, to do whatever they are able to do and are interested in doing, be they of lesser talent or none.

Hobbes's Third Law simply calls upon us to keep our agreements. Whether this is relevant to the ensuing discussion is, as we shall see, a somewhat difficult question. Hobbes claims that this Third Law is the "fountainhead of justice"; and if the Social Contract was literally an *agreement*, then we could argue that the injustice that is attributed to acting inconsistently with it would be unjust by virtue of being literally the breaking of an agreement. Hobbes helps himself to that gambit in proclaiming a duty for us all to obey the government no matter what it tells us to do, on the ground that we have agreed, or at least that we would rationally agree, to that – a gambit for which I, for one, have no sympathy at all. But that particular issue will not, again, figure in the forthcoming discussion. Our question is whether the Social Contract calls for a welfare state (in effect), and if it does, then the ground for accepting it will not be the duty to obey the law, but rather the duty to help people out to the degree and in the ways called for by the Social Contract, if indeed it does call upon us to do that. In other words, if we have that duty it will not be because we literally agreed to it, but rather because we see ourselves to be in such a position that we rationally accept, given appropriate reciprocation by the rest, a duty that entails the duty to support the welfare state to the relevant degree and in the relevant way. Still, questions of *particular* agreements and their reach may possibly arise in our discussion.

Hobbes's Fourth Law says that we should be grateful for benefits voluntarily provided by others, that is, by others who were not under any obligation to provide them but did so anyway. More importantly, it commands us not to do what would make people come later to regret that they extended this benefit to you. Some minor reference to this "law" will also be made later. Thus, those benefiting from the welfare state, if it is justified, do not need be and typically, one should note, are not grateful to the rest of us for this because it is a matter of right which they can claim; but if it is not justified, then whatever the rest of us do for them is a voluntary benefit and they should be grateful for that.

Finally (for our purposes), there is a Fifth Law calling upon us to "accommodate ourselves to the rest." Hobbes himself makes heavy use of this rule in his discussion of something partially approximating the welfare state. I am sympathetic to this "law," but obviously it is far less precise than the others, and its implications much less definite. There is, indeed, reasonable question in what sense this is a "law." Hobbes, to be sure, says of *all* the "Laws of Nature" that they are strictly speaking not laws, but only *virtues*, on the ground that only the enacted laws of the Sovereign, that is of the state, are literally laws. I do not accept that part of his philosophy, of course. Or at any rate, I do not accept this terminology, since I take it that we literally are morally required to do the things his Laws says we are to do – they are not *just* virtuous things to do, although to be sure it *is* virtuous to perform well by them, and we ought to encourage people to do so, by among other things holding up the tendency to abide by them as recognizedly virtuous.

This short excursion into Hobbes is indulged in not for reasons of scholarship, but because Hobbes seems to me to provide the cleanest and most promising account of morals from the classical liberal point of view. Others may think that Locke, for example, improves on Hobbes, but in regard to the content of the "Law of Nature," I think that an error. Locke tells us that "Reason, which is that Law, teaches all Mankind, who will but consult it, that being all equal and independent, no one ought to harm another in his Life, Health, Liberty or Possessions."[24] Here Locke spells out somewhat the content of what constitutes aggression: harm to the victim's life, health, liberty, or possessions. No problem there – those are all, indeed, aggressions and so they are all actions that Hobbes's First Law, like Locke's, tells us to avoid. Locke's version of the Law is precisely like Hobbes's version in

---

24 John Locke, *Second Treatise of Civil Government*, in *Two Treatises of Government*, ed. Peter Laslett (New York: Cambridge University Press, 1988), #6.

that it only tells us to avoid certain actions. It imposes no positive requirements. That brings us to the next point.

The Hobbes/Locke formula is clear that our basic duties are all *negative*. We are not to aggress, but there is no requirement to help, on the face of it. They amount to a proclamation of a general right of liberty for all. Locke's law provides a list: we are not to "harm another in his life, health, liberty, or possessions." Taking my life is certainly equivalent to divesting me of all liberties whatever; making me sick impedes me in all sorts of things that I want to do; taking my possessions, likewise, disenables me from doing whatever I intended to do with them. If this were an excursion in Hobbesian and Lockean exegesis, we would then have to consider that Locke talks very strongly about our duties to provide for our neighbor if he is in really tough shape and we can afford to do so.[25] But his formula, as it stands, is not apparently consistent with *compelling* us to do that – or at least, not unless, somehow, it can plausibly be argued that in cases such as this, my inaction amounts to action, and aggressive action at that. Do I, by failing to help you, *harm* you? If not, then the First Law of Nature as it stands cannot be invoked to yield this particular positive duty.

Part of the background of this discussion consists in the point that the answer to this latter question, *on the face of it*, is in the negative. I "harm" you if I *make you worse off* than you would have been had I not acted – had I, for example, not even been anywhere in the neighborhood but instead, say, in Bolivia at the time. Of course you are worse off if I do not help you than you would be if I *did* help you. But the question is whether I am supposed to help you at all, in the first place. Obviously we cannot simply assume that and then appeal to it as a baseline for further analysis. To argue that I harm you if I do not help you on the ground that my not helping you leaves you worse off than

---

25 Locke does this in the "First Treatise," sect. 42 (in ch. 4): "God ... has given his needy Brother a Right to the Surplusage of his Goods; so that it cannot justly be denied him, when his pressing Wants call for it ..." (in *ibid.*, p. 170).

you would have been if I *had* helped you is, of course, to beg the question – as it, alas, very often is begged. That way, indeed, lies madness. For no matter what I do for you, if I could have done still better for you, then the theorist who commits this fallacy would infer that I "harm" you to the extent that I fall short of the absolutely best I could possibly do for you. And that is absurd: the fact that I am not right now making out a cheque to you, the reader, for ten thousand dollars does not mean that I have robbed you of ten thousand dollars. Prima facie, then, as I say, my harming you is one thing, my helping you is a second option, and there is also a third alternative different from either: simply doing nothing, one way or the other, which leaves you right where you are, wherever that may be. That is the relation almost all of us have to virtually the whole of mankind at any given time. Now, negative rights are the sorts of things that are, necessarily, fulfilled by that third alternative *as well as* by the second. If the Hobbesian/libertarian view of rights is correct, then the situation is that we are being just in relation to almost everyone almost always, since we almost always do no harm to them. If there were an *antecedent* duty to provide, of course, that would be another matter. However, we have, as yet, no ground for asserting that.

Meanwhile, Sterba has helpfully accepted the challenge, saying

> Let us begin by interpreting the ideal of liberty as a negative ideal in the manner favored by libertarians. So understood, liberty is the absence of interference by other people from doing what one wants or is able to do.[26]

So far, so good – except that I think we must say, "wants *and* is able to do," and not the weaker "or." For if you are *not* able to do it, but still want to, our question is whether, at least in a subset of such cases, your liberty would be being interfered with if we did

---

26 James Sterba, "Our Basic Human Right is a Right to Liberty and it Leads to Equality," delivered at a colloquium between Sterba and myself at Albion College, Michigan, April 2006.

not provide you with the means to do this thing. That cannot be assumed. And if it is not being interfered with in this way, then inference from inability to do x to positive right to do it is blocked. When we talk of liberties being abridged, denied, or violated, they are the liberties to do what we would and could otherwise do, not what we cannot do. (There are things you cannot do right now but will be able to at some point in the future. My acting now so as to prevent your doing it then would, of course, be an infringement of your liberty too.)

To remind about our project, the universe of discourse here is *general moral principles*. And these are *general*. So the characterization of liberty supplied underdetermines our issue, by a very long shot. The general thesis that people have a right to liberty is advanced (and advanceable) *only* under a covering assumption that the liberties we speak of are generalizable, which entails that they are *compossible*. Here, for example, is Kant's formulation.

Universal Principle of Right

Every action is right which in itself, or in the maxim on which it proceeds, is such that it can coexist along with the freedom of the will of each and all in action, according to a universal law.[27]

That the right in question "can coexist" with any other rights, and with all other persons' rights, is the nub of the matter. A "right" to do what negates the liberty of someone else is, obviously, ineligible to serve as a universal right, since liberty is being claimed as a general right. So when we say that liberty is "the absence of interference by other people from doing what one wants or is able to do," the focus has to be on *which liberties are excluded*. As we have seen, *all* moral principles in some way *reduce our permitted range of action*, and, so, our permissible liberty. The liberty to invade, despoil, aggress, undercut others' liberty, is excluded if the liberty principle is to serve as a universal rule. It is

---

27 Kant, *Rechtslehre* (*Doctrine of Right*), Part I, Introduction, section C (trans. Hastie).

a strange misreading of the principle of liberty that makes it a free-for-all. Free-for-alls, indeed, are not matters of "principle" but, really, of lack of principle. Principles impose restrictions – they do not leave us free to do simply whatever we want. But making *liberty* into a principle means that we *restrict our freedom in the interest of freedom*; thus, it is the freedom to undercut or destroy or impair other people's freedom that the liberty principle deprives us of. It does so in order to make it possible for us all to be as free as possible – for freedom to be truly universal.

Sterba's central argument

That said, let us have a look at what Sterba proposes as a bridge for getting from the negative right to liberty, to which he has agreed, to the positive right to it, to which I do not agree. His proposed liberty is this:

> Now in order to see why libertarians are mistaken about what their ideal requires, consider a typical conflict situation between the rich and the poor. In this conflict situation, the rich, of course, have more than enough resources to satisfy their basic needs. By contrast, the poor lack the resources to meet their most basic needs even though they have tried all the means available to them that libertarians regard as legitimate for acquiring such resources. Under circumstances like these, libertarians usually maintain that the rich should have the liberty to use their resources to satisfy their luxury needs if they so wish. Libertarians recognize that this liberty might well be enjoyed at the expense of the satisfaction of the most basic needs of the poor; they just think that liberty always has priority over other political ideals, and since they assume that the liberty of the poor is not at stake in such conflict situations, it is easy for them to conclude that the rich should not be required to sacrifice their liberty so that the basic needs of the poor may be met.[28]

28 James Sterba, "Presidential Address to the APA," *Proceedings and Addresses of the American Philosophical Association* 82, 2 (November 2008), p. 59 (hereafter, "APA Address").

Nevertheless, Sterba holds that this liberty *is* "at stake":

> In fact, however, the liberty of the poor is at stake in such
> conflict situations. What is at stake is the liberty of the poor not
> to be interfered with in taking from the surplus possessions of
> the rich what is necessary to satisfy their own basic needs.[29]

It will have been noticed, I trust, that Sterba's formulation contains notions lacking entirely from libertarian formulas.
Nowhere does the libertarian distinguish between "desires to
have one's basic needs satisfied," and any number of other
desires. That the desire of the "rich" is a "luxury desire" is beside
the point, so far as the libertarian is concerned. That is because
he is indeed a *libertarian*: what matters is not the particular
content of the liberty in question, but the sheer fact that it *is* a
liberty, one that is not in itself invasive of anyone else's liberty.
What is not beside the point, however, is that (a) the individual
in question actually has the desire; and (b) the means he might
employ to promote this desire are *all voluntary* on the part of
affected persons – they are all realized either by the person's own
independent actions, or by making agreements with, and not by
coercion of, those who are to supply the means in question, or
else they simply do not affect third parties. Yet what Sterba holds
is that needs of person A trump luxuries of person B, as it were:
that the sheer fact that what the poor would be promoting when
they take, without permission, from the rich, is the satisfaction of
their "basic needs." Those, we are to understand, are enough to
outweigh or undercut the fact that what they would be taking
from the "rich" in question are things that those well-off persons
have acquired in perfectly voluntary ways (as we are assuming
they have, in the relevant cases; of course, one who has become
rich by theft is another case altogether).

---

29 [Sterba's footnote:] "Basic needs, if not satisfied, lead to significant lacks or
deficiencies with respect to a standard of mental and physical well-being.
Thus, a person's needs for food, shelter, medical care, protection, companionship, and self-development are, at least in part, needs of this sort. For a
discussion of basic needs, see my *How to Make People Just*, pp. 45–8."

What this amounts to seems to be a denial that people *have* full rights to their possessions: there are, on this view, no real property rights. Rights permit the possessor of those rights to exclude others from the use of what they have a right to. But Sterba claims, in effect, that what satisfies "basic needs" overrides the exclusionary right normally held by those who have the things that would satisfy those needs. Why is this supposed to make such a difference? Why, that is, in terms fundamental to considerations of *liberty*, rather than, say, welfare? For it is a presupposition of this inquiry, common to both of us, that we do not assert welfare rights simply as such. But Sterba's claim is that these can be derived from the accepted standpoint of liberty rights. That is the claim I am disputing.

"Conflicts" of liberties?

Sterba says that there is a "conflict of liberties" in these cases. The rich wish to keep a superabundant amount of food on hand so as to be able to choose, at whim, what they and their friends will have for dinner; the poor wish to have some of that same food too, and face severe malnutrition if they cannot get it. But of course, if you say nothing about how the food or other goods in question happen to have been acquired by those who have it in the status quo *ex ante*, you can call any conflict by that name, no problem: the murderer's interest in taking the life of his victim is in conflict, no doubt, with the victim's desire to remain alive. This indeed is a conflict of liberties: if one person, the victim, does as he wants to do, then another person, the murderer, thereby cannot do as *he* wants to do. But the murderer's desired liberty would itself, obviously, be *a liberty to reduce other people's liberty* (to zero), whereas his victim is (we assume) innocent. How is *that* supposed to show that the libertarian's objection to the murderer – viz., that he is aggressing against the life of someone who in his turn has aggressed against no one – is beside the point? And if it does not, then why isn't the similarly liberty-removing activity of the thief subject to the same response, namely, that it is not a liberty that the libertarian wants to require us to respect, since it would be the liberty to harm (= to violate the liberty of) someone else?

To shed some more light on this matter, consider a criticism of libertarianism advanced by G.A. Cohen, long ago. Cohen observes,

> If I now try to do this thing that I want to do [the case: pitching a tent in your back yard], the chances are that the state will intervene on your behalf. If it does, I shall suffer a constraint on my freedom. The same goes, of course, for all unpermitted uses of a piece of private property ... But the free enterprise economy rests upon private property: in that economy you sell and buy what you respectively own and come to own. It follows that libertarians cannot complain that a socialist dispensation restricts freedom, *by contrast* with the dispensation that they themselves favor.[30]

But no such thing follows. Cohen observes, prior to this passage, that his colleague John Gray had protested that he was "unable to believe that something so banal could be polemically consequential" – a complaint Cohen says, parenthetically, is "misplaced." This "banal truth" is that "if the state prevents me from doing something that I want to do, then it places a restriction on my freedom."[31]

But banal it indeed is. Apparently Cohen did not appreciate just how banal it was. The subject of normative principles, and especially, as we saw at the outset, of those normative principles classified as principles of *justice*, is the subject of *restrictions*: what is it that people *are not to do*, and what on the other hand they *may* do, and in both cases, why. Obviously, the fact that they are *ruled out* of doing something is a restriction on their liberty. True. The libertarian, who proclaims a general *right* to freedom, is of course maintaining that the ground on which we may *restrict* someone's liberty is that what that person is doing is, in his turn, aimed at restricting the antecedently definable liberty of someone else, that someone else being one who is not, in his turn, doing that to anyone else. To complain that the libertarian is thus

---

30 G. A. Cohen, *Self-Ownership, Freedom, and Equality* (Cambridge: Cambridge University Press, 1995), p. 56.
31 *Ibid.*, p. 55.

"restricting someone's liberty" is to make a point that is banal indeed – banal to the point of being jejune. The question is whether it makes sense to advance as the only permissible ground for restricting a certain liberty of person A that A is in the process of restricting the liberty of some further person, B. And it does make sense: one individual's restricting of the liberty of another individual who is not, in turn, acting so as to reduce the liberty or some other is a matter of *attacking*. If the person attacked is not in his turn guilty (as the libertarian would describe it) of, in turn, restricting the liberty of some further person, say C, then there is no difficulty understanding the libertarian's thesis. The thesis is that persons who invade and aggress against those who in their turn are doing no such thing are in violation of the principle declaring general liberty to be a right. And so far as the control of coercive actions is concerned, that is the *only* principle the libertarian advances. Prima facie, then, the case is closed. Killers and assaulters and robbers all act so as to harm, and thus to destroy the liberty of, those they attack, they being presumed here to be innocent. The attackers, therefore, get no protection from the liberty principle in respect of those actions. On the contrary, that principle condemns them, as it is intended to. Their victims, on the other hand, *are* entitled to such protection. Their actions are (we presume here) innocent; the assaulters' actions are not.

To argue that this distinction is either incoherent or impossible is to argue that morals is incoherent or impossible. Morality criticizes, blames, and calls sometimes for punishments or defensive measures. It cannot do this without distinguishing the good guys from the bad guys, the guilty from the innocent, those in the wrong from those in the right. If it must refrain from any such interferences with the liberty of those claimed to be on the "bad" side of this line, then morality is impossible. The libertarian's criterion for drawing this line is respect for liberty. The line is drawn for everyone in relation to everyone. Those whose actions essentially interfere with the liberties of others are deemed to be in the wrong and to be eligible for restrictions on their liberty to engage in those interferences. Those whose

actions do not are eligible for the benefit of being left free, by
others, to proceed in their various courses of action. That those
actions do not, as may be, consist in feeding the hungry or
freeing the enslaved or otherwise helping someone who in some
way needs help is nothing to the point. What he has the right to,
in the libertarian view, is to do what he wants, provided *only* that
he is not *harming*, that is, *worsening the situation of*, someone else.
If the person he is not thus worsening the situation of is in fact in
very bad shape now does not change the description. He may be
dying, but the agent is not killing him. His unhelpfulness may
indeed be morally objectionable, as I would agree in serious
cases; but it is not unjust, not a violation of the sufferer's right,
if all he has is the right to liberty.

A short excursion on property

To be sure, my criticism of Sterba's argument above does assume
that liberty, in effect, implies property. Someone who owns
something that has been acquired by effort, by voluntary
exchange, or by sheer luck rather than by taking it from someone else who is already in possession of it, possesses that thing in
such a way that we may properly describe the actions of someone who would, without seeking his permission, remove it from
his possession, as *attacking* or, in Hobbes's words, "despoiling" the
owner. In Sterba's hypothetical example, that is the position of
the "poor" in relation to the "rich." Yes, the poor person acts
under the influence of need, but still, what he does is to *take*,
against the will of the legitimate owner, what he needs. We may
hold that the owner ought to be nice and let the poor man take
what he needs. But by being the owner, he is in the position of
the one who is despoiled if the poor person in question takes
without asking, or takes despite the refusal of the wealthier
person to help out. Victimhood is not a status reserved for the
poor. Just as there can be poor murderers as well as rich, so there
can be poor thieves as well as rich, and rich victims as well as
poor. For the libertarian thesis, what matters is not whether you
are a rich victim or a poor victim, but only that you are *a victim*.
Then and only then is your assailant eligible for the defensive use

of liberty-restrictions by others, including, if need be, the use of physical force in support.

Sterba, we might note, characterized the libertarian idea thus: "the ideal of liberty as a negative ideal in the manner favored by libertarians." But it is quite misleading, as we have just seen, to attribute to libertarians a general "ideal of liberty" in the loose and unanalyzed sense in which the murderer's liberty would be just as legitimate a liberty as your freedom to go to the movies. Libertarians propose to make liberty into a *right*, which means, a ground upon which people's actions may be criticized, and, in some cases, coercively *restricted*. They are restricted if they consist in denying, undercutting, attacking other persons' liberty – in attacking people who, since they are not in turn guilty of any such attacks, have, on the principle in question, the right to be left in peace.

Writers of socialist persuasion, such as Cohen, tend to argue that *property* is somehow assumed, without argument or reason, to be a special and restricted part of the libertarian panoply of liberties, quite unrelated to the rest. But while libertarians do indeed take violation of property to be a violation of liberty, it is not without argument or reason. The reasons are remarkably simple, in fact. The legitimate owner of property (as distinct from the thief) has, we are supposing, either simply found what he owns, in a situation in which no previous possessor exists, or created it, using materials which in turn are previously unowned by others (which can arguably be made out to be a sort of special case of the previous category); or else he has got it by voluntary agreement from someone else. In all of those cases, the possessor in question has not come by his possession by means of dispossessing some present or previous possessor. No one's liberty, therefore, has been violated by any of these actions. The Cohen argument completely ignores these essential points. So too, in a more restricted area, does Sterba's.

Some indeed insist that people's liberty *has* been "violated" in such cases – at least, in the case of possessing land.[32] Those who say

---

32 This is a common view. Among modern writers, see, for example, Eric Freyfogle, *On Private Property* (Boston: Beacon Press, 2007).

this have in mind that, after all, they are no longer able to come into possession of what the first-comer acquired by getting there first. Are not their liberties thereby decreased? Thus, for example:

> let's consider what really happens when a person becomes first owner of a trace of land and puts up no-trespassing signs around the perimeter ... The landowner, to be sure, has gained greater freedom over this exclusive piece of land. The owner's liberty has gone up. At the same time, everyone else's liberty has gone down.[33]

The reply to this is straightforward: anyone who is prevented from doing a violence or aggression against someone else does indeed "have his liberties decreased" – in just the way that any assertion of rights necessarily, logically entails this. Then we need to point out that it is logically impossible for a material item to be fully possessed by more than one person: either they split it, agreeing on joint ownership, or else, if one gets it, the other does not. When this is so, the claim that second-comers have been denied something they might have had is seen to be wholly misleading, for if one person has it, no other person *can* have it and therefore no other person can be "denied" it.[34] The earth and its natural contents belong, intrinsically, to no one. When we use those contents, we do not thereby prevent others from using whatever there is to use, but we do prevent them from using what we are then using. To be free to act is to privatize. In declaring murder to be wrong, we privatize our selves: this body – "mine" – is *not* available for *your* use, at your complete discretion. Instead, you must ask me first, gain my permission, if you wish to do something with it. The same goes for anything else

33 *Ibid.*, p. 7.
34 I have written frequently on the topic of property as have many others. See my "Property and Rights." See also the articles by Ann Levey ("Liberty, Property, and the Libertarian Idea") and Peter Vallentyne ("On Original Appropriaton"), and my replies to them ("Social Contract, Game Theory and Liberty: Responding to My Critics"), in *Liberty, Games, and Contracts*, ed. Malcolm Murray (Aldershot: Ashgate, 2007), pp. 129–46, 173–8, and 231–7, respectively.

I am using, with of course the usual restriction that I in turn must not have come to my possession of it by means that take it from others. But in order for it to be an invasion of others' liberty, they have to be in possession of it: it cannot be merely something they would *like* to have.

In the preceding, I used the word "possession" rather than "own." This is deliberate. We possess things if they are within our grasp, within our power to use, legitimate or otherwise. But possession acquired without thereby depriving others of possession is, according to the libertarian, converted into ownership: we have the right to do whatever thing is innocent, including innocent in the respect of not depriving others of what they have. They may not "own" it in a legally recognized sense, but nonetheless we damage them if they are in possession of it or use it in the same innocent way. Thus the common forest land, long used as routes of travel, cannot simply be taken; nor can the famous last waterhole in the desert, used since time immemorial by all passersby. (It is another matter if there has never been water hereabouts, and I dig a well or discover a way to desalinate water from the sea or whatever, by some not hitherto known process or route, and by my ingenious labor. I then do get to sell it for what the market will bear.)

Thus what others have in the way of liberty to use things is not the right to possess any *particular thing*, apart from the particular thing that all of us must already have in order to be who we are, namely, our own bodies. So far as all other things are concerned, all they logically can have is a right to *try* to come to the possession of something, with the condition that they will fail if someone else is already in possession. And someone's new possession of something does not deny *that* liberty. We can all try. But so far as any particular thing is concerned, we cannot all succeed – indeed, only one of us fully can. Or, if it does, then the acquisition is indeed wrongful: I cannot properly come to own x by pushing you into a pit on your way to it. But I can do so by outrunning you, or just happening to be there at the time and you not.

Analogously, we are all free to compete in the marathon race, but we are not all entitled to win. Rather, we are entitled to be regarded as the winner if we have outrun all the others. At that point, the prize is not the property of all competitors, but only of the winner. That winner has abridged no one else's liberty to compete for the prize, but the race organizers do thereby abridge the liberty of anyone else to have the prize. The acquisition of things via a prearranged competition is not the normal case, but they are, as I put it, analogous: those who "get there first" are the natural possessors in the non-prearranged case, and the stipulated possessors (of the prize) in the case of an artificial competition.

But if now someone comes along and proposes to take what this person now has – the prize, in the race, or the piece of land, in the case of one who occupies it first, then he is, obviously, attacking the possessor – this being what Hobbes's Law disallows. Robert Nozick emphasized that property rights are *historical*: you own what you do not by virtue of the pattern of "holdings" you now exemplify being of one sort rather than another, but rather by virtue of the history of your acquisition: you did not aggress against any others in the process of coming to have it.[35] Cohen, in his writings, seems incapable of grasping the distinction, though it is surely pretty obvious to all, including Cohen in his nonprofessional moments. We have little difficulty distinguishing thieves from legitimate possessors. The distinction is not that some government somewhere has made a rule from which it follows that what the possessor has is legally his and not the attacker's. Rather, it is that the possessor came by his possession without attacking anyone else – in short, by peaceable means.

First comers

It might be claimed that first comers have only an arbitrary claim to what they find. Why should we award land, or whatever, to them rather than to, say, the deserving, or to everyone equally, or some further among the innumerable possibilities of distributive systems? Those who take such questions seriously must,

---

35 Nozick, *Anarchy, State, and Utopia*, esp. pp. 153–64.

I think, be supposing that somehow, someone, or some institution, is in a position to *do* the "distributing" in question. But
this is not usually so. David Schmidtz makes the point, with his
characteristic elegance:

> However, we lack a right to distribute mates. Thus we have
> no right to distribute mates unfairly, and neither do we have
> a right to distribute mates fairly. They are not ours to
> distribute.[36]

Similarly, the hitherto unoccupied land is not ours to distribute,
nor anyone's. Once we occupy it, indeed, we are then in a
position to "distribute" it if we should wish to. But we may not
wish to: we may want to use it ourselves.

Critics of natural acquisition must think that it simply does
not matter that people are particular entities, operating in time
and space. In the real world there are people who are standing
on particular bits of land or other supportive platforms, or
grasping with their hands various material items in particular
environments.[37] If social philosophy is to pay attention to
these actual people, doing actual things, it can hardly help
noticing that from the point of view of such people, the claims
of others who come on the scene present themselves as threats.
After all, here we are, peaceably making or trying to make our
livings from this particular bit of stuff, this part of our environment. If others are to acquire it, they can do so only by *displacing*
us. Our claim is the claim of existence: of *here we are*. The new
claimants are, of course, no better than we are, true: but they
are, meanwhile, in a worse position, so far as the acquisition of

---

36 David Schmidtz, *Elements of Justice* (New York: Cambridge University Press,
   2006), p. 213.
37 Here, to be sure, I gloss over the very interesting question of how to assess
   ownership of what is not immediately under, say, one's feet but merely within
   the intended and actual compass of my directed activities. A (surprisingly,
   given the title) short essay by John Roger Lee, "Libertarianism, Limited
   Government, and Anarchy," in *Anarchism/Minarchism*, ed. Roderick Long
   and Tibor Machan (Aldershot: Ashgate, 2008), pp. 15–20, nicely presents
   the problem, if not what I would accept as a solution.

these things is concerned, because *we* were *here* when they *weren't* – we got here first – came here when they didn't. Why must *we* move over to let *them* use these things that we have taken into our care and made our own? If we do not want to move – as no doubt we will not want to – then they will have to push us off, and, in doing so, they use force against us; but we did not use it against them by simply remaining where we already are. We pushed no one off to be where we are. So, as I say, the question is, why should they be thought to have a case against us? Questions like this will recur when we turn to the Social Contract idea. They will not be easy to answer in relevant ways.

Returning now to Sterba's complaint: those who propose to acquire what someone else has come into possession of without attacking anyone in the process, are now in the position of attacking that person, and *therefore* of violating his liberty and thus, in the libertarian view, of violating his *right*, which is, we are hypothesizing, a right to liberty. Obviously, libertarianism is in no way inconsistent in declaring the attacker to be in the wrong, despite his claim to "need" what he is proposing to take. Need simply is not one of the relevant concepts in the libertarian's theory of justice. Should it be? If it should, then libertarianism is an erroneous theory of justice. If it should not, though, Sterba's complaint is improperly advanced under the aegis of liberty. He is, in that case, into a different agenda. Maybe we do not have the "general right of liberty" to which we libertarians appeal. Who is right, and how do we decide? To determine this, we must look into the foundations of morals. In the case of Sterba and myself, we think we know where to look: we are agreed that they are to be found in the general idea of morality as a "Social Contract." We proceed to that, after one further point concerning Sterba's arguments.

"Ought" and "can"

Thus far, I claim that the libertarian's position is wrongly described as a preference of one kind of liberty for another. It is, rather, a denial that people ought to be at liberty to impose losses of liberty on others. Still, it is fair to ask whether the moral system proposed is reasonable. Sterba claims that it is not:

> I submit that the liberty of the poor, which is the liberty not to be interfered with in taking from the surplus resources of others what is required to meet one's basic needs, is morally enforceable over the liberty of the rich, which is the liberty not to be interfered with in using one's surplus resources for luxury purposes. To see that this is the case, we need only appeal to one of the most fundamental principles of morality, one that is common to all moral and political perspectives, namely, the "ought" implies "can" principle. According to this principle, people are not morally required to do what they lack the power to do or what would involve so great a sacrifice or restriction that it is unreasonable/contrary to reason to ask them, or in cases of severe conflict of interest, unreasonable/ contrary to reason to require them to abide by.[38]

In an endnote to this passage, he goes on to explain:

> The combined predicate "unreasonable/contrary to reason" in my version of the "ought" implies "can" principle is meant to suggest that the unreasonableness of the sacrifice or restriction being assessed here is not to be determined simply by an assessment of the magnitude of the burden imposed on the agent in and of itself, but rather also requires an assessment of the reasonableness of imposing this burden in light of related burdens and obligations imposed on others.[39]

This is an important distinction, for the assessment of "magnitudes of burdens" would surely be both difficult and insecure. The psychopathic criminal, for example, may be quite unable to prevent himself from murdering and raping – but we do not, for all that, think that he therefore should have the right to murder and rape with impunity. Likewise with the poor, who no doubt would be under considerable psychological incentive to satisfy their desires even if, in the circumstances, they would be doing so at the expense of others, by theft of their resources. But no doubt, if it is *morally unreasonable* to impose this duty to respect the liberty of others

38 Sterba, "APA Address," p. 60.
39 *Ibid.*, note 58.

on them, then we shouldn't do it. After all, the word "morally" is pretty strong stuff: morals is about what is right and wrong, and the morally unreasonable sounds as if it is wrong. But is it? And what would determine this?

The social contract idea is in fact a theory about finding the answer to that. The rules of morals are to be for the good of all – not just some. They are to play no favorites: impartiality is a *sine qua non*. In so doing, they of course will work what some will take to be hardship on some people in some circumstances. It is notoriously expected of us that we must do our duty, even if it hurts. Socrates preferred death by hemlock to escaping, as he easily could have done, but which he claimed would be a violation of his duty to Athens. And it could be that morality requires us to put up with starvation in some circumstances. So the question is whether it does.

Consider an example, the Western tourist in Cairo. He emerges from the airport into a sea of beggars, most of whom look miserable indeed, and many of whom, very likely, actually are. His first impulse is to provide for them – until he realizes that doing so in any serious degree, considering the level of demand for his largess, will spoil his trip. Do I see the Great Pyramid, or do I expend all my cash on the needy – who are clearly very much needier than I have ever been? Typical tourists act as my friend did – they answer with their feet, in favor of seeing the pyramids and contenting themselves with a sad shrug of the shoulders for most of the supplicants. Do those poor beggars think the tourists are *unreasonable* in this preference? I doubt it. Hungry they may be, but they can see perfectly well that people coming from thousands of miles away to see the wonders of their country are not about to change their itineraries, even the course of their whole lives, for their sakes. Indeed, it is *unreasonable* for them to think otherwise. The calls of the hungry stomach are strong, to be sure; but those calls are not the calls of "moral reason." Our "agreement" with these people is that we decide what we will do with our time and money, and they, after doing their best to induce us to help them out, will leave us unmolested, contenting themselves with the hope that they will, some of them, emerge a bit better off than if we had simply stayed at home. After all, they do get the first few of my dollars, if I am a typical Western tourist. Besides, many will surely gain when their cousins who drive the taxis, or guide us around the wonders of the ancient world, or work in the restaurants where we enjoy their interesting cuisine, come home and share with their needy neighbors. That is the way of the global market. But there is simply no room to argue, as Sterba does, that the sheer fact of their hunger is enough to trump our interests as tourists or businessmen or whatever we may be.

Academics seem to have a penchant for the hair shirt. Like Peter Singer, they are all ready to lay upon us the duty to part with enormous amounts of income in order to help our suffering brothers and sisters in Central Africa or wherever.[40] But these are not sacrifices that most people expect others to make for them, even if they are enormously needy. The poor about whom they are so concerned think that such demands on us are unreasonable, and it is surely not unreasonable to suggest that even softhearted academics *ought* to see the point. People are people. They are different people, coming from various backgrounds and circumstances. Some are more fortunate than others, some are cleverer than others, or harder-working, and in innumerable respects in very different situations from others. A decent respect for these differences dictates that our cries for help may reasonably go unheard or unheeded, unhappy though that may be in particular cases. The claim that we have a *duty* to impoverish ourselves for the sake of others, simply because they are in fact less fortunate, is not one that human nature puts up with readily or for long.

2   The "social contract" approach to moral philosophy

Social contract: some general observations

Why ever would we conceive of morals in this way – as the subject of a "contract"? To answer this, we first need to answer

---

40 Peter Singer, "What Should a Billionaire Give – and What Should You?" *New York Times* (December 17, 2006) at www.utilitarian.net/singer/by/20061217.htm (cited by Sterba, "APA Address," note 77).

a logically prior question: what is morals all about anyway? Why do we or would we have such a thing as a "morality"? Many theories of morals appear to assume that somehow morality is just "there," part of the structure of the world, or of our genetic profile, or some such thing. (Neo-Aristotelian theories of natural law, understood as claims that things and people have various natural purposes built into them, are accounted in the latter group, for present purposes.) Theories of that kind have serious and by now familiar problems. A claim that a particular moral view reflects the "nature of reality" will be met with denials by those who do not share that view; and if they request some kind of evidence, it will not be forthcoming in a way that satisfies the questioner, since it is wholly unclear what is to count as "evidence" with such a view. A plausible answer to our question about the foundation of morals is going to have to do better than that. Particular people espouse this or that moral outlook, or in some cases perhaps *no* moral outlook. They can consider their view and possibly reject it, or alter it in some way. Such alterations can come about by various means – unaccounted changes in the subject's interior having no direct relation to the ideas in question, for instance. But the means of special interest to us is *rational* change: that is, where the individual in question considers arguments, either put to him from without or perceived by himself, and finds them convincing in some direction.

Many think, of course, that reason is too weak or too quixotic to have any serious effect in these matters, though I am hard put to see what the point of philosophical thinking about them might be if that were so. Meanwhile, the question is whether there are premises plausible to all from which, by valid reasoning, we may infer conclusions of serious normative import that the persons concerned will thereby be constrained to accept as plausible for their part – to the point, even, of affecting practice. The social contract theory, so far as I can see, has the best chance of succeeding at such an effort. For it appeals only to the *interests* of all individuals, as viewed by those persons themselves, without assuming any real uniformity to them and without assuming any prior moral views. The assumption is only that people do have interests, which they wish to pursue, and that among those interests will be some whose pursuit will bring them into contact with others. Almost all of those others will have a capacity to respond in various ways to the contacts in question: there will, in short, be *interaction*. That interaction will be modulated by the interests of the other people with whom the subject comes into contact. All will have two things to consult: (1) their interests, and (2) what appear to be the facts about their situations. These, taken together, yield practical conclusions about what to do. (Both sorts of premises, one apparently needs to add, are subject to indefinite reappraisal, scrutiny, supplementation. But while not fixed, at any given time, still, we must act with what we have at that time.)

Self-interest and the interests of selves

Contractarians are typically accused of holding to a narrow and rigid view of human nature, according to which people are obsessively self-interested. But this should be firmly rejected. The contractarian should make no special assumptions about the character of human interests. Obviously humans vary enormously from one person to another. That they are exclusively self-interested in any interesting sense is, as Bishop Butler pointed out, simply not true – even to the point where, he adds, they would likely be better off if they were more self-interested than they are. Being "self-interested" is here taken to be understood *narrowly*: that is, referring to being interested in achieving certain states *of oneself* that are definable independently of relations to others, or even of the existence of others, for instance in keeping one's own stomach filled, whatever may happen to anyone else. So understood, Butler's denial is clear and well supported. Many people devote their lives to promoting the well-being of groups going very far beyond themselves, and, indeed, sometimes groups of which they are not even themselves members. But there is, nevertheless, good reason for awarding a certain analytical priority to self-interest. That reason is found in the basic idea of the social contract. The idea is that we are all to come to agreement on the basic principles by which we will appraise each other's behavior, and hopefully conduct ourselves, in society. We cannot "all" do this unless our basic assumptions hold for all persons, and they will not do that unless wide variation is allowed for. Will we be left with a basis on which any "agreement" would be reached? That is the challenge facing such a theory.

Now suppose that A is interested in B: A wants B to behave in various ways. Very well: but what does B have to say about it? In the social contract, the answer is: everything! Each of us is taken to be a free agent, making agreements in light of our situations as we see them. The fact that A is interested in B in some way may or may not be of positive interest to B. If it is, then B will agree to some proposals from A that affect or involve B; if it is not, B will not so agree. And if he does not, then there is no deal, for *all*, according to the social contract idea, must agree before something can pass muster as a principle for all. But presumably B in the end evaluates A's proposals on the basis of *how they affect B*. To be sure, B's utility repertoire might include love for A – but then, of course, it also might well not. The reason for proceeding as if self-interest was fundamental stems from that point. What really matters from the point of view of social contract is that each individual has the decision-making authority in his or her own case. It is the interests *of* each self that counts for that person's behavior – but there is no necessity that all such interests be ultimately analyzable in terms of interests *in* the self in question. It is a matter of experience how self-interested or other-interested any given individual may be, and the safest assumption is that it ranges all the way from virtually zero to virtually all self-interest.

Reasoning from wherever we are to morals

Historically, social contract theorists have begun with an idea of a "state of nature." That is the social condition antecedent to government, in familiar versions. But we are trying to get, not to government, but to morals. And therefore, we must begin "prior" to morals. There is no need to suppose that, historically, society or societies existed without any sort of moral controls. Indeed, it is a considerable part of the support for the social contract idea that such a society is unlikely to endure long if at all. But nevertheless, there is a conceptual need to consider, somehow, how things might be in the absence of morals of any sort.

The absence of *morals* does *not* mean the absence of *values*, however. No human goes without anything answering to the description of "values." Their values may be rudimentary, uncouth, bizarre, certainly barbaric; but, still, they make decisions on the basis of considerations about how various actions might advance or retard what matters to them, and that is all we need to understand by "values" here, even though, of course, some people's values will be very much more fully worked out, and, as some of us will think, more sophisticated, more subtle, and – *better* – than others'. But for purposes of the social contract, criticisms we might launch concerning someone's value system are beside the point. We must take people as they are. In the status quo prior to morals, people as they are is the bottom line.

Should that be, as they are, minus whatever they have in the way of specifically *moral* values? Yes and no. No, in that we must not exclude any values they may have, whether they view those as moral or not. But, certainly, yes, in the sense that we are trying to go *from* wherever we might be antecedently to having a morality, *to* where we will be *with* such a thing. What their moral values are antecedently to our "contract" procedure has no moral significance. Jones may *believe* that x is wrong when he goes "in" to the social contract, but since Smith believes that x is right and Robinson that it is indifferent, none of those views taken as items of belief in the status quo can be regarded as what our output – morality, as the theorist thinks – will contain. What it contains, rather, is what is, somehow, able to be agreed upon by all in light of their situations, interests, and relations to their fellows.

Sterba, in his account, suggests that "the question at issue here is what reasons each of us should take as supreme." And he suggests that the basic issue is whether those reasons are to be egoistic or altruistic, or some mix of the two:

Notice that in order not to beg the question, it is necessary to back off both from the general principle of egoism and from the general principle of altruism, thus granting the prima facie relevance of both self-interested and altruistic reasons to rational choice.[41]

To this we should comment that it is not for us, the theorists, to decide whether the one or the other sort of reason is "supreme." For if by supremacy is meant determinative of choice ahead of all other considerations, then the question is, determinative of *whose* choice? We should not say, "the rational individual's," for that assumes that they are all the same in this respect. But why assume that? A given individual will have a choice function such that, at any given time, something or other will be determinative in the required sense. In a given case, it might be self-interested – but the next individual, most likely, will be different in that respect. Sterba is rightly concerned to avoid question-begging, but we will not avoid it if we suppose that somehow one person's rationality will head him the same direction as another's. The contractarian project begins with minimal premises, and hopes to get somewhere from there despite this meager starting point.

The output of our procedure is to be a principle or set of principles such that all will have reason to support those, provided others do as well. Now, whatever that outcome is, the contractarian does think it has the imprimatur of reason: the reason of each, given how things are and in particular how the others stand.

Input and output

The social contract idea, then, is that we start somewhere, viz., with each individual's decision-making apparatus, whatever it may be. Call this the "input." We are trying to work from there *to* something, namely morals. Morality, we propose, will be the *output*. In so saying, what we intend is that our negotiated agreement will *constrain* us in various ways. It is a universal

41 Sterba, "APA Address," p. 50.

constraint, seen to be advantageous to all provided all comply. By the right kind of reasoning, and attention to relevant facts, whatever they are – but *not* "moral facts" since those are either just another name for the very thing we are trying to come up with, and thus, in context, question-begging, or else controversial and so useless. Facts in the usual sense in which we contrast facts and values, however, are certainly relevant and what we need.

In fact, the "input values" for our purposes are also facts, in the sense that it is a fact that Jones values x over y, Smith values y over z, and so on. That someone values something in some way is, we suppose, a fact: we can discover it, be mistaken about it and correct our mistakes in light of further investigation, and so on. Thus our reasoning is based entirely on facts, including both facts about what people value and also facts about the connections between proposed courses of actions and the outcomes to which such choices would lead in various circumstances. For the latter purposes, there is in principle no upper limit to what might conceivably be relevant. But various familiar facts about people and their environments are, at any rate, available and we suppose they will get us pretty far.

We can sum up the situation in terms of a sort of generalization of Aristotle's "practical syllogism." It will look like this:

(1) premises about what the agent wants – his personal "values" or interests;

(2) premises about (a) what he is able to do, hence what his options are among which he can unilaterally choose to put into effect, and (b) the facts that determine what the outcome will be of any particular choice;

(3) reasoning that assesses the prospects of available options in terms of their promotion of (1), utilizing the agent's overall measure of value in view of his whole set of relevant interests;

(4) (a) action, or (b) commitment to action, as in adoption of a general principle. (Where the actions lie in the future, as most will in the present case, where we are attempting to choose a general principle, then commitment, intention to act in the appropriate circumstances, is the output.)

What, then, is the "output"? What is morality? What determines this is primarily the information in (2b): how the actions of others would affect the agent, and his them, with appropriate adjustments to his calculation of overall benefit.

Morals

Our project here is to define "moral" for present purposes. Now, there has been a general division about the subject matter of morals, down through the ages. On the one hand, morals has been taken to be about our theory of life. Aristotle, for instance, takes the arena of morals to be control over the "passions." That such a subject is important and interesting is clearly true. But it is one of two quite different subjects, and there is, as we will see, a serious question how the two relate. This other use of the term "moral" is intimately bound up with the *interpersonal*, that is, the *social*. Robinson Crusoe on his desert island will have Aristotelian questions to solve: he can certainly have need to control his passions in various ways – to "aim at the mean," perhaps. However, since there is no social environment on his island (until Man Friday comes along), he simply does not have an issue about morals in the sense of concern here. That sense is, then: *interpersonal rules*, or, more generally, interpersonal *directives*, whether or not they are cast in the form of "rules."

Many moral theorists of late have been down on the subject of rules, and propose instead that we deal for these purposes in talk of virtues and the like. My characterization above is meant to be neutral on that matter, rather than to load, by definition, the notion of "rules" in any narrow sense into the very meaning of morals. Nevertheless, the talk here will be rule-like. We will be looking for principles, for a reason that steers us rather strongly down that dialectical track. For our problem is disunity at the "start"; what we are attempting to do is come up with a single, interpersonally authoritative set of directives – ones that *anyone* will rationally subscribe to.

The spirit here is to define a project: a uniform set of require-ments for all. Perhaps this is impossible, as I am sure many will think. But it will be agreed, too, that it would be nice to have such a thing. If we did, then a dispute between anyone and anyone else about anything lying within the reach or ambiance of the rules or principles in question would be capable of settlement, objectively, dispassionately, and relevantly. The social contractarian's strategy here is to find a basis *within* the already acknowledged value framework of each person, despite those being very different from one person to another, for supporting, nevertheless, this uniform, same set of principles. If this is possible, then the problem in settling a given issue is one of good reasoning and solidly supported facts, rather than of differences about the ultimate relevant evaluative premises. Those "relevant premises" are to be the outcome of our philosophical deliberations, and they are relevant for *these* purposes. But not for *all* purposes. We each have our own homework to do about how to run our lives, and the contractarian moral theorist is to make no assumptions about these, and, especially, no assumption that one of us has it right and the others wrong. Any given individual may indeed think that. (I, for example, suspect that *your* tastes in many musical matters are quite in error ... and if you are also interested in music, you almost certainly think the same of mine!) But your thoughts along such lines are irrelevant for moral purposes. We look, rather, to common ground.

We may even think of the hoped-for common ground as the "common good" sought by Aquinas and so many others. But being common, it is not something about which one person's opinion is "as good as another's." For there is a control, and that control is the social contract itself. The social contract theorist holds that the principles of morals are just those principles such that all will have reason to accept precisely those and no others, given the stipulation that *everyone else* must also agree.

What is the status of this output? Sterba puts it as follows:

> This question is not about what reasons we should publicly affirm, since people will sometimes publicly affirm reasons that are quite different from those they are prepared to act

upon. Rather, it is a question about what reasons it would be rational for us to accept at the deepest level – in our heart of hearts.[42]

But this, alas, is in a way idealistic. Of course we want commitment at that deepest level. That is because we want *compliance* – we want people to follow through, to *act* conformably to our mandated results. Indeed, action in social contexts is what it is all about. However, that is what it is *all* about, and hearts of hearts go farther than we need. Do we know whether the person who apparently acts on moral principle really does so? Kant shrewdly pointed out that the answer to this would seem to be forever in the negative.

> It is in fact absolutely impossible by experience to discern with complete certainty a single case in which the maxim of an action, however much it may conform to duty, rested solely on moral grounds and on the conception of one's duty.[43]

The best we can do is get the individual into a reliable groove of socially useful activity. If we had to depend on notions of the heart of hearts, we are, as Kant insists, doomed, for that is something we cannot ever know for sure. But it is a mistake to think that we must have that. If, deep down inside, our agent's heart is not really in it, that may be too bad, but so long as his actions are reliable, that will do. For the same reason, we should not be too quick to dismiss public affirmation, as Sterba appears to do. For after all, what we have in our model is, in the first instance, *all* "affirmation." There is, of course, no "moral conference" at which we negotiate the terms of the moral contract. But on the other hand, much of the modus operandi of morals is verbal. We *say* things to each other, and we must make a judgment how seriously to take what a given person says. But what a person *says*, in public, has the extremely important property that it can be a matter of record, and used against him next time there is a problem, if his actions deviate from his words. We can hold

---

42 Sterba, "APA Address," p. 50.
43 Immanuel Kant, *Foundations of the Metaphysics of Morals*, trans. Lewis White Beck (Indianapolis: Liberal Arts Press, 1959), p. 23.

people to their word, because it *is* their word. And we can put pressure on people on that basis. We can lambast them with further words, and also we can alter our own courses of action in light of what they say and then of what they do. And some of those alterations – say, a one million dollar lawsuit – will not be easy for the miscreant to ignore.

Morals is in essence a set of internalized social behavior controls. It has the extremely important feature that it is *decentralized*. Anybody can play, because everybody must. Each comes up with his own rules and engages in his own levels of mutual enforcement. But because we are dealing with *other people*, who have minds of their own, and whose behavior can and does impact on us, there are, as I put it above, controls. If what you say will not hold up in the public court of deliberation, you do not have a case. For that public court is, simply, social life, and like it or not, we are *in* that life, inextricably (until, at any rate, death does us part; but after that, the departed individual is no longer able to affect anyone else's actions by his or her own decisions).

Thus it is not hopeless to address the question of what a rational person could say and do in light of this or that consideration, and to infer some common principle that all can see to be for their good provided that others do so as well.

The common good

The social contract requires commonality in the output: that is the target, the job. What can possibly get us there? Consider the expression "the common good." Many doubt that this is a useful expression, on the plausible ground that, after all, we are each different. And of course we are, but that is not the end of the matter. In various ways, we can nevertheless have common interests. We must be very wary of this phrase, however. You want food; I want food. Common interest? Indeed not: what you want is food in *your* stomach, while what I want is food in *my* stomach. Should there be only one serving available, our interest, so far, is not common – indeed, it may set us at odds. The common interest has to be an interest that is common in the sense that each person is interested in *it* – shares, then, an interest in that *one* state of affairs. Since everyone figures in this state of affairs, it is a hugely complex object, in one sense. And if, as is probably almost always the case, there is a divergence between some individual's interest and the common interest, which way will the individual go? Why will he care? Clearly, if a common interest is what we seek for present purposes, it must be one important enough that everyone can agree to defer to it when it collides with his own interest. That is a tall order.

But we have something of an ace up our sleeves: conflict. When our interests diverge, they may or may not lead to conflict. Where they do not, we have no problem, and we need no principles to iron things out. But then there are the cases in which it does so lead: now what? Conflict can be costly. It may be better to settle for a peaceable outcome, even though not as much to your liking as some other would be. But this other one may be unavailable. If so, you may do best to go the peaceful route.

Or not. And then what? Now the stakes rise. But this matter of conflict and its control leads us to the proposal that is central to our inquiry here: the making of individual liberty into a socially recognized *right*.

The interest in liberty

While people's interests vary enormously, there is an abstract kind of interest that can safely be ascribed to all: the interest in being free to do one's thing, to pursue one's interests. If Jones wants that his actions bring about p, then it *follows* that Jones wants, insofar forth, *not to be prevented* from bringing about p. For being *prevented* means, by definition, that you *do not do it*. Yet the assumption is that Jones *wants* to do it. True, we sometimes change our minds in midstream, or we find ourselves acting rashly, or we discover that we miscalculated or made some kind of mistake. And for most of us, there are certain specific people – our spouses, for example – whose intervention in a given case is likely to be welcome, or, at least, of serious weight with us. Yet it is plausible also to say that the individual concerned wants to be the judge of such things (marriage, for example, is voluntary). Of course, we can judge any intervention, by anyone, possibly finding it satisfactory in the event. But *we* will be that judge and will want to be able to overrule interventions as *we* see fit. Attribution of this general disposition to all is called for because of the basics of action. To want is to want to succeed, not to be hindered. As Alan Gewirth puts it,

> Since his action is a means of attaining something he regards as good, even if this is only the performance of the action itself, he regards as a necessary good the voluntariness or freedom that is an essential feature of his action, for without this he would not be able to act for any purpose or good at all.[44]

From this, Gewirth moves to the conclusion that freedom is a right – though too quickly, as I have elsewhere argued.[45] For my granting you a right to freedom imposes a cost on me – forbearing interference with your free actions, which I may well not find to be in my interest, in a given case. What is needed is the social contract: that is, an agreement by each, based on the perception that one's own interest in freedom is great enough that it is worth getting even at the cost of acknowledging and respecting the freedom of others.

Contractarians historically have come to the same result: to a general principle of proscription of harm, attack, hindrance to others, except only when those others are themselves harming, attacking, or hindering others. Such unwanted intervention is sometimes gathered under the heading of *coercion*, although the immediate purport of that term is somewhat narrower than the others. Coercion is usually specific and practical: A wants B to do a quite specific kind of thing, and attempts to induce him to do it by a plausible threat of evils inflicted on B in the event of noncompliance.

44 Alan Gewirth, *Reason and Morality* (Chicago: University of Chicago Press, 1978), p. 52.
45 Gewirth also holds that well-being is such a right, construing this in a positive sense. See *ibid.*, pp. 63–75. I do not accept his reasoning toward that end, which depends on a noncontractarian procedure. See Jan Narveson, "Alan Gewirth's Reason and Morality – A Study in the Hazards of Universalizability in Ethics," *Dialogue* 19, 4 (December 1980), pp. 651–74.

It is not clear that all harms and attacks are of that specific a kind, though. Harms from sadists or the extremely negligent or careless are as unwanted as coercions, since what they do to us is similarly unwanted. No matter: this point needn't be pressed, for the upshot is the same: let us agree to refrain, mutually, from inflicting evils on each other; we therefore agree that considerations of responsibility matter, since the principles are there for the guidance of our actions. If we agree that we are to avoid harm to each other, then we agree also that we have to act with care, where possible, so as to avoid causing such harm even when we do not directly intend it.

Because the individual's *will* is what determines an agreement, the question of what constitutes "harm" to an individual is also determined essentially by his or her agreement, so far as that can be discerned. People can choose to undergo what to others would be tortures; but if it is really their choice, then we are not in a position to object. Voluntary consent will be the fundamental determinant if there should be any serious question. (For example, euthanasia, when genuinely voluntary, is something the contractarian will not be able to prohibit as a matter of principle, at least so far as its direct consequences are concerned.)

Social contract theory

These ideas bring us back to the subject of social contract theory. For present purposes, it is clearly essential to spell out more about the idea of the social contract. Much has, of course, been written about this and different ideas developed, and I have somewhat developed what I take to be the preferred version above. But a somewhat more thorough exploration is required here. We need to discuss, especially, two things: first, what is meant by the "agreement" – purely hypothetical, after all – of which we rather loosely speak? And second, what sort of conditions does the social contract impose so as to yield a meaningful agreement of the sort in question?

"Agreement"

Although we make a great number of agreements in society, and in many more cases have unspoken understandings with others about various matters, it is rare indeed, outside the halls of philosophy, to utter sentences to the effect that one regards, say, killing innocent people as wrong, much less to *say* to anyone that you will not kill him provided only that he does not kill you. Nevertheless, the social contract theorist wants to claim that we do "agree" to such things in just that conditional way. The agreement is behavioral: I in fact refrain from things like killing, and I do so conditionally upon my belief that others will reciprocate. It is an interesting question what our prospects would be if we were to bring up the subject, at the verbal level to which philosophers are accustomed, in hopes of securing, by argument and persuasion, someone's similarly behavioral acceptance of the prohibition of killing, in cases where it wasn't pretty obvious that he did already accept that prohibition.

Morals has two aspects, needing distinguishing. On the one hand, and primarily, one *has* a certain moral principle if one actually has the disposition to do what it tells people to do. Morals is about conduct, and if what someone professes to be a moral principle does not affect his conduct, then something has gone wrong. Prima facie, we have to side with Socrates: to profess, sincerely, that something is wrong is to imply that one will not do it.

But there is also another aspect, which we might call "administrative." In addition to doing right ourselves, we may and on many occasions should attempt to induce others to engage in morally acceptable behavior (or better). The two aspects should, and perhaps usually do, go hand in hand: we *say* that this or that is right or wrong, and we in fact do, and intend to do, and, should it prove difficult, at least try to do what is right and to refrain from what is wrong. But as we know, words and deeds can diverge, and every so often do.

Of course, in one sense, they will certainly diverge, for as philosophers have become keenly aware, it is extremely difficult if it is even possible to spell out, with anything close to completeness and precision, the principles we suppose morals to consist of. Killing is wrong, except ... Well, except when we must kill if we are to keep someone else from killing some further person, say. But what about the innocent victims who get accidentally caught in the crossfire, or get blown up by bombs aimed at persons who arguably we were justified in aiming at? And so on.

Despite all this, criticism of both our own and others' behavior is not only expected, but essential. If morals as a device for social behavioral control is not capable of verbal formulation, the hoped-for social control will be impossible. We must be able to say that this or that or the other particular action was right or wrong, and also that some contemplated act *would* be one or the other, in the interests of attempting to promote, *in advance*, prospects of the right ones being done and the wrong ones avoided. Generalization in morals is unavoidable, essential, even if framing perfect generalizations is all but impossible.

So the idea is this: that we can identify, in words, principles, rules, and maxims, types of behavior that are to be encouraged and approved, and, of course, *done*, and others to be discouraged, disapproved, prohibited, and, of course, *not done*. In the case of explicit promises and contracts, the behavior in question is fairly precisely specified, and detecting divergence between word and deed is, within limits, fairly easy in typical cases. But in the case of underlying principles, such specification may be more difficult. Still, it is what we aim to do, and if we nod heads in agreement, the expectation is that the nodder will in fact do what he agrees to. One second-order principle of great importance in ethics, indeed, is that those whose deeds do *not* accord with their words are problems, and need to be corrected in some way.

Morals, in the sense addressed here, is interpersonal. It is not a set of valuations of impersonal states of affairs; it is, rather, a transmissible, discussable set of valuations of conduct, and at base, of the conduct of essentially anyone. The social contract idea is that the presence and natures of other persons in our environs makes a difference to what we ought to, and therefore, hopefully, *will* do, and that it makes this difference because others are capable of taking significant action towards ourselves, wanted or unwanted. Morals, in our view, is a program of optimization: each is to act toward others in such a way that all relevant parties will do better, or, at least, as well as circumstances make possible, if they all live up to the sorts of principles that would be generated by mutual agreement.

Starting points

The other question concerns the sort of assumptions or conditions to impose on the "agreement" in question. While there have been many variants, I think that we may, for present purposes, reduce the variety to just three general options:

(1) First there is the ur-idea: I'll call this the out-and-out Hobbesian view. In this version, the social contract is made against the background of *no morality at all*. Hobbes, as we noted, famously theorizes that such a condition will be chaotic, a "war of all against all." The Social Contract is seen as the optimal way out of that condition, given the natures – the interests and powers – of each of us.

(2) Next is what we will dub the "Lockean" view. According to it, the social contract is made among persons conceived to be *free and equal*. This forms, as we may put it, the moral baseline for any further discussion. Since Hobbes also claims that we are in fact free and equal, there is a need to explain the difference. That difference has been nicely characterized by Paul Viminitz as the difference between bargaining with, or without, "guns on the table."[46] On the Hobbesian view, we have to persuade each other to put our guns away by arguments based on our interests; on the Lockean view, we get to put the guns aside with a sweep of the moral upper hand. Freedom and equality as a baseline is a basic moral assumption in the Lockean view, but not in Hobbes.

(3) Finally, there's Rawls, more or less. Here the theorist makes free to add explicitly *moral assumptions* to the procedure; specifically, we re-rig our starting situation in such a way as to guarantee certain moral results. Just which assumptions we add will, of course, make all the difference. Nor, in the Rawlsian framework, is it very easy to sort out which is which. Rawls is ready to proclaim equal opportunity, for example, as a fundamental principle of justice. But how this

---

46 See Paul Viminitz, "Getting the Baseline Right," in *Liberty, Games, and Contracts*, ed. Malcolm Murray (Aldershot: Ashgate, 2007), pp. 129–46.

would be derivable from the Hobbesian or Lockean framework is impossible to say. One concludes that it is one of the morally basic assumptions that Rawls feels we are entitled to help ourselves to in the process of arriving at what he calls Reflective Equilibrium – the mix, or balance, of moral intuition with foundational theory from which the theorist is not willing to depart and which seems to him comfortable.[47]

The original idea of the "social contract" is to provide a genuine explanation of morality or political institutions, or both. The explanation in question is to be foundational in the sense that (1) it is intended to provide the basic ideas from which the rest follow, and (2) that these foundations are explainable prior to and independently of the notion of morality itself. We are concerned here only with morality, and with political institutions only insofar as they are to operate under moral constraints, or of achieving certain antecedently accepted moral aims. Genuine *foundations* are ones that presuppose no morality. A *morality* is a set of general requirements and prohibitions on behavior, intended to apply to *all* who are capable of responding to moral-type requirements. (Or, to all in some more limited group whose moral code is in question. But the special case of group variance is not directly relevant in this inquiry. Confining a morality to a given group simply puts off the question of what is to be done when members of another group, initially professing a supposedly different morality, are encountered.) Unanimity, of a sort, is therefore written into the idea. Given all relevant facts, the basic principles are to be viewed as ones that all parties will find it rational to accept – on the crucial condition that others accept them as well.

So we are attempting to build moral outputs on nonmoral inputs. In particular, we try to show that rational people would accept certain requirements or constraints, and we take the fact

---

47 The primary Rawls source remains his majestic *A Theory of Justice* (Cambridge, MA: Harvard University Press, 1971); but an important and much shorter source is *Justice as Fairness: A Restatement*, ed. Erin Kelly (Cambridge, MA: Harvard University Press, 2001).

of their rational acceptability to be what confirms them *as* moral requirements. Of course, each individual needs to have a normative personal basis on which to proceed: it is that individual's *preferences* or, indifferently, *utilities* that provide this. The social contract does not commit the "Naturalistic Fallacy." Any individual will have an array of personal values that he does in fact accept, and at least some of those, at any given time, will have been "accepted" not on the basis of argument but as a matter, perhaps, of instinct or genetic wiring. The "output" values that we call moral are to be based on these in the sense that the individual's concern in moving to a morality is nevertheless to do better in terms of the values he already holds. But those values themselves are not moral. They are, simply, his values – the things that individual does in fact prefer, or does in fact hold to be valuable. We need, of course, to make assumptions about the general character of these, but the assumptions need to be empirically responsible. We may not assume anything we know to be false, and what we do claim must be known to be at least broadly true, in real-world cases. So, for example, we cannot assume much in the way of altruism; neither can we assume that people are altogether, narrowly self-interested. On the other hand, as previously argued, we can certainly assume that they are *at least* self-interested, even if not exclusively so. (Recall that being "self-interested" here is understood narrowly as explained above: to mean, interested in achieving certain states *of oneself* that are definable independently of relations to others, or even of the existence of others, such as keeping *oneself* fed, whatever may happen to anyone else.) Thus when a "deal" – that is, a formulated principle calling upon all to accept a certain set of restrictions on their actions – is proposed which has the expected potential to prohibit the doing of certain acts that may well be otherwise in the interest of the agent in question, an expectedly necessary condition of its being accepted is that it appeals, given our general relations, on balance to *all of* the other persons to whom it is proposed. Everyone must expect on the whole to do better living under the regime defined by this principle if complied with by all, including that person himself. But others will have such reason only on the basis of *their* interests. Interpersonal comparison of utilities is not, as such, employed. What A thinks of B's utilities is agreed to be up to A, and expectedly quite variable.

For this reason, what has generally been taken to be a major issue, and a sore point in contract theory – namely, the supposed assumption of self-interest at its base – is in fact nothing of the sort. It does not matter whether our contractors are narrowly self-interested or not. What does matter is whether the others who are also in on the "deal" are ready to accept their roles in the moral system proposed by the others. If those others, call them the A's, are other-directed, and their sentiments or preferences are directed at individuals B, C, and D, then whether their proposals in the way of moral principles and restrictions will be accepted depends on how they affect B, C, and D – not just on how they strike either individual A or, more to the point, the moral philosopher doing the theorizing. At some point, people must appeal to their own independent interests, in deciding whether to accept the proposals of others that affect them in various ways. And so self-interest has a certain conceptual priority. But it is not that we must assume that people are either purely or even largely egoistic in our "input" considerations.

Problems with the Rawlsian and Lockean options

Of the three theoretical options, then, as will be clear by this time, I reject the Rawlsian one as being foundationally useless. That is because either everyone does accept the various ideas proposed, or they do not. If they do, perhaps because they are programmed by nature in that way, then the social contract device is redundant, and we might as well just be natural law theorists. If they do not, however, then they will not accept the proposals that require them, and thus those proposals are defeated as outputs of the social contract, and so are useless for present purposes. And the overwhelmingly more plausible supposition is the latter: that they *do not* all already accept any particular principle regardless of its merits in terms of their personal values.

To be sure, finding the right set of conditions from which to begin is a difficult and controversial matter. In principle, however, we should here be under control of the facts about people. This includes, specifically, facts about (1) what they want, and (2) their powers to realize those wants. (Many other facts about people feed into those two categories. Almost anything can turn out to be relevant in some way, by virtue of their effect either on our interests or our powers.) Experience provides plenty of information of both types – though whether it is enough to get us to an actual moral conclusion is the (very difficult) question.

John Rawls's categories of "primary goods" are contributions to this part of the theory, and all proposals on the matter encounter the problem that seemingly no entry on it is truly universal. A plausible general claim, for instance, is that, whatever else, they want to continue living – though even that has problems: what about suicidal people? But again, the social contract machinery can tell us that this will not necessarily matter either, for those who wish to kill *themselves* are not ordinarily a problem to the others (apart from friends and loved ones who do not want to see them go); where they are a serious problem is when they insist on taking others along with them, as with contemporary terrorists. But that is a serious practical problem, rather than a serious theoretical one: it is obvious that we cannot expect agreement on the proposition that certain parties should be allowed to kill other people virtually at random. The example does suggest the line of reasoning that helps the social contract to a substantive and meaningful conclusion.

The lack of true universals has understandably been regarded as a major problem for contractarians. But whether it is so depends on what we are trying to achieve, and that in turn depends on what we want. What each of us wants is formally characterized as "maximization of utility" – a phrase meant only to capture the fact that we have wants and that they need to be somehow commensurated and estimated, along with appraisals of our capabilities, if we are to make any decisions. *Agreements* come into this as means of advancing one's interests overall. The aspiration of contractarianism as a theory of moral foundations is to show that we would all accept certain restrictions on our voluntary behavior, provided others do so as well. But at least notionally, we suppose that there are some who will accept no agreements, no restrictions. In relation to such persons, if there really are any, the theory is clear: we act as best we can, extending no rights to the recalcitrants. We remain, to put it in terms familiar to the theory, in the "State of Nature" in relation to them. Logically, of course, the only alternative to agreement is no-agreement. But the question is what the no-agreement condition would be like, and here the classic assumption is by no means a purely logical point: the claim is that the no-agreement condition would be chaotic – chaotic enough to motivate all to escape it. How bad this chaos might be, and especially whether it is bad enough to motivate the agreement we seek, is an interesting question. The claim of Hobbes is that this condition would amount to a "war of all against all," the hypothesis being that this would be terrible for all. Is he right?

In the no-agreement condition, we are to take it, people would never keep and therefore would never bother to make promises or contracts. They would use any amount of force they could muster whenever they supposed it would be effective in attaining their ends, whatever those ends might be. Hobbes's assessment of the consequences of such a condition are famously stark:

> In such condition, there is no place for Industry; because the fruit thereof is uncertain; and consequently no Culture of the Earth, no Navigation . . . no Knowledge of the face of the Earth; no account of Time; no Arts; no Letters; no Society; and which is worst of all, continual fear, and danger of violent death; And the life of man, solitary, poor, nasty, brutish, and short.[48]

No one we know could be unimpressed by his list, if he is right. But might some very unusual characters – psychopaths, megalomaniacs, or the like – remain unmoved?

Let us suppose that some would be like that. So, we consider instead a mixed scenario, in which almost everyone "accepts"

---

48 Hobbes, *Leviathan*, ch. 13.

and only a few "reject" the "agreement." How does this affect matters? Few of us civilized types are in practice ready to make unlimited war against sociopaths, just as such. Yet the terms of the social contract idea *entitle* us to do just that, and of course those few holdouts would be overwhelmingly outnumbered by the many who do accept conditional restrictions on themselves in the interest of enormously greater gains from social cooperation. Given this point, it seems to me there is little reason, as a matter of theory, to be concerned about "holdouts." Those who do not agree to refrain from inflicting evils on us are our enemies and to be treated accordingly. Those who do agree but in practice break the terms of the social contract will be subject to penalties and punishments, and the theory concerning what sort of penalties and how severe these may be is, of course, an important one in its own right. But it is subsidiary to the main project, which is to work out the reasonable general principles on which we can all expect everyone to proceed in adjusting their mutual relations. The libertarian proposal is that the most general principle is to respect everyone else's general liberty. That is the one that everyone has an interest in, no matter how diverse their interests.

Contract requires a baseline, and the original baseline is the complete absence of the sort of restrictions that we are supposing morality to be made up of. (It is a matter of definition that it is made up of such: "morality" refers to interpersonally authoritative requirements/restrictions and recommendations/inducements.) The plausible assessment of this situation is that its special problem is the prospect of interpersonally inflicted evils: bodily injury and death, in the first instance, and, more generally, obstacles to our pursuits of our various ends. But once we have an *agreement*, in real life, the baseline changes for those party to it. If I agree to purchase your used car, then a certain amount of my money becomes part of your reasonable expectation from me, and the future use of what used to be your car my reasonable expectation from you. Changes to that baseline would have to be by further mutual agreement: unilateralism is not acceptable. Unilateral departures from agreed terms are then further impositions of evils, since they leave the other party worsened as a result of participating in the agreement up to that point. Such behavior, then, makes the imposer liable to correction or penalty.

So far, then, the situation looks highly conducive to supporting Hobbesian Law No. 1, which prohibits the use of violence for promoting one's interests, except for the interest of peace itself. For that purpose may require the use of violence against the previously violent, that is, *aggressors*. So far, it is very difficult to disagree with Hobbes.

More?

Now, I have characterized the situation in recognizably "negative" terms. St. Augustine anticipates me (and Pareto) by proposing "that a man, in the first place, injure no one, and, in the second, do good to every one he can reach," these being the terms of the "well-ordered concord" of "The earthly city, which does not live by faith," but which nevertheless "seeks an earthly peace, and the end it proposes, in the well-ordered concord of civic obedience and rule, is the combination of men's wills to attain the things which are helpful to this life."[49] Augustine, to his very great credit, observes that these general terms hold between those adhering to his preferred Faith *and* those who do not adhere to it but nevertheless are interested in getting on in life. What I want to call attention to is the ordering of the two major requirements: *first* noninjury, and *second*, doing good to others. Of course, if we *equate* the doing of noninjury and the doing of good, we could not even raise this question. But to make that equation is to cheat; nothing is gained, and much lost, by tiresome begging of questions. But we are above that, I take it, and recognize a generic difference between action from A toward B which leaves B *worse off* than if A had not acted, and actions that leave B *better off* than if A had not acted, thus leaving a third area in which A's actions simply *do not affect* B one

49 St. Augustine, *City of God*, XIV (first quote), XVII (second quote).

way or the other – this being the presumptively normal case between essentially any given individual, A, and nearly all of the six billion or so of the rest of those currently in residence on this planet. Betterings and worsenings from the baseline of *non-action* are, as Gauthier encapsulates them in his version of the "Lockean proviso," the stuff of the most general level of the "social agreement," and St. Augustine's formula, recapped by innumerable moral philosophers and economists since, is the plausible proposal about that agreement. In the absence of any special relation of friendship, on the one hand, or enemyship, on the other, between one person and any miscellaneous other, it is abstractly rational that they agree to refrain from making each other worse off. Each person's concern for his own well-being assures that.

So – to return to our major issue – the question is whether a universal social agreement can include any *further* requirement than mutual non-harm. Saying, as I recently have,[50] that we would agree also to mutual aid, does not get us very far. For mutual aid extends to those with whom it would be genuinely mutual, and this hardly includes the whole of mankind at large. It includes, rather, those nearby with whom we interact closely enough that it can be expected that we might have similar need of assistance from them, and so can honestly say, "You'd have done the same for me!" Expectation of real reciprocation from very distant persons (both physically and culturally) is not reasonable. All the same, aid to anyone, if it genuinely does aid them, is of course to be encouraged, and this too, I think, is part of the social contract. But that contract is not a contract of requirement to *do* such things. It is, rather, a contract of requirement to *encourage*, to *recognize as a virtue*, the doing of more, with of course the expectation that many will be moved by such encouragement and recognition to actual

---

50 Jan Narveson, "We Don't Owe Them a Thing! – A Tough-minded but Soft-hearted View of Aid to the Faraway Needy," *The Monist* 86, 3 (July 2003), pp. 419–33. Further discussion of the issue in light of that article is found below pp. 233ff.

performance. Benefiting strangers, in short, is admirable, but it is not a duty of justice as such.

We can now return to our opening question: can liberty and equality be reconciled? As I said at the outset, this is too imprecise a formulation to admit of direct answer. Of course they can in the sense that it is *possible* for Jones to be disposed to give of what is his to give, equally to some set of persons. But issues of justice are not about that. Those issues, rather, have to do with what we may all reasonably *require* of each other. May we reasonably require everyone to respect everyone else's *liberty*, to act as he will, produce what he will, and promote his life as best he can, provided only that he in turn respect the same in relation to all others? The libertarian, following the "classical liberal," answers this in the affirmative. But for that very reason, we can*not* reasonably require everyone to "distribute" whatever he can produce equally to all others, or to randomly selected subsets of those others, or indeed to anyone. As requirements, they are clearly incompatible, and the two *cannot* be reconciled. If we require the one, we cannot require the other.

If they cannot, it remains to ask which of the two is to be preferred: requirements to respect liberty, or requirements to give equally? The social contract, I think, speaks clearly to this point. There is no reason why any individual should accept the latter requirement, and every reason why he should accept the former. We will not want to be slaves to anyone, whether richer or poorer than ourselves. Consequently, the social contract calls for the former – for liberty for all – and declares against the latter, coerced welfare assistance from all. Once we are clear about the terms of this question, I do not see how any other answer can be forthcoming.

Does it work?

There are two important questions about this in the context of contractarian reasoning. The first is whether we will succeed in getting this result, in view of the real disparities of powers among individuals. The second is whether we might get something further – not only the nonharm agreement, that is, of general

negative rights, but perhaps in addition a right of mutual assistance – or even, as so many recent philosophers assume, of
unilateral assistance – roughly, positive rights, leading perhaps
to the welfare state.

Before opening discussion on this crucial matter, we need to
revert to our opening definitions to note an important distinction. We are discussing, in this book, *rights*, as specifically *enforceable*. But we need to be clearer about the kind of enforcement
that is in question. John Stuart Mill argued that all moral claims
are enforceable in one way or another:

> The truth is that the idea of penal sanction, which is the
> essence of law, enters not only into the conception of injustice,
> but into that of any kind of wrong. We do not call anything
> wrong, unless we mean to imply that a person ought to be
> punished in some way or other for doing it, if not by law, by
> the opinion of his fellow-creatures, if not by opinion, by the
> reproaches of his own conscience. It is a part of the notion of
> Duty in every one of its forms that a person may rightly be
> compelled to fulfill it...[51]

But punishment in the form of verbal admonition is a long
way from punishment by execution or incarceration, or even
from compulsory extractions from one's income. It is the latter
two especially that are in question here. It is not that there are no
controls whatever on the use of less stringent reinforcements.
There are various reasons for arguing that severe restrictions on
our use of such devices are not in general warranted. But it is
important to recognize that a contractarian argument can be
mounted in support of use of some such less stringent reinforcements in a certain range of cases. Among these, for example,
could be the admittedly important category of attending to the
needs of others. We will recur to that topic later. What is important here is only that our issue is not whether neglect of one's
fellows may be reasonably held to be generally *wrong*, but rather,

---

51 John Stuart Mill, *Utilitarianism*, ch. 5: "On the Connection between Justice
and Utility."

whether such neglect is *punishable*, as it would be if its potential recipients actually had a *right* to our services in that respect.

Why welfare rights are a problem

To resume our main line of discussion, then: above, I used the word "unilateral" in my description of the category of positive welfare rights. If we have such rights, then the situation is that others are required to supply the things in question to the right-holder even if he does or can do nothing in return. On the face of it, one would not expect a "contract" to have such a feature. After all, contracts are made in the interests – and ultimately, as explained above, the self-interests – of the parties to them, and it is unclear how it can be in the interest of Jones to accept a positive right for Smith, whom we shall assume to be a perfect stranger, with no reciprocity envisaged.

Now this could be argued to be a misunderstanding. For the theorist who holds that the social contract includes positive rights will want to point out that we *all* have these rights: For all persons, person A undertakes to provide x for B if B is in need, and B to provide it to A if A is in need. And are we not all on occasion in need? But it is the latter that is the problem. On which occasions and how many do we need what? Most con-temporary Americans will never be in a position where they must rely on the charity of others for basic income. The things typical ones of us might possibly need are things which private charity and general good-neighborliness can supply, and govern-ment simply cannot: helping me clear my driveway on a particu-larly snowy day, changing my tire if my back hurts too much, providing directions to an address I do not know... But the sort of positive rights that the welfare state envisages are not the kind where a real likelihood of reciprocity is to be envisaged. Govern-ment-supplied welfare will certainly transfer resources from people who will never need or want them supplied to them-selves, to people who are not capable of reciprocating and many of whom will never be. Private insurance will cater to the needs of almost all of us, and charity, as I shall argue below, could readily handle the rest. To resort to compulsion for these purposes, even if they were on the face of it supportable by compulsion, is unnecessary, and because it is unnecessary, so the libertarian argues, it is also wrong.

Positive rights enthusiasts want to apply these rights to all, from birth up. Yet it will certainly seem to some, with good reason, that they are extremely unlikely to benefit, and meanwhile are certain to incur serious costs, from such provisions. The enthusiasts in question – Dworkin comes to mind – want the "contract" to happen, it seems, prior to birth. He talks of taking insurance out against being born with Down syndrome, or whatever.[52] In such an application, clearly, the idea of the contract has been taken well beyond the limits of the concept as normally understood. For once we are born and on the way in life, it will be obvious that we will never be sufferers from certain genetic conditions. There was no time in the life of any real person at which he or she could have rationally moved to insure against the likelihood of being born with Down syndrome, or two heads, and so on.

To be sure, the whole idea of social contract might be accused of doing something very like that, so the question is whether this particular way of doing it is any more objectionable than the general idea in any of its forms. In response, the first thing to say is that the central idea of the contract theory is not so hard to state. Namely, we begin with individuals and their values and powers, whatever they may be; and then we ask whether they are such that certain general constraints on their behavior, provided all others agreed to them as well, would yield a positive return for everyone. And if some proposal does appear to do that, is there any other that does yet better? In principle – in contrast to the now-popular procedure of Rawls who puts his individuals behind a "veil of ignorance" – we ask real individuals, not metaphysically possible individuals before they exist. We cannot, of course, literally ask each person, one by one, and so we must consult our general knowledge of people, and work out plausible

---

52 See Ronald Dworkin, *Sovereign Virtue* (Cambridge, MA: Harvard University Press, 2000), pp. 80–3.

answers on that basis. And there we can certainly go wrong. But not, I think, so wrong as when we resort instead to metaphysics.

In this we have no sensible alternative to using Pareto reasoning. Pareto's general idea concerns what he calls "efficiency," a possibly misleading term. But the main idea is clear enough. A certain social situation shows a "Pareto improvement" if some action leaves at least somebody better off in the society *ex post*, while no one is worse off than in the status quo. If we put this idea into normative terms, we have the familiar general strictures of the medievals and many others: do not harm anyone who is himself innocent of harm to any other, and within that restriction, try to do some good. The lower limit of acceptability is where no harm is done to anyone even if no good is either. That is because when we claim that someone has done wrong, we are, as Mill says, in effect either calling for some or other punishment, or are actually delivering a sort of verbal punishment – either of which will leave that individual somewhat worse off. But doing those things to innocents, on the other hand, would violate the Pareto criterion. Confining negative reinforcement to the infliction of evils solves that problem: evildoers have already violated the criterion anyway.

How does this apply to social contract? Well, since everyone is in on it, there is no point in proposing a "deal" that is contrary to the interests of some. Any costs accruing to anyone had better be compensated by commensurate benefits. On the other hand, it is impossible that everyone should be literally benefiting everyone else, in the sense of himself doing what would raise the other person above the latter's status quo share. The obvious alternative is to agree *to leave each other in peace*, supplying, perhaps, no benefits but at least imposing no costs. That, in short, is *freedom*: A leaves B to his devices, and B does likewise for A. Everyone, necessarily, benefits (in his own view of what constitutes benefit) from freedom. Not everyone, even foreseeably and probably, benefits from an across-the-board imposed requirement to bring or keep all and sundry others above some prescribed level. Human variability, both situationally and physiologically, is much too great. The appropriate price of freedom is, then, freedom. Each benefits from the noninterference of the other(s), relative to the chaos of the (moral) "state of nature."

If some insist on a higher price for allowing the other to live in peace, why should the others agree? My "service" of refraining from taking the opportunity to invade and despoil costs you little: it leaves you free to do as you like, within the limits imposed by granting that same right to all others. Why, then, shouldn't I be left similarly free, *instead of* needing to add costly burdens in *your* case? Why should your basic rights cost me something extra? In particular, how can it be reasonable for one person, who happens to be born with a reasonably good physical constitution and the standard allotment of mental agility, emotional stability, and so on, to be *held responsible* for someone else's being less fortunate? Especially when the "someone else" has no direct and possibly no indirect relations to the individual whom we are proposing to saddle with this responsibility? A does nothing to cause B's defects: it simply happens, alas, that B got a less desirable package at the hands of the "natural lottery" – to use Rawls's perspicuous phrase – genetics, parentage, and local environment. Suppose that A is ready to let B go his way in peace? This is normally no problem – after all, in almost all cases it is supremely easy for A to do this. The cost is almost always zero. So why should B and his political supporters be conceptually permitted to insist on something more at the hands of A? Positive rights of the envisaged kind are not impartial. They load the dice in favor of the needy, the incapable, the naturally shortchanged, and against those able to provide for them.

Rawlsians and Dworkinians seem to think that it can be appropriately made the responsibility of all of us to repair the "injustices" of Nature, equalizing where Nature has made us unequal. But, let us remember, Nature simply is not one of the parties to this discussion. Each of us *people* must do our best in the face of nature, taken as it is, and of each other, taken as we are, but also as we can be with careful discussion and reflection. The cosmic problem of inequality, like the similarly cosmic problem of evil, is not ours to deal with. The local problem of our potential evils to each other, on the other hand, most decidedly *is* our problem. Happily, it is a problem that moral dispositions can help to solve.

It can also solve the other problems, however. For it is indeed an important part of morality that we be disposed to help our fellow. But it is a part for which we should be positively rewarded rather than coerced.

Force

The question is whether anything that imposes more costs on us than the libertarian "contract" can be justified. We will consider some further ideas about this, but there is, straight off, one important, and apparently credible answer to this: individual A might have no choice. B and his friends may be able to threaten A with evils sufficient to induce the A's of this world to accept these otherwise unfavorable terms. That, certainly, has been the way of politics from time immemorial. Politics is power, after all. And democratic politics, in particular, marshals the power of the majority, which might well be held to be irresistible. As a late colleague of mine used to say, "What democracy proves is who would win in a fair fight!"[53] So if the majority votes, say, for welfare measures, then why does not that make welfare measures morally acceptable?

Now, we usually think that morality is not quite like that. With morals, there is an extremely strong presumption against resorting to force. Everyone is to recognize and respect rights of others, and interactions are to proceed by agreement rather than coercion. That the force is yielded by 50.5 per cent of the population is, on the face of it, neither here nor there. The majority is *not* always right, and certainly it is not *necessarily* right. (Moreover, most members of majorities agree with that. They do not think that if the majority should like to torture the members of some group, then it is perfectly OK to do so.)

53 The colleague was Richard J. C. Burgener. I don't know where he got it.

But we cannot just assume our way out of this. If the idea of social contract is to make contact with the real world, then the reality that people often are in a position to exert compulsion on others is to be taken properly into account. But "taking account" of it does not necessarily mean simple acceptance.

Here we can instructively compare the Hobbesian view with that of John Locke, who tells us that the "state of nature" is "A *State* also of *Equality,* wherein all the Power and Jurisdiction is reciprocal, no one having more than another."[54] The question is, what justifies Locke's bold generalization? For as we know, people are not equal in any significant respect, including that of coercive capability. They are not born equal in that regard, and they do not stay equal. How, then, can we philosophers presume to cancel out these differences, especially when we do not also cancel out the enormous differences in *productive ability* of which they are also so manifestly possessed? But there is a classic reply, found in Hobbes – the only one, I think, who faces this problem squarely. According to Hobbes, "when all is reckoned together, the difference between man, and man, is not so considerable, as that one man can thereupon claim to himself any benefit, to which another may not pretend, as well as he."[55] Here he appears to be not just chiming in with Locke, but offering an explanation. We assume that people are roughly equal in this very important respect because, he suggests, in one very basic way they actually *are* so, or near enough to do. Hobbes is well aware that people differ in their powers, coercive and otherwise. Yet, his claim is these differences are not such as would justify a wholesale acknowledgment of a *right* of the stronger. And why not? Because it will be in the interests of the supposedly weaker to get together and become stronger than that supposedly stronger party – or strong enough to assassinate him, at any rate. For Hobbes, the bottom line is that "as to strength of body, the weakest has enough to kill the strongest."[56] It does not take

---

54 Locke, "Second Treatise on Civil Government," #4.
55 Hobbes, *Leviathan*, ch. 13.
56 *Ibid.*

much, after all. Any normal person who really wants to kill some other relatively normal person would likely be able to do it. And Davids can kill Goliaths, come to that.

But if there is wholesale approval of such methods, we make might into right – and we thereby bring society to its knees, a chaos of violence with no end in sight. Temporary ends, perhaps, yes: but not permanent ends. By contrast, Hobbes thinks, we can all benefit from peace, because practically anybody out there can kill us. In today's world, with lethal inexpensive weapons available to all, the possibility that literally just about anyone could in fact kill just about anyone else, given inclination and determination, is uncomfortably real. Given the incentive and the excuse, they not only *can* kill us, but there is rather too much of a chance that they *will*, even on fairly flimsy excuse – religious fanaticism, to take one popular example.

The idea that a morality should sanction such behavior rather than condemning it is not credible. That violent behavior is morally prohibited, condemned, is one of those ideas that, as T. M. Scanlon puts it, "no one could reasonably reject."[57] At any rate, the libertarian makes a proposal about the content of morality that looks plausible. To any who would prefer violence, we have to say: not, at any rate, with *our approval*; and then, we will do our best to make sure you fail in your attempts, or at least suffer severely if you persist in them – which is what is in question here. To the man already on the battlefield, there's not much to do but try to have superior weaponry, training, courage, and the rest of the military virtues. But to the citizen able to cast his vote for or against violence, can there be any reasonable question? Along with all the classic philosophers, we will say: the minimum for socially acceptable behavior is the disposition to refrain from violence in the pursuit of one's interests, whatever those interests may be. We will instead say, with Grotius, that "war is undertaken for the sake of peace," and that

---

57 T. M. Scanlon, *What We Owe to Each Other* (Cambridge, MA: Harvard University Press, 1998). Space does not permit detailing my agreements and disagreements with this important book.

"Thus for instance, to deprive another of what belongs to him, merely for one's own advantage, is repugnant to the law of nature..."[58]

To be sure, this is a very large question, with either a very complex answer, or perhaps none. The contractarian project is intended to provide foundations for general morals. We start with man as he is; we appraise his interests and capabilities. We then look for the possible set of restrictions on everyone's behavior that would be rationally accepted by all, as being in their interest. Those will be the basic principles of morals. All writers have supposed that we will emerge with a general condemnation of violence. Hobbes depicts the horrors of the "state of nature" in colorful terms, and finds that the root cause of all this is violence, the tendency to "invade and despoil." If his analysis is right, it surely looks as though a general proscription on violence is what is needed to do the job – the job of getting us from those horrors to the blessings of civilization. The blessings are due to the freely productive efforts of each. What makes it possible is the absence of violence, which in turn is due to its rational condemnation by all, with participatory forbearance.

Equality of vulnerability

The Lockean version *assumes* "equal liberty" in the sense we have carefully defined: that no one gets to push anyone else around. But how did we get to that as a *starting* point? If it is a normative assumption, then what makes it work? It does not seem reasonable simply to assume it. What, if anything, makes it a reasonable assumption?

What we need for this purpose, evidently, is the aforementioned Hobbesian thesis, that whatever disparities among us as individuals there may be, they will not be such that the "strong" can *reasonably claim* any benefits from the basic principles of morals at the expense of the weak. And this, as we have just

58 Hugo Grotius, *The Rights of War and Peace*, trans. A. C. Campbell (New York: M. Walter Dunne, 1901). Accessed from http://oll.libertyfund.org/title/553. The first quotation is from ch. 1.I; the second from ch. 1.III.

noted, in Hobbes's notable summation is because "as to strength of body, the weakest hath enough to kill the strongest." So if we ask, why will we join with others in renouncing violence as a permissible way to make one's way in the world? the answer is: because those who live by the sword are asking, in effect, to die by it, and making it in the interest of others to advance the date at which they do so as much as possible. Violence obviously makes it more difficult, or impossible, for its victims to pursue, and thus to achieve, their ends. If virtually everyone is capable of inflicting harm and loss on virtually anyone, then since it is to everyone's benefit not to have such losses inflicted on themselves, the way forward is to overrule violence in general, except, of course, as it may be needed in order to counter the proffered violence of others. Aggression, then, is what is condemned. Aggression is war, for it is the infliction of injury and loss on the peaceable.

That, I think, was Hobbes's reasoning in proceeding to this "first Law of Nature." David Gauthier, who comes as close as anyone (unless perhaps myself) to being Hobbes's contemporary disciple, entitles his celebrated exposition of the point of view, *Morals by Agreement*.[59] Indeed, he might well have called it "morals *as* agreement." Those who seek advantage over others by using and threatening force are clearly not "agreeing" with those others – and thus, not proceeding morally. To be moral is to proceed in another way: the way of mutuality, whereby we proceed by peaceful means to go our various ways, thus to *mutual* benefit. The benefit is the absence of the evils that will certainly prevent us from getting ahead.

Is such a morality rational? It is, if its presumptions are right: *that we all have more to gain from peace than from war.* What makes that plausible is the prospect of loss at the hands of our fellows if we choose war. If this prospect is similar for all, then the presumption looks very promising: we each, then, have an interest in supporting peace above war.

---

59 David Gauthier, *Morals by Agreement* (New York: Oxford University Press, 1986).

But this loss from battle may not be *net* loss. Might not our violent forays yield gains enough to justify their costs? We must admit that in many particular cases, it might appear to be by no means certain that some violent individual will not reason that way. When it is not, we victims of aggression will have to resort to force – we will have no real choice but to do so. And predictably, at least many of us, very likely by far most of us, will be worse off from the situation that forces us to make that choice. If we play our cards right, the defensive violence that we can muster will make the aggressive violence of those we defend against sufficiently unprofitable to make them back down. In the age of the easily carried firearm, and other equalizers developed in the course of the evolving technology of war, the Hobbesian assumption is not so implausible. Moreover, the prospect of victimhood provides a motive for potential victims to band together in defense against those who think they can gain from violence. Since we are all potential victims, there is a very strong inducement to join the ranks of the peaceable. Indeed, at the very abstract level at which we are considering this matter – namely, the level at which we are attempting to find general principles to be advanced by all in relation to all – the case is surely closed. Advocacy of war as a way of life is irrational. Advocacy of peace is thoroughly rational – so long as it is not advocacy of *pacifism*, which is quite another matter. Hobbes's Law of Nature has *two* branches, not just one: (a) always to seek peace, and (b) when you cannot get it, to defend yourself by all means, including as much violence as necessary. Abandoning the right of self-defense is as irrational as – and not far from equivalent to – advocating a general right to use violence for any purpose whatever.

A social contract will not, then, give us slavery, nor will it justify aggressive war as a way of achieving our ends. It will instead bring us general voluntary cooperation and, therefore, peace. That is to say, it will give us these *as principles*, relevantly invoked whenever there is deviation from them. Those who defraud and despoil, invade, aggress, are to be criticized and faulted. What they do is unjust, as being contrary to the terms on which humans can live successfully together.

Coerced assistance?

But what of those who do none of those things – who avoid all aggression – but are nevertheless *unhelpful*? Is that also "contrary to the reasonable terms of human association"? And especially, is it so to the point that we may turn to coercion in order to induce people to be helpful?

There is, of course, a question of what constitutes "coercion" for these purposes. We usually think of reinforcement by threat of jail terms, or financial takings, or more rarely of physical attack or execution. But much moral reinforcement is accomplished by responses well short of that. We can threaten our future noncooperation in various ways, or we can cuss people out, or look askance at them, or "cut" them in public ... The present issue has to do with *coercive* methods, which notionally at least are a proper subset of these ways of attempting to influence behavior. Neither governments nor anyone else, I argue, may *coerce* people into helping those in need. The assumption underlying that is that there is something special about coercion. What is it?

It is normally supposed that coercion deprives us of liberty. In some sense, coercion does not *let* us make up our own minds. Now, of course, in one sense there is no way to prevent someone from "making up his own mind." We are not robots, after all. The coercer does not achieve his purpose if his victim is a robot: rather, he *induces* compliance. What the coercer has is the power, in the circumstances, to *alter people's payoffs*. The coercer proposes to make the coerced person's life *worse* relative to the status quo, if the latter does not comply with the directives of the former. He changes our world: he compels us to make our choices in a world made worse by his actions.

There are difficult issues about coercion which we can hardly get into in this essay. Sometimes individual A is a past and ongoing provider of benefits to B. On occasion x, A proposes to cease this helpful activity unless B does something he would rather not do. Is this coercion? It is likely to be effective in many cases, and it might well feel like coercion to someone long accustomed to being the beneficiary of A's good services. Yet B, we suppose, was not entitled to that stream of benefits in the first place: A, we will suppose, was providing the benefits out of the goodness of her heart. That goodness will be reduced a bit unless B does x, yes: but then, it does not literally seem that B's *freedom* is reduced by B's decision not to comply and instead to accept the proposed reduction. But suppose instead that A proposes to take, by force, some of B's money if B does not do x. This does feel like a reduction in B's freedom, if, as we will assume, B's money had been honestly come by and also not come in the form of a gift from A.

We shall have to leave aside such interesting questions for present purposes. Welfare *states* are coercive in a quite plain sense of the term. They tax without consent of the individual person whose money is taken (though, in democratic countries, perhaps with the consent of his neighbors who voted the program into office). Taxation is not a matter of *withholding favors*, but of *imposing costs*. And it is the welfare *state* that is in question here. Voluntary charities do not have the option that states do. They solicit money from us, and we can choose to help out, or not, as we prefer. The consumer is king, and that includes the consumer, as we might describe him, of charitable services. He shops around, or may do so, at any rate, and he chooses the one that will give his money for what he judges to be the best purposes. Those who do not buy go elsewhere, or stay home, or whatever.

What is at issue here is whether the needs of the needy are such as to justify compulsion in supplying them. This is understood here as a pure question of principle. The Contractarian holds that general normative principles are set by agreement, issuing from a hypothetical bargain. The question at issue, then, is: will a principle calling for compulsory service to the needy secure the universal agreement that is the hallmark of the social contract? It seems to me that it will not.

After all, the alternative available to almost everyone is to form associations, not just for mutual defense against aggression, but also to pursue all sorts of other benefits. All commercial life is like that: consumers and producers form a voluntarily acting group, often very large, of persons who supply each other with various things on terms of exchange agreed by the respective parties. Among the many goods and services available in this way is insurance. Here the provider provides a guarantee: your house burns down, you get x per cent of the costs; you get sick, you get taken care of, perhaps cured, by persons whose knowledge and skills are now devoted to you, the customer. In contemporary America, that is how most people get their medical care. But not all: for a very large minority, care comes from publicly funded resources – from "social insurance," which is out of the voluntary association loop, being compulsory in its source. The point, however, is that there is nothing impossible about voluntary insurance schemes. And it seems clear that many people will see themselves as doing much better if they confine themselves to private sources, rather than enlisting in a compulsory regime. It is hard to see why they are not right about this. And if they are, it is very hard indeed to see how the "social contract" with its requirement of unanimity in principle is going to underwrite publicly funded schemes for these ends.

3   The grounds for welfarism considered

Why would it be thought that people do have a *right* that their neighbors, or indeed anyone who can, must come to their aid when they are in states of deprivation? One very urgent question for the welfare theorist, of course, is just *how* "deprived" they must be before such action is due. Another is, how much of a cost is to be imposed on the helping party. All of us, after all, have needs. Jones might need a faster car now that his neighbor, in an effort to "keep up with the Joneses," has one equal to his present vehicle in that respect. Multimillionaire Helena might need a condo on the Mediterranean so that she can better pursue her passion for painting Van Gogh-like sunflowers. The welfare theorist proposes to draw the line far, far below those. But where? In practice, as we know, contemporary G8 states draw a "poverty line" below which people are not to be allowed to stay, or at any rate below which they are considered eligible for public, that is, compulsorily financed, support. The line in question, as drawn in the USA and Canada at least, is astonishing by world standards. Poverty in America would be at least middle-class status in any number of Third World countries. To defend such public largess as a matter of staving off "needs" is to stretch the notion of need to somewhere beyond the breaking point. A different theory is needed, such as an egalitarian one, where we need not worry about "needs" but focus merely on the sheer fact that some have a good deal *less* than others.

It is clear that the contractarian will not go for equality in the relevant sense. Those who are subjected to taxes for the purpose of narrowing a gap between themselves and putative recipients are not going to be moved by this project. No doubt it might appeal to the relatively poorer – though even with them there is a question. For the poor, especially in North America, notoriously tend not to stay poor. As the decades go by, they move up, from the bottom quintile to the fourth, the third, or even the second or first.[60] The thought that they will never be able to get anywhere because the political system prevents anyone from doing so, however useful the services of those who made more, is going to deter the aspiring welfare recipient. People want to get ahead, and a rigidly egalitarian system will make it impossible for them to do so. Its effects on general productivity are foreseeably adverse. David Hume was among the first to point this out clearly:

> Render possessions ever so equal, men's different degrees of art, care, and industry will immediately break that equality. Or if you check these virtues, you reduce society to the most extreme indigence and, instead of preventing

60 The US Treasury Department says that 86 per cent of people in the lowest income quintile in 1979 had moved up at least one quintile by 1988; of those, 65 per cent had moved up *more than* one (quoted in Schmidtz, *Elements of Justice*, p. 133).

want and beggary in a few, render it unavoidable to the whole community.[61]

Our concern, to be sure, is not with the egalitarian as such. Sterba does not advocate egalitarian policies, nor do most theorists today. Instead, they call for *safety-net* policies, intended to guarantee that those at the bottom are nevertheless far enough above it to enable them to live a life at some level of satisfaction. Of course, this raises the very vexed question just what that level is to be. And on that point we again encounter substantial differences among advocates of welfarism. A vague notion of "basic needs" tends to be invoked, but just which are they? Presumably having enough food to sustain life at all will be included whatever else is – typical proponents of welfare states invariably invoke the dread prospect of *starvation* as if *it* is the only real condition that the welfare state aims to prevent. But that is a very low level indeed – indeed, below the level of reality, as I will point out later in this essay. Any actual theorist on this subject will quickly expand the list. The minimum will include not just enough calories to remain alive, but health, clothing, and shelter to some "decent" level.[62] In North America, no one with a domicile goes without hot and cold running water, indoor toilets and bath, and, if only because of the plethora of Salvation Army and other providers, it is really impossible for anyone to be unable to afford enough clothing to keep out the elements and be presentable in public. Yet those are luxuries in the world's poorest countries. And again, by implication, this raises the question how the welfare theorist can avoid extending taxed benefits to all of the world's worst-off – not just those in the theorist's own country.

61 David Hume, *Inquiry Concerning the Principles of Morals*, Section III, Part II.
62 For a careful treatment of the situation in Canada, see Chris Sarlo, *Measuring Poverty in Canada* (Vancouver: Fraser Institute, 2001). For further interesting discussion, see Rudy Pohl, "Poverty in Canada," www.streetlevelconsulting. ca/homepage/homelessness2InCanada_Part2.htm

How much is the minimum?

That perceptive student of society Alexis de Tocqueville, in his 1835 "Memoir on Pauperism," opens his essay with the interesting observation that in the Europe of his day, the poorest countries had the fewest "paupers" whereas England, by far the richest, also had by a considerable margin the most. That seems a paradox, and of course is grist for the leftist critics who deplore the huge disparities in wealth engendered by capitalism. But Tocqueville provides the solution:

> The more prosperous a society is, the more diversified and more durable become the enjoyments of the greatest number, the more they simulate true necessity through habit and imitation ... Along with the range of his pleasures he has expanded the range of his needs and leaves himself more open to the hazard of fortune. Thus the English poor appear almost rich to the French poor; and the latter are so regarded by the Spanish poor. What the Englishman lacks has never been possessed by the Frenchman. And so it goes as one descends the social scale. Among very civilised peoples, the lack of a multitude of things causes poverty; in the savage state, poverty consists only in not finding something to eat.[63]

Thus when we come to proposing a right to a social minimum, it obviously makes a very large difference what we are counting as that minimum. Sterba's case looks strong because he talks, often, of *starvation*, and more generally of the "basic needs" of the poor. Any list of basic needs of humans would include minimal nutrition, to be sure, and if someone is literally going without his "basic needs" fulfilled, he is soon dead. But if we move to modern levels, such as a budget sufficient to keep the recipient in hot water, indoor plumbing, a decent used car, and the capability of renting at least one DVD per week, we have surely moved from

---

63 Alexis de Tocqueville, *Memoir on Pauperism*, trans. Seymour Drescher, intro. Gertrude Himmelfarb (London: IEA, Health and Welfare Unit, 1997), p. 24.

the social minimum concept of welfare to something nearer an egalitarian concept.

Thus when we discuss grounds for welfare, a problem is that there are many different notions of the levels of welfare that ought to be aimed at in public programs, and consequently a different set of "grounds" would have to be found. However, certain arguments can cut rather substantially across these distinctions, and, moreover, cut across the differences between Sterba and myself. Two in particular need some discussion here: (1) that the peculiar interdependency generated by modern economies calls for welfare measures independently of specific social philosophy; and (2) that welfare measures control crime and civil unrest. In either case, if those arguments work, the welfare theorist would have premises enabling him to cross the gap between negative and positive rights.

Arguments from economic interdependency

We would all, let us assume, like to make as much income as possible.[64] But now, suppose that certain macroeconomic conditions are such that everyone's doing this simply requires that everybody, regardless of work, ability, or lifestyle, be able to continue spending and consuming. The argument requires that this latter "propensity to consume" is able to be economically effective despite unemployment at useful productive activities by the consumer in question. Indeed, the effect, let us imagine, is such that it *pays* people in the middle and higher income groups to accept higher taxation levels, because without these, their *net* earnings (that is, their earnings after taxes) would actually *fall*.

It is hard to see how such a scenario could be realistic. Money is a medium of exchange, not a good in itself. Our interdependency

---

64 That is a very rough generalization, and a very imprecise one as well. Assume that what is meant is that *nearly* everybody would like to do this, and also that "as much as possible" means, short of extraordinary changes in lifestyle, number of working hours, and various other things too numerous and inchoate to mention here. Still, I take it to be all but a sheer truism that people would be glad to have much higher incomes than they do, if the cost to them of doing this was quite small.

is a large nexus of mutual exchanges, large or small. Every trans-action in it is in some way negotiated by the parties to it, and each receives because he gives, gives because he receives. How can it improve matters that some give involuntarily, others receive without giving?

But that is not something we can determine here. Rather, it may be agreed that if such a thing as that just described really were to happen – frequent involuntary transfers required in order to maintain the voluntary system – then it would indeed be irrational to oppose welfare measures: the case would be closed in their favor, however much disagreement remained at the high level of abstract principle where our disagreements are being discussed. I assume that Sterba and myself would agree on this point, and that it would render our discussion of principle, insofar as it had any role to play, practically irrelevant. I do not think that the economics behind the scenario sketched do make sense, in fact. But still, strange things do happen out there in the real world, and the point here is just to take cognizance of the possibility. It would, of course, shift the debate right out of the realm of philosophy, except that there would still be an abstract question of principle. Only, it would be one that did not need to be resolved so far as practice is concerned.

The argument from "class wars"

The other argument is a bit different, and of rather more rele-vance. Here the idea is that if we do not look out for the needy, they will take matters in their own hands and turn to theft, either of food or of other things that they can exchange for food or further essentials. Thomas Hobbes, in illustration of his Fifth "Law of Nature," commending every man to "strive to accom-modate himself to the rest," says:

> For seeing every man, not only by Right, but by necessity of Nature, is supposed to endeavor all he can, to obtain that which is necessary for his conservation; He that shall oppose himself against it, for things superfluous, is guilty of the war that thereupon is to follow; and therefore doth that, which is

contrary to the fundamental Law of Nature, which commandeth to *seek Peace*. The observers of this Law, may be called SOCIABLE. The contrary, *Stubborn, Insociable . . . Intractable*.[65]

In this interesting passage, the motive for attending to the poor seems to be to prevent them from trying to get what they need by force. The passage raises a serious question. Hobbes's First Law of Nature was to seek peace, this being a dictum addressed to all. But now it appears that the very needy are exempted from this rule. *They* get to take what they need from the rest of us who have "more than enough." That looks inconsistent, on the face of it. And since Hobbes is a very careful writer and an able thinker, I am guessing that he does not quite mean that by it – but this is not a paper about Hobbes and the issue can wait.

Things get more complicated when Hobbes switches from the language of law and right to the language of virtue and sociability. The uncharitable, we are now told, are to be regarded as "stubborn, unsociable, intractable." OK. But such language does not ring the same as the more imperious language of rights. Hobbes says that those among the more affluent who do *not* help out with the poor are "guilty of the war that thereupon is to follow." Well – why? Aren't those who *start* the war – namely, the poor, in this case – the guilty ones? The better-to-do may indeed feel "guilty," but that seems like an appeal to sentiment rather than reason. And sentiment is indeed a powerful force. A major point in my argument in this essay is that the generous, sympathetic, and benevolent among our sentiments are things to be socially promoted and approved of. But still, that is not a command on all fours with the rule against murder and violence.

Besides, on the face of it if we expect that the poor will make war on us, we would appear, logically, to have two options: try to buy them off, or else defend ourselves against them. Is it obvious that we must choose the former rather than the latter? Some might think it somehow obvious that the second option is immoral. But if someone attacks me, I do not see why I should

---

65 Hobbes, *Leviathan*, ch. 15.

care what his level of needs-satisfaction is: I do care that he is trying to kill me or steal my goods, and I claim the right to defend myself, just as much as if there were instead a millionaire at the other end of that barrel.

Certainly the poor man who proposes to despoil the wealthier one is not operating on a basis of mutual advantage: instead, he is taking advantage, if he can, of the wealthier person's goods, by helping himself without getting the victim's leave. As we saw, Sterba claims, about this situation, that "What is at stake is the liberty of the poor not to be interfered with in taking from the surplus possessions of the rich what is necessary to satisfy their basic needs."[66] No doubt it is "at stake," just as the murderer's liberty to take the life of his victims is "at stake" when we declare that particular liberty to be one that they are not entitled to. People are entitled to their lives and thus to their liberty to do whatever they can do without aggression against others. But how is it an *aggression* on the part of the rich man if he decides not to part with some of his goods to help out the poor man? What the rich man does to the poor man in that case – namely, nothing – does not make the poor man worse off; it merely leaves him as badly off as he already is – which is by hypothesis pretty badly off. And of course, relentless nature makes the poor man still worse off as the days go by during which he gets no sustenance. But that is not the rich man's doing – it is nature's. On the other hand, if the poor man robs the rich man, then of course he does intervene into the rich man's life and leaves him worse off than he would have been had the poor man not done this. That there is, in Sterba's phrase, a "conflict of liberties" is, as we saw before, beside the point. What is in point is whether the interpersonal situation between the two is infected with aggression. And it appears that it is. Nonhelp does not aggress; robbery does.

To be sure, there is an important likelihood that the amount of the rich person's possessions that would really be needed to slake

---

66 Sterba has iterated this example in various places. The most recent is in his "APA Address," p. 59.

the thirst or quell the hunger of the poor man would be small, even to the point of indiscernability. Among the standard sources of sustenance for the homeless are the "Dumpsters" in wealthy neighborhoods. Here indeed is a "surplus" whose loss to the rich is zero. In fact, it is perhaps less than zero, since probably the rich are happy to have their level of waste products, for whose removal they need otherwise to pay for, reduced by the efforts of the indigent. There are points on the indifference curves of every person where what is of benefit to someone else is either of no cost at all to himself, or even a modest benefit. In a very wealthy society such as that of contemporary northern North America, it is a good guess that such no-cost sources of minimal existence would be enough to take care of the whole problem, if set out purely in terms of the minimal caloric needs of the poorest people. And at that point, again, Sterba and I would have, so far as I can see, no practical issue. We would both prefer to see the poorest kept alive, and we would both prefer, I believe, that it be done by voluntary methods if those will work.

Sterba argues that "the liberty not to be interfered with in taking from the surplus resources of the rich what is required to meet one's basic needs is morally preferable to the liberty of the rich not to be interfered with in using their surplus for luxury purposes."[67] But is it? Well, that is *his* preference. But then, what are the sheer *preferences* of a few, or even those of a great many, worth for purposes of moral theory? Morality has no business expressing preferences of that kind. What it notes is that the poor man's action intervenes, negatively, into the life of another person; the rich man's actions do not, in the stipulated case. Sterba correctly observes that "the libertarian's right to property is not a right to receive from others the goods and resources necessary for one's welfare, but rather typically a right not to be interfered with in regard to any goods and resources that one

---

67 From "Our Basic Human Right is a Right to Liberty and it Leads to Equality." In his "APA Address," p. 60, however, Sterba says that the liberty of the poor to take from the "surplus" of the rich is "morally enforceable over the liberty of the rich."

has legitimately acquired either by initial acquisition or by voluntary agreement."[68] That seems admirably clear, though the word "legitimately" should really be deleted, since the thesis is that those possessions of goods and resources that are got by voluntary agreement or initial acquisition are *thereby* legitimate. His statement surely seems to make it clear that the acquisition of goods, however much one may need them, by taking them from someone else *without* that person's agreement, is not similarly legitimate. Yet, as we have seen, he goes on to say that "since [libertarians] assume that the liberty of the poor is not at stake in such conflict situations, it is easy for them to conclude that the rich should not be required to sacrifice their liberty so that the basic needs of the poor may be met." But this is wrong. The libertarian is *always* calling for "sacrifices of liberty." However, this is not so that the needs of some group, such as the poor, may be met, in *whatever way may be possible*, nor is it the expression of a preference for one sort of liberty over another. It is, rather, in the interests of defending everyone's general right of liberty, a right which entails the wrongness of *attacks* on people, including their activities and products. This extends to any and all attacks on any and all people, so long as those attacked have done nothing to attack yet others.

As Sterba spells it out, then, his argument would seem to be either irrelevant or question-begging. The libertarian defends only compatible liberties, not all liberties. The essence of libertarianism is to proclaim a general *right* of liberty, and thus to disallow any and all actions done at the expense of others, thus leaving us free to engage in any other actions. The point of any moral theory is to identify sets of actions that are to be permitted or encouraged or required, and others that are to be discouraged or forbidden. It seems clear that the actions of the "poor" in Sterba's paradigm are of the type not allowed within a libertarian theory, and so there is no question of deciding which liberties are to be preferred to which. In the libertarian's view, therefore, the

---

68 Sterba, "Our Basic Human Right is a Right to Liberty and it Leads to Equality."

proper arrangement is that the rich do not attack the poor and the poor do not attack the rich. The fact that the poor are poor, or even starving for that matter, does not alter things, in that view.

Liberties and compatibility

This is perhaps the place to observe that it is something of an advantage in the libertarian position that its proposed prohibitions are intrinsically all compatible with each other. For what it says is that there is a general type of action which one is not to do. One can in general succeed in acting as it prescribes by doing nothing whatever. But not doing one thing is easily compatible with not doing another. As we sleep, we are not killing anyone, nor are we assaulting them, lying, cheating, stealing, or, in general, doing any of the things that their negative rights require us not to do. And we are not worried about whether obligation x conflicts with obligation y, because, in the cases where x and y are positive actions, the libertarian's claim is that we have, at base, no such obligations.

This is, indeed, largely a dialectical point, since it concerns only *fundamental* duties. But we, most of us, quickly contract into all sorts of obligations, and then indeed there are likely to be conflicts. You agree to meet Henry for lunch and you agree to get your wife to her office, and then there's a delay and you cannot do both, and now what? We use our liberties to get ourselves into jams. OK: but that is not the *theory's* fault – it is our fault, or, perhaps, the fault of the Pernickityness of the World.

We are fallible, the world is hard to predict in various respects, and the exigencies of life require decisions, some of which are sure to go wrong. However, there is no posited obligation to feed the poor, etc., to pose a continual conflict with our general right to liberty.

It might be suggested that, after all, we will sometimes be inclined to do some things that are not obligatory, but in certain circumstance are at odds with other things that *are* obligatory. Now, such inclinations, in general, the liberty theory would regard as presumptively immoral. We do not rob B in order to help C, even if B is rich and C is in great need. We are not to do evil, and if we want to do good by evil means, we are still not to do it. Thus we take seriously the constraint against doing evil. But it must be admitted that sometimes the wrongs are small and the goods large. In the spirit of St. Thomas Aquinas's principle of "double effect," we might weigh the ordinarily wrong against the right and if there is a great disproportion – trivial wrongs, enormous benefits – we will feel justified in going ahead.

Thus, for example, philosophers bring up examples such as the skier or hunter caught in a blizzard and making free to enter a cabin in the woods, availing himself of its shelter and perhaps local food supply in order to keep himself, and perhaps suffering companions, alive. Is this not permissible? Surely it would be hard to say that it was not.

Mutual aid

More generally, we may well think that in addition to our general libertarian requirement to avoid doing evil to our fellows, that there is at least some positive obligation at the base of moral theory: especially, to be ready to assist our fellows when things are tough. A plausible general category here is the Duty of Mutual Aid, as we may call it.

Just how does this work? Familiar cases come readily to mind: the child is drowning in fairly shallow water; you have but to wade in and you can save her, even if you are unable to swim. Should we do this? Of course we should. On the other hand, Sally has left her purse in the burning building. Must you rush in and retrieve it, at great danger to your life? Surely not. Some reflection on such cases suggests a general – though of course very imprecise – formula: help others when the cost to the helper is small and the benefits to the beneficiary are large.

People often invoke the Golden Rule for these cases: do unto others as you would have them do unto you. But as it stands, this is implausible: I can think of all sorts of things I would be glad to have done unto me, but I certainly wouldn't be prepared to do them to all and sundry, and I would certainly not expect them to do so either. What I would *like* is one thing; what I am *owed* or can reasonably expect, quite another.

A better rule is what I have called the "Silver Rule":[69] do unto others what you not only would want done to you if you needed it, but also what there is some chance that you *will* need it, and could get it, from them; and do not insist on more than that. So understood, it is an application of Hobbes's Second Law, calling upon us to demand no more liberty for ourselves than we are willing to grant to others.

And how much is that? A general formula is available. When you can render great help to your fellows at small cost to yourself, and provided that the frequency of helping behavior called for is not inordinate, then you should indeed supply the help. The tenderhearted tourist, stepping off the tarmac into a sea of beggars, supplies a dollar to the first few, but after that, there's a limit to his generosity. Peter Singer's proposal, that we be prepared to part with as much as will leave us nearly as impoverished as our beneficiaries, is very far beyond the pale of reason. Within it, on the other hand, are the sort of assistances which we know that we ourselves are likely to need some day – it could easily happen to us, and, if it did, we'd be very glad of others' assistance. This is what makes the aid *mutual*. It is not just that if I *were* in your shoes, I'd want the help. It is that there is actually some nonzero chance that I *will* be in similar shoes in the foreseeable future. Under those circumstances, we can expect a net benefit by submitting to a rule of mutual aid. We're willing to help, because we know you would do the same, and that we are liable to the same calamities from which others can save us at small cost to them. It's a deal! But beyond that, we are outside of the realm of duty, and into the realm of benevolence.[70]

The general idea applies not only to cases of great need, but to trivial ones as well. Someone on the street, obviously flustered,

---

69 The idea of the "Silver Rule" is developed in my *The Libertarian Idea* (Philadelphia: Temple University Press, 1988; republished at Peterborough, Ont.: Broadview Press, 2002), pp. 242–4.

70 I have addressed the question of world poverty and our relation to it in "Welfare and Wealth, Poverty and Justice in Today's World" and "Is World Poverty a Problem for the Wealthy?" *Journal of Ethics* 8, 4 (2004), pp. 305–48 and 397–408.

asks where the Hotel X is, and, since you know, you pause to tell him. His life is not at stake, but it is a very useful bit of information for him at the time, and it takes you five seconds to impart it. We should do it. But there's no serious moral urgency here, either. One could easily be too busy, or preoccupied, and so on. It would be wrong for him to threaten you with violence if you do not impart the information; it would be, not wrong but certainly below moral par, for you to refuse to tell him in the absence of plausible suspicion of his motives (he could be a terrorist, after all, identifying the location of his target).

Even then, what kind of "should" is this? Here we have a crucial question. For the subject of this essay generally is duties enforceable by compulsion. Do we not only think we ought to save the child, and would rightly complain of someone who did not, but also that the nonactor should be punished severely for his nonassistance? Some perhaps do think that. But should they? Would it be rational to support a moral outlook making people in general liable for this? Arguably not. Of course we want people to help. But do we really stand ready to *compel* them to do so?[71] Do *we* want to be subject to compulsion in this respect? Perhaps some would. But this is where the contractarian idea dominates: would *everyone* want this? Surely not. Indeed, provably not: for *I* do not, for one.

Reality: voluntary resources

From this point on, the libertarian needs to decide how to answer the many writers who claim that a system that would permit some to starve while others have plenty is "grotesque" or words to that effect. Here, for example, is Jonathan Wolff:

> For many – the old, the sick, the poor; generally those unable to fend for themselves – the minimal state, inevitably accompanied by the purest possible free market, is not so much a dream as a nightmare. Critics of Nozick point out that he has depicted a utopia in which some might starve as a consequence

---

71 See Narveson, "We Don't Owe Them a Thing!"

of their lack of rights to food, while others legitimately let their surplus rot. Thus they claim that Nozick's assertion that the minimal state is inspiring as well as right is grotesquely wrong on both counts.[72]

What are we to say to this? Many things. In the first place, Wolff simply *assumes* that the "critics" are correct in thinking that "some might starve as a consequence of their lack of rights to food." But is this true? Libertarians, as a class, are generally fairly well schooled in economics, and to some degree also in history as well as in how politics works. From all these sources, we might well put together a very different story. This story says, in the first place, that Wolff's "critics" have things exactly backward. For it is precisely the claim to *guarantee* against starvation, to declare a *right* – that is, in the above terminology, a *positive right* – to Aquinas's "sufficiency" that can lead in practice to starvation. The greatest known starvation in history took place in Meo Tse Dong's China, with some thirty million estimated victims – though all of those people had the sort of "rights" the critic seems to think we need. Meanwhile, in wealthy North America (north of the Mexican border, anyway), nobody starves, and this has been true since long before the "welfare state" came on line. It is not that nobody was ever in need of food, or unable to earn enough to supply his or her needs in that respect. Rather, it is that for those few who were in that unhappy position, there were many well-fed people standing by, ready to lend a helping hand – *voluntarily*. "Agreed," said these generous people, "they *don't* have a *right* to what we produce. But nevertheless, dammit, they *need* it, and common decency impels us to help them out." Which they did. The record of American (and others') generosity is plain and pretty well told, though it seems to have gone unnoticed by contemporary American and British social philosophers, who seem unable to conceive that their picture of human nature, as a

---

72 Jonathan Wolff, "Robert Nozick, Libertarianism, And Utopia," from his "Critiques of Libertarianism" site: http://world.std.com/~mhuben/libindex. html

set of cold-hearted, grasping Scrooges, is very far off the mark. But it is. How many do they know who do not stand ready to provide *voluntary* assistance? Even to people far away, as in the great tsunami of 2004, where I found myself one of the many thousands who, immediately upon hearing the news, went to their computers to see how they could help, sending a hundred dollars, twenty dollars, whatever. By two days later, the problem was how to most effectively spend all that money, how to organize the relief systems, and how to circumvent the heavy hands of interfering bureaucracies at the other end so that the needy might actually be reached by those of us trying and ready to reach them.

Philosophers will say that reliance upon generosity and voluntary means is "chancy." One might ask just what they think the "chances" actually *are*. True, the sun might not rise tomorrow, but I do not recommend worrying about it. And there might be starvation in the streets, but if there is, you can place a far safer bet on the proposition that it is because somebody in a position of political power is putting obstacles in the way of those who would like to help, rather than that nobody can be found who can and would like to extend the help in question.

And of course, the melancholy history of socialisms, of which Mao's is only the worst example rather than an isolated one, remains as testimony to the point that stirring pronouncements are not the solution to human problems. Philosophers can declare rights until they are blue in the face, but it will do not a stick of good unless and until some people out there are willing to do something to support and cater to those rights. Since so many of us already are disposed to extend care to the needy, without the threat of imprisonment by officials carrying out the dictates of superiors, these proclamations are not only counterproductive, they are also entirely unnecessary.

In the second place, we might ask these very philosophers whether they are ready to declare, literally, that *all* men owe *all* others these duties, taken in the way they are meant in the local case. Should Americans be shouldering the burdens of *all* the starvelings *everywhere* in the world – "shouldering" in the political sense, that those burdens will be forcibly imposed on every one of us? I have at various times noted how advocates of welfare states invariably confine the reach of compulsory "giving" to those in the same political state, rather than to mankind at large, and yet it is welfare as a *human right* that we are discussing here, is it not?

Finally, it has to be pointed out that those Wolff has in mind are assuming that the fact (if it is one) that some starve would impute the theory's claim to be the best theory of justice. To do so is to assume the very thing for which proof is needed. We can agree, without begging any questions at issue here, that the fact that someone dies young, say, is *a bad thing*; it would, of course, be better if no one did. But our question is whether the fact that someone dies young is not only a bad thing, but a thing that we may hold someone responsible for, with threatened penalties for noncompliance, is just as it stands. That no one is to kill or otherwise harm any innocent person may also be chalked up as common ground, perhaps. But someone's dying of some curable disease is not common ground. Wolff does not offer arguments of the contractarian type for his position, and in the absence of convincing argument, the fact of starvation amidst plenty – if it were one – would not as such impugn the justness of the system in which he does so.

Few hold to the Utilitarian view of morals any more, though no doubt some do. In that view, perhaps, it is generally supposed, at least, that it would follow from the fact that someone dies when someone else might have been able to prevent it that an injustice has occurred. But we have no business taking such a controversial theory as a working assumption here. It is not.

Meanwhile, what the libertarian does do, and what the other views cannot do, is to put the blame on individuals as such for the rectifiable misfortunes that befall our fellows. A welfare state demonstrates the democratic voter's readiness to compel his fellows to promote the voter's own sentiments. It does not demonstrate that person's morality in relation to his needy fellows. But if we relied on voluntary charity, then those who help would get the credit, and those who do not, the blame. Surely that is as it should be.

Effects of the welfare state

We may turn to Tocqueville again to put the case:

> At first glance there is no idea which seems more beautiful and grander than that of public charity ... It asks some to give of their surplus in order to allow others the basic necessities ... certainly a moving and elevating sight...

> [C]ould work be imposed as a condition on the able-bodied indigent who asks for public pity? ... [S]ome English laws have used the idea ... they have failed ... Nothing is so difficult to distinguish as the nuances which separate unmerited misfortune from an adversity produced by vice ... Who would dare to let a poor man die of hunger because it's his own fault that he is dying? ... The laws may declare that only innocent poverty will be relieved; practice will alleviate all poverty.

> ... Any measure which establishes legal charity on a permanent basis and gives it an administrative form thereby creates an idle and lazy class, living at the expense of the industrial and working class...

> ... [N]othing ... elevates and sustains the human spirit more than the idea of rights ... But the right of the poor to obtain society's help is unique in that instead of elevating the heart of the man who exercises it, it lowers him ... Ordinary rights are conferred on men by reason of some personal advantage acquired by them over their fellow men. This other kind is accorded by reason of a recognized inferiority ... The more extensive and the more secure ordinary rights are, the more honor they confer; the more permanent and extended the right to relief is, the more it degrades.

> ... But this is still not all: individual alms-giving established valuable ties between the rich and the poor. The deed itself involves the giver in the fate of the one whose poverty he has undertaken to alleviate. The latter, supported by aid which he had no right to demand and which he may have had no hope of getting, feels inspired by gratitude. A moral tie is established between those two classes ... and although divided by circumstance they are willingly reconciled. This is not the case with

legal charity. The latter allows the alms to persist, but removes its morality...[73]

Money does not grow on trees; there is no such thing as a free lunch. The welfare state appears to deny this, and makes people think that the world *owes* them a living. It does not, and it is surely more honest to have a system in which those in need are supported by those whose hearts are large enough to provide for those needs. One can plausibly argue, too, that it is also going to be enormously more efficient. Indeed, it is going to *be* efficient, in the Paretian way: some are not going to be made better off simply at the expense of others. But with people as they are, this is also a job that is going to get done.

The place of private charity

It seems to be a familiar theme among philosophers that welfare *should be* a right because private charity is not up to the job of providing the kind of certainty that the welfare state would provide. This is an interesting phenomenon: a public philosophy dedicated to the proposition that most people are hard-hearted and miserly. I doubt if many of the moral philosophers who make this extravagant accusation against their fellows actually know anyone like that. I do not think I am in any way atypical when I point out that I am ready, when the situation demands, to help keep the people around me alive. Furthermore, as I have elsewhere pointed out,[74] if the welfare-staters' accusations against typical mankind were true, it is hard to see why a great majority of people would vote in favor of welfare policies, seeing that they do, after all, get taxed to support them. The interesting question is why academics are so readily persuaded that there are not enough other people like themselves to "get the job done" – and that the remedy for this is

73 Tocqueville, "Memoir on Pauperism," pp. 36–7.
74 Jan Narveson, "A Dilemma for Would-be Liberal Defenders of the Welfare State," presented at the Canadian Philosophical Association meeting, Laval University, Quebec, May 26, 2001. It is to be published, in German, in *Analyze und Kritik* in 2009.

compulsion, the social method to which the politically inclined so naturally resort.

Social contract theory, as I have argued, can make no controversial assumptions about the parties to the proposed social agreement. All, notionally, are to agree. I have allowed that variability among humans is the indicated assumption. This accords with reality: it takes all kinds, as we say. Yet all, I have argued, have in common the desire not to be molested by their fellows. Of course, this leaves open the empirical question of the actual incidence of human sympathy and sociability. There is, as I have insinuated above, much reason to believe that this must be fairly high. Human societies have survived through thick and thin, and a society is not going to manage that if its members are not fairly frequently helpful rather than the reverse. We need not go quite as far as Hume, who insists that

> It is sufficient for our present purpose, if it be allowed, what surely, without the greatest absurdity, cannot be disputed, that there is some benevolence, however small, infused into our bosom; some spark of friendship for human kind; some particle of the dove, kneaded into our frame, along with the elements of the wolf and serpent. Let these generous sentiments be supposed ever so weak; let them be insufficient to move even a hand or finger of our body; they must still direct the determinations of our mind, and where every thing else is equal, produce a cool preference of what is useful and serviceable to mankind, above what is pernicious and dangerous...
>
> The notion of morals, implies some sentiment common to all mankind, which recommends the same object to general approbation, and makes every man, or most men, agree in the same opinion or decision concerning it. It also implies some sentiment, so universal and comprehensive as to extend to all mankind, and render the actions and conduct, even of the persons the most remote, an object of applause or censure, according as they agree or disagree with that rule of right which is established. These two requisite circumstances belong alone to the sentiment of humanity here insisted on. The other passions produce, in every breast, many strong sentiments of

desire and aversion, affection and hatred; but these neither are felt so much in common, nor are so comprehensive, as to be the foundation of any general system and established theory of blame or approbation.[75]

Whether the existence of a universal sentiment of the kind Hume describes is either necessary or sufficient for the foundations of morals is questionable, and the social contract idea essentially denies this. On the other hand, if Hume is taken to be asserting that without at least a very widespread such sentiment, morals is unlikely to take much hold in a large community, he is surely right. In this, as one would expect from this philosopher, he argues from common sense. People are typically at least somewhat sympathetic and at least somewhat helpful to their fellows.

We can be helpful, and applaud helpfulness in others, without going so far as to make it compulsory. And in the case of the welfare state, the helpfulness being exacted, we have a case of A being "helpful" to C by threatening evils to B in order to induce him to go along. That is objectionable, and in this book I am objecting to it. The objection thus far has been at the level of general principle: we should not do good to some by doing, or even threatening, evil to others, and this, I claim, is what would be recognized in the social contract.

But at the same time, there is no objection whatever to holding up helpfulness, generosity, benevolence, compassion, fellow-feeling, as virtues. And this, I think, will also be upheld by the social contract. For even the very egoistic can see that they have nothing to lose from a social practice in which benevolence is encouraged and rewarded, for it leaves them free to be as unhelpful as they would wish, and at the same time makes it likely that they themselves will benefit from the generosity of others on various occasions. Upholding generosity as a virtue is a win–win proposition. Thus the social contractarian, who after all wants the social rules from which all of us will do best given that

---

75 David Hume, *An Enquiry Concerning the Principles of Morals*, Sect. IX, Conclusion, Part I.

all others are to agree, will be ready to join in pronouncing it to be the virtue that it so universally is in fact regarded.

No one can be against the offering of aid to the needy, when the offering is voluntary, and at least so long as the needy in question are peaceable persons rather than criminals on the make. Our question, then, is one of means rather than ends: are our means to be peaceable, like the ends we hope to promote? Libertarians answer this in the affirmative. Thus they disapprove of the welfare *state*, but they strongly approve of the voluntary provision of welfare, when needed.

Just business

While charity is an enormous resource, it is not our only one. On the contrary, its role must be and normally is comparatively minor by comparison with the other voluntary means of promoting welfare: free-market exchange.

The essence of the free market is that parties to exchanges act with a view to promoting their interests. This is usually and somewhat misleadingly characterized as "self-interest," but as we have seen, that is quite unnecessary, and fairly frequently false. Parties to free exchange can certainly be, and very often are, acting in the interests of others: of loved ones, of fellow believers in some religion or social cause, and of course of needy persons near and far. What matters is that each is indeed free to use his or her efforts, or products, in accordance with the exchanger's own interests, not those imposed by others. And the ethics of business are such that those persons are likewise constrained to respect the similar rights of their business partners and associates. Business persons are to make their way by agreements with others – not by robbery and fraud. To be sure, persons purporting to be engaged in business are often in fact engaging in fraudulent practices as well, but their fraudulence negates their participation in business as a legitimate social practice.

The power of free-market business has been widely recognized and needs only a reminder here. Business participants are presumed to be "in it" for the money, for profit. They make those profits by offering services to others which those others find beneficial to themselves. Nothing constrains either party other than the prohibitions on force and fraud; thus deals are not accepted unless seen as beneficial by the taker.

Business methods are, then, inherently cooperative, in the social contractarian's minimal sense of being matters of mutual interest. They capture the self-interests of diverse parties – parties who need not be motivated by Humean sentiment at all, and yet whose actions make for the good of others. Whatever we may reasonably presume about the extent of Humean sympathy, the extent of potential human benefit made possible by free-market exchange is very much greater. It is, indeed, so great that we may reasonably expect just what we have actually achieved in the past many centuries of human exertion: a general degree of prosperity, in the countries where the market has taken hold and been able to operate. This should surprise no one. What should surprise us is the continued extent of incursion into the workings of this extremely useful human arrangement.

Critics love to excoriate the inequalities generated, as they suppose, by market activity. It is debatable to what extent the inequalities observed in recent years in America, in particular, are due specifically to the market, and to what extent they are due instead to the special character of the many interventions brought about by well-intended (or not-so-well intended!) government action; but in principle, of course, the charge – if it is such – that markets are not respecters of egalitarianism is perfectly true. What is also true, however, is that very large incomes and wealth holdings by a relatively small part of the populace can, and do, generate a great deal of beneficial activity. It is not just the Adam Smith principle (that the "invisible hand" leads to very widespread general wealth) but also in the narrower sense exemplified by Bill Gates and Warren Buffet, in recent times, who are only the most spectacular cases in a long-familiar trend toward philanthropy by the very rich. The generosity of the likes of Carnegie, Rockefeller, Mellon, Ford, and many others has funded art and architecture, universities and scientific institutes, along with research facilities and hospitals for promoting health, and charitable undertakings for the relief of poverty. It takes a jaded and myopic acquaintance with the social world we live in to fail to see the social efficacy of the business system in both these ways. That such resources are much more than capable of handling the objectives of the welfare state, insofar as those are legitimate, is surely undeniable.

In practice

A final reflection. Welfare expenditures make up, I am told, a minute fraction of the Federal budget, and a very modest fraction of most city and state budgets. Let us suppose that the amounts devoted to the subject in dispute here are indeed quite tiny. Very few people will really complain at being separated from $100 per year to keep the very poor in rags. What, then, is the big deal? Indeed, isn't it simply handier to have the money deducted from one's paycheck instead of having to face an army of solicitations from well-intentioned charities? I must admit that I am sympathetic to this, in practice. It is not worth putting up a big fuss about it, especially given the difficulty of fighting City Hall. But of course, it is similar reasoning that gets us The State anyway. The libertarian might well insist that these are all straws contributing to a short life for the camel's back. As well, there is the point that what we currently call welfare expenditures are actually part of a much larger set of government undertakings that include health care, retirement, and various other things. And there is nothing trivial about those as a whole. But their funding is essentially different. Various payroll deductions make these systems more or less self-funded: benefits to workers paid for, over the years, by workers. Those differences take such subjects beyond the terms of reference of this inquiry.

The modern welfare state raises two kinds of issues. Only one is an issue of justice: are some people being wrongly compelled to contribute to the welfare, security, etc., of others? That is the issue that has been discussed at such length in this essay. But the other issue is whether the welfare state is an effective, useful, workable institution as compared with alternatives. The answers to these could diverge. We might insist that it is unjust, but agree it is doing a pretty good job in general. Or we might think that justice is not the problem – but that the rigging of government programs and institutions is such as to create huge inefficiencies and counterproductive side effects. While these latter questions are real, they too lie somewhat beyond the province of our discussion here.[76]

A more important afterthought

The wider macroeconomic issue concerns the Free Market. The hallmark of this institution – if that is what so natural an arrangement should be called – is, as the name implies, the freedom of the participants. In markets, people buy and sell, but nobody is compelled to do either. The terms of exchange are set by the parties to it, each consulting his or her own interests, whatever they may be. The controlling rule is that participants respect each others' libertarian rights: they do not proceed by violence or fraud, but by negotiated exchange. Of course, in the background lie consumption and, therefore, production. If sellers are to have anything to sell, and thus buyers anything to buy, someone must produce. And if the free-market idea is extended, as libertarians hold that it should, then production should be similarly free. Within the limits of what they can produce, they produce what they judge of most benefit, to themselves or whomever they intend to provide for. And if they are to do that, property must be respected. We produce for reasons, and rarely is that reason to provide, without recompense, for strangers wanting simply to take from us. Property and liberty are inseparable.

Now, it is true enough that while we all have a property in our own selves, many have little property in anything else. It should be more than a little strange that that is so. Everyone consumes, and virtually everyone is able to produce. If the terms of exchange are freely negotiated, then it should be a matter of

---

76 Two strong negative statements are found in Charles Murray's modern American classic, *Losing Ground* (New York: Basic Books, 1984), and for the British situation, James Bartholomew, *The Welfare State We're In* (London: Politico's Methuen, 2004).

astonishment that anyone ends up with too little even to maintain himself in being. It will always be in someone's interest to
purchase the labor of someone able and willing to work, and that
leads to property, on the part of that someone. We benefit each
other by exchange, and if we all engage in it, we all do better.
That is the idea, and it is a good one.

Unfortunately, there are often people ready to take advantage
of others: to rob, to enslave, to defraud. And there are not always
people ready or able to take measures to prevent this, nor institutions to enable the victims of these activities to get proper
redress. Indeed, with the advent of government among men,
there are often people who are not *allowed* to take those measures. And with government, fully free markets are rare. Taxes,
regulations, prohibitions, compelled production, are the stuff
of government. The legally imposed minimum wage is an
example. If you start a business which cannot be profitable
at the minimum wage, those who might have worked at
the wages you could pay will likely be without work. Then
a question of justice really does arise: should the public be
depriving people of work, and then try to make up for it by
paying them to be idle, at the expense of the others who do
work, and who might have benefited from the labor of those
prevented from work by the minimum-wage program? The same
question can be asked of innumerable government initiatives –
not just the minimum wage. But again, these issues take us
beyond the terms set for the present inquiry – though not
entirely, for the proposal to leave welfare issues to empirical
analysis raises the question of how we are going to assess the
findings for normative purposes.

Useful employment is the basic welfare program. It needs no
bureaucracy, no central committee. Achieving that in the non-
Soviet way – that is, by having everybody do useful things for
their incomes – requires a good monetary system and true free
trade. These things are not easy to come by in these highly
politicized days. Special interests have little difficulty persuading
those with political power to turn the law into a support mechanism for those interests.

The welfare state, many libertarians hold, is essentially a byproduct of bad economic policies by governments. Paying people to do nothing who could be doing something is poor policy. Putting them in a position where doing nothing is their best alternative is part of the problem. And giving people good reason to think that the government is always there to cover their mistakes is perhaps the most fundamental problem of all.

A major problem for a discussion of this kind is that the world does not offer clear-cut test cases to enable a decisive experiment. If in a given case there is inflation, or deflation, or some other economic malady, is it, as critics of the market are sure to insist, due to flaws in the free-enterprise system? Or is it due to some of the various interventions that relevant governments may have imposed? In the absence of cases in which the rights of all concerned are fully respected, and yet the problem persists, we must turn to theory. But theory leaves us with controversy. Defenders of the market ask the interventionist just why or how the market might "fail" if left to its own devices, and how there could be reason to think that intervention could help. And when presented with standard cases, such as the Great Depression of the 1930s in America, we have a fine example of how interventions introduced with the best intentions in fact prolonged the Depression far beyond what it need have lasted.[77] (As this is written, America is again in the midst of a severe and expectedly prolonged recession. The new government is gearing up to take measures – like FDR after Hoover, measures initiated by the existing government – that we may expect, likewise, to make a bad situation worse. That the situation was crucially initiated by well-intended government measures is also by now a matter of record.[78])

But here the non-economist runs out of resources. No doubt these are controversial matters, and we had best follow the

---

77 The case is spelled out in detail and at length in Gene Smiley, *Rethinking the Great Depression* (Chicago: Ivan Dee, 2002).
78 See Stan J. Liebowitz, "Anatomy of a Train Wreck: Causes of the Mortgage Meltdown," in *Housing America: Building Out of a Crisis*, ed. Randall G. Holcombe and Benjamin Powell (Oakland, CA: Independent Institute, 2009).

strategy used in the preceding pages: grant the possibility that macroeconomic policy might be needed for coping with economic downturns, etc., and that it might in the process provide a case for shoring up the incomes of those who, as we might well think, do little or nothing to earn them.

Most importantly for our purposes here, it has to be pointed out that this kind of reasoning does not support the claim that contractarianism makes a case for *basic rights* to welfare. Rather, it would make a very indirect case to the effect that the welfare state might serve macroeconomic ends that really are recommended for all. Instead of a *basic right* to welfare, the argument would have given us all a right to the use of good policies for the maintenance or promotion of economic growth in unusual circumstances. The effect, as also previously noted, might in its results be indistinguishable from what we would have with a genuine right to charity – but still, it would not have given us that genuine right.

On the other hand, an additional dialectical benefit from this kind of support for welfare programs might be that it can make sense of confining them to one country, instead of imposing on its own citizens the obligation to provide welfare for the world's needy wherever they are. At the same time, however, it also makes it questionable why the welfare should be *state* managed. After all, the sensible thing for workers to do in an uncertain economy is to join in insurance arrangements. Moreover, those arrangements should be independent of their particular employer, since – as is obvious now from the case of General Motors – any particular employer, even a very large one, could go under. If you make these arrangements via government, there will certainly be counterproductive requirements. The American system, for example, hooks health insurance very closely to employers, binding the worker to his particular employer and leaving him adrift in the period between employers if he should move from one to another job.[79]

79 For a careful critique, see Daniel Shapiro, *Is the Welfare State Justified?* (New York: Cambridge University Press, 2007).

4 Conclusion

The argument of this essay has been narrow, to the point, as some will no doubt suppose, of myopia. My question has been whether the social contract idea would support an enforceable right to assistance in time of need, which Sterba and I both take it would justify the welfare state. And my answer has been in the negative. Free persons in the pre-moral "state of nature," the "Original Position" – in its Hobbesian, not its Rawlsian, version – would not commit themselves to open-ended, nonreciprocal transfers toward persons in need, even if that level of need was life-threatening. They would, on the other hand, accept a general prohibition on violence and fraud – in short, what has become known as the libertarian principle. The "Social Contract" requires unanimity, and we all stand to benefit from nonmolestation and noncoercion by others simply in order to promote their own purposes. Rather, each is to be free to promote his or her own purposes, his or her own life, on the restriction that the like freedom of all others is to be respected. Thus our rights are fundamentally negative, not positive. They say: *do not* harm peaceable others. They do not say: *help* those others.

On the other hand, the right in question certainly allows people to be as helpful and generous as they are inclined to be – with their own resources, that is, but not those of nonconsenting others, as in the welfare state. Moreover, I argue that it is part of the social contract to *approve* such altruism; we are to encourage such activity, on the ground that it can only serve mutually acceptable ends – those of both the donor and the recipient – while doing no harm to anyone else. So generosity is greeted with the moral carrot, as it were, rather than its absence being punished by the moral stick.

General liberty and general equality, understood in their narrow and normal senses, cannot both be required, and in that sense, liberty and equality are not compatible. If the state compels us to help various people though we have done no harm to anyone, then it does not leave us free to run our lives and expend our resources as we ourselves see fit.

But even if positive welfare rights were endorsed, that would not be the end of the issue. For the next question would be whether freely undertaken activity should not be *preferred* over coerced activity, other things being equal. And surely it would. Again: the original position free agents would always prefer freedom to coercion where freedom is possible without real harm to others. If, as I claim, the aims of the welfare state would be adequately realized by a combination of proper government economic policy and private activity, of both commercial and charitable types, then even if we granted such a right to welfare, in practice we should still avoid having the government try to cater to it.

Arguments of a technical kind in economics have been treated here as beyond the limits of purely moral discussion. I have granted that if macroeconomic considerations should be decisive in moving toward a system with much more extensive redistribution, then the welfare state could be a part of the called-for system for economic equilibrium. But that would not have established welfare as a basic positive right. Rather, it would serve to table the issue in principle, since practice would simply bypass it. Like Plato's "noble lie," which he supposed would be justified by the legitimate ends of government, so welfare rights would be justified in effect by the exigencies of economic policy.

On the main issue, therefore, I believe we are left with the conclusion that fundamental positive rights to welfare are not forthcoming from the social contract idea. And since – as I have not argued, but only presumed[80] – the social contract idea is the only foundational idea of any real promise in the field of moral philosophy, that would seem to settle the matter at this level of principle.

---

80 Space to argue for this large claim is obviously not available in this endeavor. For a substantial argument in that direction, see Jan Narveson, *The Libertarian Idea* (Peterborough, Ont.: Broadview Press, reissued 2001), chs. 9–13.

Part III

4   Response to Narveson

James P. Sterba

Engaging in this debate with Jan Narveson has been a valuable experience for me. I know of no better way to defensibly hold a moral and political perspective than by testing one's arguments out against one's philosophical opponents. In this regard, Jan Narveson has proven to be a worthy adversary. In this brief reply, let me see if I can add just a bit to our debate by making the choice between our two perspectives even clearer and starker.

Surprisingly or maybe not so surprisingly, there is a parallel structure to the main arguments that both Jan Narveson and I advance in our essays. We each begin by specifying what negative liberties we think are morally justified. We then go on to claim that our support for those negative liberties cannot rest on morality alone but must have an even more basic foundation. We then attempt to provide that more basic foundation for the negative liberties we support.

Narveson's main argument

Accordingly, Narveson begins by arguing that we all have a morally justified right not to be harmed, hindered, have costs imposed on us, or be made worse off by the actions of others unless we have first inflicted such acts on others.[1] Narveson thinks

---

1 Jan Narveson, "The Right to Liberty is Incompatible with the Right to Equality," pp. 132–3, 171–2 and 193–4.

that this captures the basic right to liberty or noninterference we all possess. He further argues that those who are first to appropriate something do not thereby harm, hinder, impose costs on, or make worse off those who come later.[2] He also maintains that those who make something out of things they justifiably possess do not thereby harm, hinder, impose costs on, or make others worse off if they act to prevent others from benefiting from the goods that they have made.[3]

Narveson then goes on to argue that this very same right to liberty would also be affirmed from a social contract perspective that "appeals only to the interests of all individuals, as viewed by those persons themselves . . . without assuming any prior moral views."[4] Nor are these contractors assumed to be altruistic or narrowly self-interested.[5] But they are understood to be seeking "unanimity in principle" and looking for "principles to be advanced by all in relation to all."[6] So understood, Narveson contends that his social contract perspective leads to a general principle that prohibits harm and hindrance to others, except only when those others have harmed or hindered. In other words, Narveson contends that his social contract perspective leads to the very same basic right to liberty or noninterference to which he claims we all are morally entitled.[7]

My argument

I begin by giving a neutral specification of the array of possible negative liberties that are available in virtually any social context, most importantly, the negative liberty of the poor not to be interfered with in taking from the surplus possessions of the rich what they require to meet their basic needs and the negative liberty of the rich not to be interfered with in using their surplus

2 *Ibid.*, pp. 165–6, 174.
3 *Ibid.*, pp. 170–3.
4 *Ibid.*, p. 183.
5 *Ibid.*, p. 201.
6 *Ibid.*, pp. 221, 218.
7 *Ibid.*, p. 194.

for luxury purposes. This neutral specification is something that Narveson also allows can be done, although he prefers just to focus on the negative liberties that he thinks are morally justified. Having provided this neutral specification, I then use my morally loaded "ought" implies "can" principle to determine which negative liberties have moral priority such that they can be coercively enforced. Most importantly, I determine that it is the negative liberty of the poor, as specified above, rather than the negative liberty of the rich that has this moral priority and should, therefore, be enforced.

Like Narveson, however, I realize that my argument for a certain set of negative liberties (in my case, ones that lead to welfare rights and ultimately to substantial equality) should not be left with just a moral grounding. Obviously someone could reject the moral foundations on which my argument rests. So I back up from morality to an even more neutral normative starting point – a nonquestion-begging one – a starting point that I claim would be acceptable even to a rational egoist. I then argue that even from such a starting point, my same conclusion can be supported, namely, that we each are entitled to a set of negative liberties that secures for us the resources required for a decent life, but no more.

The arguments compared

So, given this parallel structure between Narveson's main argument and my own, how do they compare? Let me try to explain why my main argument works and why Narveson's does not.

First, the way that Narveson discusses the liberties that he thinks are morally justified in the first part of his argument obscures the choice that is available to hypothetical contractors in the second part of his argument. This is because Narveson basically discusses only his preferred candidate for a basic right to liberty. My candidate for a basic right to liberty that leads to substantial equality, and other candidates that lead to a right to welfare but not substantial equality, are hardly discussed as such, that is, as a candidate for a basic right to liberty. Yet given that Narveson's hypothetical contractors are imagined to be rationally choosing a basic right to liberty, they should be fully considering other candidates for that basic right along with Narveson's preferred candidate.

Second, Narveson fails to realize that one way that he has of specifying his morally preferred basic right to liberty is actually neutral between his view and my own. He claims that the basic right to liberty that we all have is the right not to be harmed, hindered, have costs imposed on us, or be made worse off by the actions of others unless we first inflicted such acts on others. But I could not agree more. This specification of the basic right to liberty formally fits my account as well as it does Narveson's. This is because, on my account, when the poor exercise their right not to be interfered with in taking from the surplus of the rich what they require to meet their basic needs, they are not harming, hindering, or imposing costs on the rich, or making them worse off by their actions because they are not depriving the rich of anything to which they are entitled.

Of course, Narveson claims that the same holds true on his own account. When the rich take action to prevent the poor from appropriating the surplus resources that the rich are using for luxury purposes, as Narveson sees it, they are not harming, hindering, or imposing costs on the poor, or making them worse off by our actions because they are not depriving the poor of anything to which they are entitled.

The difference between our accounts, therefore, is not found in the general formulation of the basic right to liberty, but rather in what we each think people are entitled to by first appropriations, legally enforced contracts, and productive activities. It is the specification of those entitlements that fixes who is harming, hindering, and imposing costs on whom in our accounts. Narveson never makes it clear that he and I are both formally in favor of the same basic right to negative liberty, but simply disagreeing about what negative liberties go into making up that basic right.

Third, and most importantly, Narveson's derivation of his favored negative liberties from his hypothetical contract choice situation is question-begging. He begins by imagining the contractors being unable to take anything from each other of what they have first appropriated or produced without provoking warfare that would be counterproductive for all. He also imagines the contractors to be self-interestedly motivated such that they would not agree to any social arrangement that involved a forced net transfer of resources to those in need. Yet while this way of imagining the hypothetical contractors does led to determinate results, it achieves those results only by begging the question against other possible interpretations of that choice situation. In particular, Narveson's interpretation begs the question by assuming away the altruistic interests that his hypothetical contractors almost certainly would have. Like many people in the real world, Narveson's hypothetical contractors might well be willing to have their altruistic interests enforced, something that Narveson's account simply precludes.

Of course, Narveson may think that he has to fall back on a self-interested-based interpretation of his hypothetical contractors in order to avoid grounding his resolution on moral premises. But that is simply not the case. One can avoid a morally based resolution without simply backing into a self-interestedly-based resolution. This can be done just by assuming that the contractors, like most people in real life, have a capacity to act on both self-interested and altruistic reasons and then determine what reasons it would be rational for them to accept. While not being explicitly committed to a moral resolution, this way of interpreting Narveson's hypothetical contractors does avoid begging the question in favor of either egoism or altruism.

Fourth, my nonmorally based argument for my preferred set of negative liberties provides just the kind of nonquestion-begging defense of those liberties that Narveson's nonmorally based argument for his preferred set of negative liberties fails to provide.

This is because, as indicated above, my argument starts with the assumption that people have the capacity to act upon self-interested and altruistic reasons and then seeks to determine what reasons it would be rational for them to accept. As I argue in my essay, this requires first giving prima facie status to both our self-interested and altruistic reasons, and then giving priority to high-ranking self-interested reasons over conflicting low-ranking altruistic reasons as well as priority to high-ranking altruistic reasons over conflicting low-ranking self-interested reasons. In other words, it requires that we support what I have called Morality as Compromise. I have also argued that Morality as Compromise, in turn, supports the coercive enforcement of the liberty of the poor over the liberty of rich, leading to a right to welfare and ultimately to substantial equality. While the set of negative liberties my argument supports can thus be given a nonquestion-begging foundation, Narveson's preferred set of negative liberties only emerge from his question-begging self-interest-based interpretation of his hypothetical social contract choice situation.[8] So why would you want to endorse the conclusion of a question-begging argument when you can endorse the conclusion of a nonquestion-begging one instead?

Let me end by commenting briefly on one puzzling oddity found in Narveson's many discussions of my argument from liberty to equality. Although at least for the last twenty years in virtually every published version of my argument, I have framed my argument as one from liberty to equality, Narveson has persisted in interpreting my argument as simply an argument from liberty to welfare, and not an argument for equality at all. For example, even in this volume, Narveson writes,

> Sterba does not advocate egalitarian policies, nor do most theorists today. Instead, they call for *safety-net* policies, intended to guarantee that those at the bottom are nevertheless far enough above it to enable them to live a life at some level of satisfaction.[9]

8 And, as I argued in my essay, Narveson's set of negative liberties is only one possible outcome of his interpretation of the hypothetical choice situation. See pp. 105–6.

9 *Ibid.*, p. 223; see also p. 146. In this volume, Narveson also quotes frequently from my recent APA Presidential Address (2008) that has the fairly transparent title "From Liberty to Equality." I also mentioned this recurring misinterpretation of my view to Narveson at a conference organized by Tibor Machan that we both attended last year at Chapman University to debate preliminary versions of our essays for this volume.

Thus, what Narveson neglects here, and elsewhere, is my argument that securing a right to welfare not only for the members of one's own society, but also for distant peoples and future generations, leads to substantial equality where each of us is guaranteed the resources for a decent life but no more.

Why, then, does Narveson continually ignore this significant consequence of my argument? Could it be that although he does claim that his account applies to everyone everywhere, he does not really think his self-interested-based view that requires no sacrifice at all for the sake of distant peoples and future generations would really be acceptable to those same distant peoples and future generations as well as to many members of his own society? This could help explain why Narveson does not want to talk about the implications of my own view for distant peoples and future generations. Still, he may have another explanation for his repeated failure to accurately represent and deal with this part of my argument. I will surely have to ask him about it.

5 Response to Sterba

Jan Narveson

Lᴇᴛ me say, first, that I am grateful for James Sterba's care in stating and restating his and my positions – and also for carefully discussing many writers whom I fail to address in my own piece. I have narrow-mindedly concentrated on developing my own position, discussing mostly the special arguments advanced by Sterba himself, and have been rather ungenerous in attending to the arguments of the many others with whom I am in such sharp disagreement. I am pleased to see that he has in general done such a good job with those writers, sparing me the need to take up valuable space for doing it myself.

The question to address in this concluding brief riposte is of course the central point of disagreement, the central issue that divides us, and thus how to identify that central issue. In my view, this issue arises from the independence of persons. However they may be linked in various groupings, whatever their degrees of affections – or animosities – toward some or many, they are individuals with minds of their own, and they act on their own motivations, their own interests. As I see it, the basic question for moral theory is to what extent this independence is to be trimmed down in response to the impingements of one's fellows. In society, we are able to address each other, to direct praise and blame and to react in more substantial ways to each other's behavior, and the question is, with what aims in view we are to do that.

I assume that when we contemplate that question, we do so from the perspective of our own interests, whatever they may be.

However, the idea of morals is that of a *unity*, "imposed," as Aquinas puts it, on the community. We look for those principles which there is reason to expect all to accede to when looming conflicts of various sorts make it sensible to look for bases of resolution. Thus, for example, we must immediately reject as a *moral* principle that of self-interest. It is absurd to ask me to address your conduct in relation to me in terms entirely of *your* interests. That would set us at odds rather than drawing us together. We need a basis in the independent interests of each person, in light of the facts, for adopting principles calling on us to treat others in certain ways.

But given our independence, what *does* "draw us together," then? For this we must look to common interests in the face of interaction. And there we of course can see that others confront us as possible enemies, on the one hand, and as possible friends, on the other. We would like to reduce the inclination to be enemies and increase that to be friends: that is to say, we hope that others will do as little evil to us as possible, and as much good. Given their independence, what can we hope for here? The short answer is that since we can all inflict evils on each other, and yet have an enormous interest in that not being done, we should renounce the doing of bad, provided that others do so too, and embrace the doing of good. But that good is not to be achieved by resorting to evil as the means of achieving it. The good is to be freely given, not compelled. Evil, on the other hand – that is, wrongful acts – may be dealt with by force, seeing that force is what the evildoer uses. Thus the social contract is to injure no one, and, second, to do good.[1] Noninjury has the *first* "place" and doing good the *second*. If we violate the first in order to bring about the second, we undo the basic purpose of the contract, which is to unite all rather than to set them apart and at odds.

My view of the social contract is Hobbesian. We begin with no morals, and ask where that would leave us. If it leaves us with general violence, as Hobbes supposes, and I agree, then we

---

1 *City of God*, Book XIX, ch. 14.

rationally impose general restrictions on our activity, provided that others do likewise – provided they are *mutual* and beneficial. The restriction on violence, on aggression, is fundamental. More generally, it is a restriction on pursuing our interests by worsening the situations of others. Any idea that we must, on pain of punishment, aid those in need, goes too far. Such aid can often be fruitfully reciprocal, and when it is so, then we are morally called upon to render that aid. But the proposal Sterba advances makes aid compulsory, on the basis *only* of a large disparity between the resources of the giver and those of the recipient. That is not *mutually* beneficial. Therefore, we cannot be thought to have voluntarily agreed to it.

The case against egalitarianism – that is, against *imposing* equality – is therefore very strong. Egalitarianism involves compelling A to transfer goods to B, simply because B has less in the status quo ex ante. What motive might A have for doing this? No doubt A can be coerced into making such transfers, should he be faced with determined and well-armed gangs of egalitarians – which apparently is what the modern welfare state comes to. But that seems an unlikely basis for regarding such transfers as *morally* called for, just as with gangs coercing transfers of the opposite kind.

The general basis for the limiting of our own pursuits of interest in whatever ways we are inclined to, on our own, is that we can often benefit from the cooperation of others, and that cooperation requires that we be ready to refrain from promoting our interests *at the expense of* those with whom we interact. This gives rise to the familiar nonharm, or libertarian, principle. It does not, however, obviously imply a further readiness not only to refrain from imposing costs on others, but also to render positive assistance, without reciprocation, to all who need it and to whom we possibly could render it. Needless to say, it does not call for our attempting to equalize levels of goods among us insofar as we can do this.

The preceding argument concerns the rather narrow part of morality known as "justice," which I take to be the part in which we are *required*, at threat of enforcement by coercive means, to do or refrain from various things. But justice is not all there is. It is a strange view of morals that all good things come from coercion. Certainly we should be disposed to approve and support benevolence. That goes beyond justice – but praiseworthily so.

More important than that, of course, is general market exchange, to mutual advantage, by persons motivated mainly by their own desire for wealth. I did not elaborate on this but took for granted that by far the main, and really in the end the only, "cure" for poverty is market exchange, by comparison with which welfare activities are a sideshow. To live well we must produce, and to produce effectively is to produce for exchange. Such is the free market: we produce freely, buying and selling in accordance each with his or her own best judgment. The hallmark in the market is *free* exchange, not any sort of compulsion. Our desire for personal wealth, pursued within the confines of respect for the rights of others to persons and property, leads us to activities greatly beneficial to all. The genius of this arrangement is that those useful activities are not compelled. By comparison with the ongoing productivity of the market, the occasional disaster, which certainly calls upon us to help each other in time of need, is a rarity. Poverty is not a "disaster," like hurricanes, though of course it sometimes is caused by them. But poverty in the sense of ongoing very low real income is due, all but entirely, to bad social arrangements which hobble the free productive activities of normal people. Compulsory redistribution is not a cure for that, but if anything a considerable part of the disease, as witness Cuba and North Korea.

Persons who are not compelled to be helpful will often be so nevertheless – and in all likelihood, much more so, and much more effectively than if exacted by compulsion. Still, the fundamental argument is the previous one. Morals is to be *by agreement*, of all with all, in respect of the very general principles we will insist on requiring or encouraging all to act by. To pass muster as such a principle, we need to show that *all* have an interest – that all will do better in a society in which all live by that principle rather than some other or, of course, none. Sacrificing the independence of some for the sake of others is not a rational element of such an agreement. We may be, and I hope typically are, appalled and saddened by the unfortunate of this world – and sometimes, to be sure, their misfortune is a result of prior injustices by other people. But they are often not, and, when not, it is not reasonable to elevate the unfortunate to the status of dictators, commanding the services of their fellows. (And even when they are, we are not required to do what we can to undo the injustices of others.)

Thus I reject Sterba's argument that in situations of what he terms "conflict of liberties" between, especially, rich and poor the liberty principle calls for weighing the relative intensities of the various interests and needs of the two parties, and awarding rights to those whose perceived needs are the greater (even relatively *much* greater). Social minima are, of course, difficult to assess and inevitably vague and variable, but wherever we set them, it remains that none of us is properly required, by respect for liberty, to see to it that those who fall below are restored to the designated level. Respecting the liberty in no case includes the liberty simply to take for oneself what has been created by the free activity of the others. We may take what belongs to none, but not what belongs to someone, as my hypothesis obtains here. So Sterba's idea that mutual respect for liberty calls upon the rich to stand aside while the poor invade their cup-boards, is a misreading of the general right of liberty. For "what belongs" to someone is, for present purposes, what that person has acquired either by his own work or by free exchange with others. Taking such things, without leave, is violating the other person's liberty. Social contract, I argue, continues to insist on respect for our mutual independence. Tempering this with pity, sympathy, fellow feeling, is most commendable; but that is not justice but charity – extremely important, yes – but *different*. The general right of liberty is fundamental and not compatible with compelling us to move toward equalities of any particular kind. In that special sense, which is the one relevant to matters of justice, liberty and equality are simply not compatible.

The aims of the welfare state, insofar as those are reasonable, will normally be met by voluntary activity. Wealthy societies have ample numbers of people ready to see to it that their fellows do not starve, and indeed in such societies starvation does not happen, bizarre accidents apart. Market freedoms create that wealth; coercion diminishes it. That wealth will reach out to the needy, without the welfare state, with its negation of liberty.

Select bibliography

Abelson, Raziel. "To Do or Let Happen," *American Philosophical Quarterly* 22 (1982), pp. 219–27.

Anderson, Elizabeth S. "What is the Point of Equality?" *Ethics* 109 (1999), pp. 287–337.

Augustine, St. *City of God*, http://personal.stthomas.edu/gwschlabach/docs/city.htm#14.28.

Bartholomew, James. *The Welfare State We're In* (London: Politico's Methuen, 2004).

Benditt, Theodore. "The Demands of Justice," in *Economic Justice*, ed. Diana Meyers and Kenneth Kipnis (Lanham, MD: Rowman & Littlefield, 1985), pp. 108–20.

Berlin, Isaiah. *Four Essays on Liberty* (New York: Oxford University Press, 1969).

"Two Concepts of Liberty," in *Four Essays on Liberty* (Oxford: Oxford University Press, 1969), pp. 118–72.

Brock, Gillian. "Is Redistribution to Help the Needy Unjust?" *Analysis* 55 (1995), pp. 50–60.

"Justice and Needs," *Dialogue* 35 (1996), pp. 81–6.

"Morally Important Needs," *Philosophia* 26 (1998), pp. 165–7.

"Just Deserts and Needs," *The Southern Journal of Philosophy* 37 (1999), pp. 165–88.

Brown, Lester. *Outgrowing the Earth* (New York: W. W. Norton & Co., 2004).

Plan B 2.0 (New York: W. W. Norton & Co., 2006).

Buchanan, Allen. "Deriving Welfare Rights from Libertarian Rights," in *Income Support*, ed. Peter Brown *et al.* (Totowa, NJ: Rowman and Littlefield, 1981), pp. 233–46.

Christman, John. *The Myth of Property* (New York: Oxford University Press, 1994).

Cohen, G. A. *Self-Ownership, Freedom, and Equality* (Cambridge: Cambridge University Press, 1995).

Cranston, Maurice. *Freedom* (New York: Basic Books, 1953).

Dancy, Jonathan. *Ethics Without Principles* (Oxford: Clarendon Press, 2004).

Daniels, Norman. "Intergenerational Justice," *Stanford Encyclopedia* (2003), http://plato.stanford.edu/entries/justice-intergenerational

Danielson, Peter. "The Rights of Chickens," in *For and Against the State*, ed. T. Sanders and J. Narveson (Lanham, MD: Rowman & Littlefield, 1996), pp. 171–93.

"Simple Games and Complex Ethics," in *Liberty, Games and Contracts*, ed. Malcolm Murray (Aldershot: Ashgate, 2007), pp. 103–14.

DeGeorge, Richard. "Do We Owe the Future Anything?" *Law and the Ecological Challenge* 2 (1978), pp. 180–90.

Diamond, Jared. *Collapse* (New York: Penguin, 2005).

"What's Your Consumption Factor?" *International Herald Tribune*, January 3, 2008.

Dworkin, Ronald. *Taking Rights Seriously* (Cambridge, MA: Harvard University Press, 1977).

"We Do Not Have a Right to Liberty," in *Liberty and the Rule of Law*, ed. Robert L. Cunningham (College Station: Texas A&M Press, 1979), pp. 167–81.

"What is Equality?" Part II, "Equality of Resources," in *Philosophy and Public Affairs* 10 (1981), pp. 283–345.

Sovereign Virtue: The Theory and Practice of Equality (Cambridge, MA: Harvard University Press, 2000).

Feinberg, Joel. *Rights, Justice and the Bounds of Liberty* (Princeton: Princeton University Press, 1980).

Freyfogle, Eric. *On Private Property* (Boston: Beacon Press, 2007).

Friedman, Milton. *Capitalism and Freedom* (Chicago: University of Chicago Press, 1962).

Gauthier, David. *Morals by Agreement* (New York: Oxford University Press, 1986).

Gendron, Bernard. *Technology and the Human Condition* (New York: St. Martin's Press, 1977), pp. 222–7.

Gewirth, Alan. *Reason and Morality* (Chicago: University of Chicago Press, 1978).

Glazer, Nathan. "Welfare and 'Welfare' in America," in *The Welfare State East and West*, ed. Rose and Shiratori, pp. 40–63.

Gordon, Anita and David, Suzuki. *It's a Matter of Survival* (Cambridge, MA: Harvard University Press, 1990).

Gould, Carol. "Freedom and Women," *Journal of Social Philosophy* 15, 3 (1984), pp. 20–34.

Gray, John. "On Negative and Positive Liberty," *Political Studies* 29 (1980), pp. 507–26.

Green, O. H. "Killing and Letting Die," *American Philosophical Quarterly* 20 (1980), pp. 195–204.

Grotius, Hugo. *The Rights of War and Peace*, trans. A. C. Campbell (New York: M. Walter Dunne, 1901). Accessed from http://oll.libertyfund.org/title/553.

Harrington, Michael. "Crunched Numbers," *The New Republic*, 193 (January 28, 1985), pp. 7–10.

Harris, John. "The Marxist Conception of Violence," *Philosophy and Public Affairs* 3 (1974), pp. 192–220.

Violence and Responsibility (Boston: Routledge & Kegan Paul, 1980).

Hayek, F. A. *The Constitution of Liberty* (Chicago: University of Chicago Press, 1960).

Hobbes, Thomas. *Leviathan* (New York: Dutton & Co., 1950).

Hospers, John. *Libertarianism* (Los Angeles: Nash Publishing, 1971).

"Some Unquestioned Assumptions," *The Journal of Social Philosophy* 22 (1991), pp. 42–51.

"The Libertarian Manifesto," in *Morality in Practice*, ed. James P. Sterba, 7th edn (Belmont: Wadsworth Publishing Co., 2004), pp. 21–31.

Jencks, Christopher. "How Poor are the Poor?" *New York Review of Books* 32 (May 9, 1985), pp. 41–9.

Kant, Immanuel, *Foundations of the Metaphysics of Morals*, trans. Lewis White Beck (Indianapolis: Liberal Arts Press, 1959).

Rechtslehre (Doctrine of Right), Metaphysics of Morals Part I: The Metaphysical Elements of Justice, trans. John Ladd (Indianapolis: Library of Liberal Arts, 1965).

Krugman, Paul. "In Praise of Cheap Labor," *Slate*, March 20, 2000 (http://slate.msn.com/Dismal/97–03–20/Dismal.asp).

Kurian, George. *The New Book of Work Rankings*, 3rd edn (New York: Facts on File, 1990).

The Illustrated Book of World Rankings (Amonk, NY: M. E. Sharpe, 1997).

Lappe, Frances and Joseph Collins. *World Hunger: Twelve Myths* (New York: Grove Press, 1986).

Lee, John Rodger. "Libertarianism, Limited Government, and Anarchy," in *Anarchism/Minarchism*, ed. Roderick Long and Tibor Machan (Aldershot: Ashgate, 2008), pp. 15–20.

Liebowitz, Stan J. "Anatomy of a Train Wreck – Causes of the Mortgage Meltdown," in *Housing America: Building Out of a Crisis*, ed. Randall G. Holcombe and Benjamin Powell (Oakland, CA: Independent Institute, forthcoming 2009).

Locke, John. *Two Treatises of Government* (New York: Cambridge University Press, 1960).

Machan, Tibor. *Human Rights and Human Liberties* (Chicago: Nelson-Hall, 1975).

Individuals and Their Rights (Chicago: Open Court, 1989).

"The Nonexistence of Welfare Rights" (rev. version), in *Liberty for the 21st Century*, ed. Tibor Machan and Douglas Rasmussen (Lanham, MD: Rowman & Littlefield, 1995), pp. 209–26.

"Does Libertarianism Imply the Welfare State?" *Res Publica* 3, 2 (1997), pp. 131–48.

"Libertarian Justice," in *Social and Political Philosophy: Contemporary Perspectives*, ed. James Sterba (London: Routledge, 2001), pp. 93–114.

"Sterba on Machan's 'Concession'," *Journal of Social Philosophy* 32, 2 (Summer 2001), pp. 241–3.

The Passion for Liberty (Lanham, MD: Rowman & Littlefield, 2003).

Machan, Tibor, ed., *Liberty and Equality* (Stanford, CA: Hoover Institution Press, 2002).

Mack, Eric. "Individualism, Rights and the Open Society," in *The Libertarian Reader* (Totowa, NJ: Rowman and Littlefield, 1982), pp. 3–15.

"Libertarianism Untamed," *Journal of Social Philosophy* 22 (1991), pp. 64–72.

MacIntosh, Duncan. "Who Owns Me: Me or My Mother?" in *Liberty, Games and Contracts*, ed. Malcolm Murray (Aldershot: Ashgate, 2007), pp. 157–71.

Macpherson, C. B. *Democratic Theory* (Oxford: Oxford University Press, 1973).

Martin, Rex. *Rawls and Rights* (Lawrence: University of Kansas Press, 1984).

Meadows, Donella H., Dennis L. Meadows, Jorgen Randers, and William W. Behrens III. *The Limits to Growth*, 2nd edn (New York: New American Library, 1974).

Mill, John Stuart. *An Essay on Liberty* (London: J. M. Dent, 1968).

Mungall, Constance and Digby McLaren, eds., *Planet Under Stress* (Oxford: Oxford University Press, 1990).

Murphy, Liam and Thomas Nagel. *The Myth of Ownership* (New York: Oxford University Press, 2002).

Murray, Charles. *Losing Ground* (New York: Basic Books, 1984).

Murray, Malcolm, ed., *Liberty, Games, and Contracts* (Aldershot: Ashgate, 2007), pp. 129–46.

Narveson, Jan. "Alan Gewirth's Reason and Morality – A Study in the Hazards of Universalizability in Ethics," *Dialogue* 19, 4 (December 1980), pp. 651–74.

"Animal Rights Revised," in *Ethics and Animals*, ed. Harlan Miller and William Williams (Clifton, NJ: Humana Press, 1983), pp. 45–59.

"On a Case for Animal Rights," *Monist* 70 (1987), pp. 31–49.

The Libertarian Idea (Philadelphia: Temple University Press, 1988; republished at Peterborough, Ont.: Broadview Press, 2001).

"The Anarchist's Case," in *For and Against the State* (Lanham, MD: Rowman and Littlefield, 1996), pp. 195–216.

"Sterba's Program of Philosophical Reconciliation," *Journal of Social Philosophy* 30 (1999), pp. 401–10.

"A Dilemma for Would-Be Liberal Defenders of the Welfare State," presented at the Canadian Philosophical Association Meetings, Laval University, Quebec, May 26, 2001. Forthcoming, in German, in *Analyze und Kritik* in 2009.

"A Critique of Sterba's Defense of the Welfare State," in *Political Philosophy*, ed. Louis Pojman (New York: McGraw-Hill, 2002), pp. 228–39.

"Liberty and Equality: A Question of Balance?" in *Liberty and Equality*, ed. Tibor Machan (Stanford: Hoover Institute Press, 2002), pp. 35–60.

"A Puzzle about Economic Inequality in Rawls' Theory," in *Respecting Persons in Theory and Practice* (Lanham, MD: Rowman & Littlefield, 2002), pp. 13–34.

"We Don't Owe Them a Thing! – A Tough-minded but Softhearted View of Aid to the Faraway Needy," *The Monist* 86, 3 (July 2003), pp. 419–33.

"Social Contract, Game Theory and Liberty," in *Liberty, Games and Contracts*, ed. Malcolm Murray (Aldershot: Ashgate, 2007), pp. 217–40.

"Social Contract, Game Theory and Liberty: Responding to My Critics," in *Liberty, Games and Contracts*, ed. Malcolm Murray (Aldershot: Ashgate, 2007), pp. 325–7.

"Property and Rights," *Social Philosophy and Policy*, 27, 1 (2009).

"Libertarianism: A Philosophical Introduction," www:againstpolitics.com/libertarian

Nielsen, Kai. *Equality and Liberty* (Totowa, NJ: Rowman & Allanheld, 1985).

Norman, Richard. *Free and Equal* (Oxford: Oxford University Press, 1987).

Nozick, Robert. *Anarchy, State, and Utopia* (New York: Basic Books, 1974).

Okin, Susan. *Justice, Gender and the Family* (New York: Basic Books, 1989).

Otsuka, Michael. *Libertarianism Without Inequality* (Oxford: Oxford University Press, 2003).

Parfit, Derek. *Persons and Reasons* (Oxford: Clarendon Press, 1984).

Parijs, Philippe Van. *Real Freedom for All* (Oxford: Oxford University Press, 1998).

Pogge, Thomas. *World Poverty and Human Rights* (Cambridge: Polity, 2002).

Pohl, Rudy. "Poverty in Canada," web: www.streetlevelconsulting.ca/homepage/homelessness2InCanada_Part2.htm

Rasmussen, Douglas. "Individual Rights and Human Flourishing," *Public Affairs Quarterly* 3 (1989), pp. 89–103.

Rasmussen, Douglas and Douglas Den Uyl, *Liberty and Nature* (La Salle: Open Court, 1991).

Rawls, John. *A Theory of Justice* (Cambridge, MA: Harvard University Press, 1971).

Justice as Fairness: A Restatement, ed. Kevin Kelly (Cambridge, MA: Harvard University Press, 2001).

Rose, Richard. "Making Progress and Catching Up: Comparative Analysis for Social Policy Making," in *UNESCO 1995* (Oxford: Blackwell Publishers, 1995), pp. 63–72.

Rose, Richard and Rei Shiratori, eds. *The Welfare State East and West* (Oxford: Oxford University Press, 1986).

Ross, W. D. *The Right and the Good* (Oxford: Oxford University Press, 1936).

Rothbard, Murray. *The Ethics of Liberty* (New York: Collier Books, 1978).

Sarlo, Chris. *Measuring Poverty in Canada* (Vancouver: Fraser Institute, 2001).

Scanlon, T. M. *What We Owe to Each Other* (Cambridge, MA: Harvard University Press, 1998).

Schmidtz, David. *Elements of Justice* (New York: Cambridge University Press, 2006).

Shader-Frechette, Kristin. *Taking Action, Saving Lives* (New York: Oxford University Press, 2007).

Shapiro, Daniel. *Is the Welfare State Justified?* (New York: Cambridge University Press, 2007).

Shue, Henry. *Basic Rights*, 1st edn (Princeton: Princeton University Press, 1980).

"The Bogus Distinction – 'Negative' and 'Positive' Rights," in *Making Ethical Decisions*, ed. Norman E. Bowie (New York: McGraw-Hill, 1985), pp. 223–31.

Singer, Peter. "What Should a Billionaire Give – and What Should You?" *New York Times* (December 17, 2006).

Starke, Linda, ed. *State of the World 2004* (New York: W. W. Norton & Co., 2004).

Steiner, Hillel. *An Essay on Rights* (Oxford: Blackwell, 1994).

Sterba, James. "Neo-Libertarianism," *American Philosophical Quarterly* 18 (1978), pp. 115–21.

"Neo-Libertarianism" (expanded version), in *Justice: Alternative Political Perspectives*, ed. James P. Sterba (Belmont: Wadsworth Publishing Co., 1979), pp. 172–86.

How to Make People Just (Lanham, MD: Rowman & Littlefield, 1988).

Justice for Here and Now (New York: Cambridge University Press, 1998).

The Triumph of Practice Over Theory in Ethics (New York: Oxford University Press, 2005).

"Our Basic Human Right is a Right to Liberty and its Leads to Equality," colloquium at Albion College, Michigan (April 2006).

Presidential Address to the APA, "Completing the Kantian Project: From Rationality to Equality," *Proceedings and Addresses of the American Philosophical Association*, 82, 2 (November 2008), pp. 47–83.

Sterba, James P., Tibor Machan *et al.*, *Morality and Social Justice: Point and Counterpoint* (Lanham, MD: Rowman and Littlefield, 1994).

Sunstein, Cass with Stephen Holmes. *The Cost of Rights* (London and New York: W. W. Norton, 1999).

Taylor, Charles. "What is Wrong with Negative Liberty," in *The Idea of Freedom*, ed. Alan Ryan (Oxford: Oxford University Press, 1979), pp. 175–93.

Tocqueville, Alexis de. "Memoir on Pauperism," trans. Seymour Drescher, intro. Gertrude Himmelfarb (London: IEA, Health and Welfare Unit, 1997), p. 24.

Vallentyne, Peter and Hillel Steiner, eds., *The Origins of Left-Libertarianism and Left-Libertarianism and Its Critics* (Basingstoke: Palgrave, 2000).

Vallentyne, Peter, Hillel Steiner, and Michael Otsuka. "Why Left-Libertarianism is Not Incoherent, Indeterminate, or Irrelevant," *Philosophy and Public Affairs* 24 (2005), pp. 201–15.

Viminitz, Paul. "Getting the Baseline Right," in *Liberty, Games, and Contracts*, ed. Malcolm Murray (Aldershot: Ashgate, 2007), pp. 129–46.

Waldron, Jeremy. *Liberal Rights* (Cambridge: Cambridge University Press, 1987).

Wolff, Jonathan. "Robert Nozick, Liberarianism, and Utopia," from his "Critique of Libertarianism" site, http://world.std.com/~mhuben/libindex.html

Wolff, Michael. *Where We Stand* (New York: Bantam Books, 1992).

Woodward, James. "The Non-Identity Problem," *Ethics*, 96 (1986), pp. 804–31.

Wright, Ronald. *A Short History of Progress* (New York: Carroll & Graf, 2004).

Index